D0502639

AN INDEFINITE SENTENCE

A PERSONAL HISTORY OF OUTLAWED LOVE AND SEX

SIDDHARTH DUBE

ATRIA BOOKS

New York   London   Toronto   Sydney   New Delhi

ATRIA
BOOKS

An Imprint of Simon & Schuster, Inc.
1230 Avenue of the Americas
New York, NY 10020

This book is a memoir that combines autobiographic details and the product of
my work and research. Some of what is found in the pages is based on extensive
interviews, the rest on reported facts or recollection; certain names have been
changed.

Photography Credits—From the author's personal collection: pages 5, 10, 72, 87,
339. Olivier Föllmi: page 99. Positive People: page 118. Courtesy of Shyamala
Nataraj: page 148. Selvi Memorial Illam Trust: page 211. Durbar Mahila
Samanwaya Committee: page 223. Maryam Shahmanesh: page 299.

First Atria Books hardcover edition January 2019

ATRIA BOOKS and colophon are trademarks of Simon & Schuster, Inc.

For information about special discounts for bulk purchases, please
contact Simon & Schuster Special Sales at 1-866-506-1949 or business@
simonandschuster.com.

The Simon & Schuster Speakers Bureau can bring authors to your live event. For
more information, or to book an event, contact the Simon & Schuster Speakers
Bureau at 1-866-248-3049 or visit our website at www.simonspeakers.com.

Interior design by Amy Trombat

Manufactured in the United States of America

10 9 8 7 6 5 4 3 2 1

Library of Congress Cataloging-in-Publication Data has been applied for.

ISBN 978-1-5011-5847-6
ISBN 978-1-5011-5849-0 (ebook)

*For Basant Kumar Dube, my marvelous father and friend,
who insisted, foremost, that we always tell the truth.*

AN

INDEFINITE

SENTENCE

ONE

SHAME

In retrospect, it's clear that the enduring themes of my life were present so many years back in that single night, which is why I recollect it all with such clarity even decades later. But I could see only with a child's eyes then, simply, directly, without interpretation, without thought of what it might mean for the future.

The year was 1971, and I was ten years old. I was at the Grand, Calcutta's sumptuous colonial-era hotel. The orchestra had burst into a rousing flourish, and everyone moved to the sides of the ballroom as a light-skinned woman, petite but full-bodied, wearing just a shimmering two-piece bikini and a veil, emerged magically from somewhere.

The woman began to dance her way slowly down the length of the vast, carpeted room, her movements languorous yet purposeful, as she removed the veil and used it as a fluttering prop for caressing and seducing. She was flaunting her near nakedness, the expanse of smooth skin and soft curves magnified by the glitter of her bikini. I was entranced.

It struck me that, unlike the other striptease dancers I had seen (my parents often brought me along with them so I wouldn't have to be left with my *ayah*), this one never pressed herself against the men in the audience. Instead, she held the gaze of man after man for a measured moment, then moved on, almost dismissively.

She is like a snake charmer, I thought to myself. And indeed, all the men, including my father, standing across from my mother and me, seemed hypnotized by the dancer in a disturbed way, almost as if they were struggling to keep themselves from grabbing her.

The dancer approached me, and I immediately pressed against my mother, finding comfort in her familiar scent and the soft folds of her sari. In the past, to my burning embarrassment and the amusement of the adults, some Park Street nightclub dancers had done a watered-down version of their bump-and-grind routine against me, no doubt singling me out because I was the only child present.

But this one just passed us by, shimmied to the end of the room, and then—to a loud, collective gasp from the partygoers—threw off her bikini top to reveal peculiarly small breasts. In another flash, to an even louder gasp from the adults, she pulled off her bikini bottom—and, as she twirled naughtily out of the room, I espied what seemed to be a penis.

There was silence for a long minute—and then an explosion of clapping and laughter from the adults. But I was in turmoil. When things eventually quietened, I tugged at my mother's arm and asked, "Mama, Mama, was that a woman or a man?"

My mother stroked my hair lovingly, and said in a voice bright with amusement, "Yes, it was a man!"

Though I was unaware of it at the time, the incident marked my first precocious introduction to some of my life's preoccupations: the beguiling possibilities of gender beyond the conventional bipolarity of male and female, and the mysterious, limitless permutations of sexual desire. It was only as an adolescent, years later, that memories of it came rushing back with unsettling clarity and I realized that I had seen something of myself in that unusual dancer.

✦

Just a year or two before that striptease at the Grand, I had become aware that I was a girly-boy, a sissy, different from other boys, and despised and ostracized by them.

I had joined La Martinière, one of Calcutta's elite secondary schools, at the age of eight. Within a few days, I began to grasp that this school bore no resemblance to my tony elementary school, Miss Higgins, still run by its elderly, eponymous British founder. While her homely bungalow had somehow made me feel at once secure and carefree, the main buildings at La Martinière were forbidding, cathedral-like edifices, over a century old. High walls and gates enclosed the grounds. The towering pillars of the assembly hall and senior classrooms only underscored my puniness. Even the steps that led up to the assembly hall were intimidating, each one so tall and deep that I couldn't climb from one to the other in a single stride. The whole compound seemed to be designed expressly to humble us children.

There were no girls here as there had been at Miss Higgins. Not one. They were all at a sister school across the street. I felt their absence as a difference in atmosphere, which seemed more boisterous yet darker than at Miss Higgins. When school ended, I would watch the girls spilling out of the gates on the far side of the street, always looking much happier than we boys did.

Soon, to my surprise, I became aware that I was not popular with my new classmates. Whenever I sat down next to someone in class or tried to strike up a friendship, I sensed I was being rebuffed. At first I wondered whether this was because our environment was so regimented.

We wore identical uniforms of white shirts and shorts, black lace-ups with knee-high socks, and a school tie of gold stripes on black, held in place with our house pin. Mine was a bright yellow, for Macaulay House, named after Lord Thomas Babington Macaulay, the nineteenth-century imperial politician who had had an outsize, enduring impact on shaping the minds of India's ruling elite, snidely known as "Macaulay's Children" and "brown *sahib*s." At morning assembly, we stood in neat rows and sang Christian hymns after we had recited the Lord's Prayer. In our classrooms, we sat at identical wooden desks and chairs, springing up anxiously when the teacher entered and singing "Good morning, sir!" or "Good morning, ma'am!" in unison, then quickly sitting down in silence. There was little time for fun before or after school hours. Perhaps my friendliness might have seemed inappropriate, given the circumstances.

However, I soon realized that the class was essentially divided into two groups: a number of studious or quiet boys like me at the front and a larger group of the rowdier kind in the rows behind. While the boys around me were cautiously friendly, the larger group in the back disliked me with a vengeance. In fact, I was the main target of their antagonism. Whenever I stood up to answer a question, they sniggered. When I turned around, I caught belligerent looks. On the few occasions when I ventured into their territory, I was shoved away by whomever I approached while the rest laughed at my humiliation.

Things continued like that for a few months. Then one day, as I stood up in class to answer a question, I heard a threatening chorus of hate-filled whispers from behind: "Sissy! Sissy! Sissy!"

A wave of shame swept over me. They were right to call me that.

I recalled how silent my parents had fallen when I had recently paraded into our living room adorned with my mother's jewelry. Not only had I had earrings, necklaces, and bracelets on, I had also secured a pendant in my hair like a Hindu bride. I pranced around like a *filmi* siren, shaking my hips, stamping my bare feet in Kathak-like movements. I had even gyrated sinuously on the floor in an imitation of the starlets of that era.

I remembered all the times my mother had found me feeding and cradling my cowboy-Indian action figures as if they were dolls. Or playing nurse with our long-suffering dogs, swaddling them in improvised bandages. With sharp shame, I also remembered how I had preened whenever my parents' friends remarked what a beautiful girl I'd have made, how I looked just like my luminous mother with my long-lashed eyes and fine skin.

Me with my first dog

At that exact moment, standing at my classroom desk and hearing the other boys calling me "sissy," I began to see myself as a freak. I was overcome with self-loathing as I realized the many occasions on which, unthinkingly, I had shown my parents what a girly-boy I was. Now, much worse, I realized that the larger world saw me as only that.

Things worsened over the next few years. Of all the boys in my class who got picked on, I became the prime target. There were other victims, who were called "fatso" or "freak," had pieces of chalk flung at them, or were shoved around when the teacher wasn't there. But that happened infrequently. I was the only one who was unfailingly the focus of hostility.

Making matters worse, I became known as a girly-boy in other classes. It seemed to me as if everyone in school had been told to despise me. Older boys shouted "Sissy!" as I walked past or stopped in midconversation to stare at me with distaste. A few times, when I inadvertently caught someone's eye, things got uglier. The taunts got louder and louder: "Sissy!" "Sissy! Sissy!" "Girly girly girly!" "Go to the girls' school!" The bullies would move threateningly toward me as I tried to beat a retreat. Though the incidents never escalated into physical violence, they were enough to make me feel constantly apprehensive.

My mother soon noticed that I wasn't enjoying La Martinière. She didn't question me about it, no doubt because she assumed that I was merely facing the routine challenges of school life. Moreover, given that she was facing struggles of her own, she probably no longer had the emotional strength to be as attentive as she had been earlier: her marriage to my father, once a powerful romance between strong-willed equals, had begun to unravel. My father relished Calcutta's cosmopolitan life and had risen meteorically in the prosperous tea industry. But my mother, ascetic and serious-minded, was a misfit in this "brown *sahib*" world of elite British mores and corporate wealth, with its constant round of parties, golf, and polo matches. Her fears that she was losing him to one or another flirtatious *memsahib* tipped over into unrelenting suspicion.

By this time I had become my mother's staunchest ally in their conflict, viewing her as the wronged victim and my father as the philandering offender. Still, in spite of my closeness to her, I couldn't discuss with her the daily humiliations I faced at school. Given my worsening antagonism to my father, there was no likelihood of turning to him. And more than anything else, I wanted to avoid drawing their attention back to my shameful problem. I felt it was I who was despicable and needed to change, not the boys who hated me.

I found my own ways of coping. I would arrive at school only when classes were about to begin. I kept to myself and avoided getting in the way of the boys who taunted me. I didn't react to their stares, their comments, or the chalk they flung at me. Shaking with apprehension, I would try to appear calm and walk away unhurriedly, as if I were doing so out of choice and not fear. That act of defiance helped me salvage some sense of dignity, despite being near tears and achingly aware that I was an outcast.

It was a difficult transition because, despite the eroding of my parents' relationship, my childhood had been happy and almost carefree until I joined La Martinière. I had not given a thought to whether I was boyish in my mannerisms and looks in the cheery mix of boys and girls at Miss Higgins, where I had found myself quite naturally at the center of most things.

Moreover, at home, I had felt no different from my brothers, Pratap and Bharat, and despite being the youngest—they were four years and one year older than I, respectively—I had confidently established my boundaries. While usually happy to follow my brothers' lead, I would get notoriously feisty whenever I felt that they were treating me unfairly. My brothers still take pleasure in reminding me that my standard comeback was "Yeah, so?!"—in other words, "What are you going to do about it?" My brothers christened me "Yaso," and though it no doubt honored my fighting spirit, it also made me sound truculent.

But on joining La Martinière my once headlong approach to life turned into an unrelenting battle with self-consciousness. To protect myself from further ridicule and shame, I began to ferociously weed out every girly trait that I could see in myself. I desperately wanted to be a regular boy, left with no damning evidence of who I actually was.

The psychological conflicts set into motion at this juncture of my life might have been even more traumatizing if, like some gender-atypical children, I had desperately longed to change my sex. But, looking back at those childhood years, at least as far as I can tell through the complexities of my own mind, I never clearly felt "that I had been born into the wrong body, and should really be a girl," as the great British writer Jan Morris—who was James Morris before a sex-change operation—wrote in her pioneering 1974 memoir, Conundrum.

Nor do I recall experiencing any of the other feelings that strongly gender-atypical children experience: disgust at their own genitals, the conviction that they will grow up to be the opposite sex, and a strong desire to do so. While I relished some stereotypically feminine behaviors—wearing women's clothing, dancing, or beautifying myself with makeup and jewelry—I never felt the urge to pursue them all the time. I was passionate about many conventionally boyish things, such as playing with model racing cars and fighter planes, for instance; my keenest desire as a child was simply to go swimming or to play with our dogs.

So, though I doubt that I ever wanted to change my gender and sex and become a girl, I am equally sure that I would have blossomed in a setting free of gender-prescriptive prejudice and fears, like the one I was in before joining the boys-only La Martinière environment—where I could be a carefree child of an amorphous, undefined gender and not have to feel ashamed and anxious that some of my actions were "girlish" and hence taboo.

Yet, even while living through those difficult years of my life, I didn't actually think of myself as unhappy or victimized. My stoicism was rooted in the childhood survival trait of attempting to live in the here and now using every psychological stratagem possible. I coped with the persecution I faced at La Martinière as well as the bitter battles between my parents by daydreaming about a peaceful enchanted place, populated only by noble wild animals (especially tigers and elephants) that lovingly protected my mother and me. Once safely back home from school, I blanked out all thoughts about my hours there, my fears returning only when I woke the next morning.

My mother was another great source of calm. After school hours, she and I spent much of our time together. With my brothers away at boarding school, we became even closer. Because of the problems at home, my father absented himself for increasingly long periods of time, touring the tea plantations in Assam and north Bengal. I savored being with my mother and was never bored, even when we spent day after day by ourselves.

It seemed to me that she had a magical way with animals. Our dogs would willingly do everything she asked of them, their eyes fixed intently on hers to see if they had succeeded in pleasing her. In the garden outside our Lord Sinha Road apartment, dragonflies seemed to choose to settle on her outstretched hands. She would tie a fine thread to their tails, so that I could hold them for a while—imagining them to be pet fairies—before she released them unhurt. At the children's section at the nearby Calcutta Club, the *chital* stag—who had been brought there when he was still a fawn—would unfailingly come to nuzzle her, though he would ignore me. Our shared love of nature kept us happy, poring over encyclopedias about pets and wildlife.

I spent a lot of time immersed in books. Every few days, we would replenish our stock from the libraries at the Calcutta Club and the British Council. I loved books about animals: Tarka, the otter in the English countryside; Flicka, the American mustang; and White Fang, the heroic wolf-dog. My two favorites were set in the wilds of India: Rudyard Kipling's *The Jungle Book* and *Chendru: The Boy and the Tiger*, an illustrated book about a real-life *adivasi* boy and his pet tiger cub.

But I also read everything I could lay my hands on—at the age of ten, I was reading Enid Blyton's Famous Five series and Frank Richards's Billy Bunter series, and, because my mother did not censor my reading, westerns by Louis L'Amour and potboilers by Harold Robbins. Jacqueline Susann became an enduring favorite, first for her tribute to her poodle, *Every Night, Josephine!,* and then for the steamy *Valley of the Dolls*.

I openly read novels by Daphne du Maurier and Georgette Heyer, thinking that my mother would assume that I liked them for their literary qualities. But in my bathroom, with the door locked, I read her Barbara Cartland and Mills & Boon romances. I loved the unceasing romance and the handsome, complicated heroes. I read them in secret because I now knew that only girls were supposed to like them. I began to spend so much time in the bathroom that my mother wrote on the door, in indelible red paint, "This is not a library!"

Our isolation was punctuated twice a year, when life reverted to a close approximation of the glorious earlier years of my childhood: before my brothers went off to boarding school, before my parents' relationship began to disintegrate, before I joined La Martinière and became ashamed of myself. Those were the holiday months, every summer and winter, when my brothers returned from school.

My parents, Savitri and Basant

All the activity at home would help revive my mother's spirits. My father would be around most of the time. My parents would fight rarely, and sometimes not at all, during those months, and I was spared the anguish of having to take sides against my father. Instead, there was once again a sense of love at home. What we children wished for desperately seemed to come true, however implausible it might have seemed for the rest of the year: our parents loved each other, they loved us, and we loved them and one another.

The company of my brothers made me feel normal once again. We would spill out everywhere together, playing cowboys and Indians and cops and robbers. We dragged our much-loved dogs into our games. Sally, our spotlessly white German shepherd, was particularly stage-worthy, seemingly born for playing the role of our indomitable protector against the threats of this world.

In the living room, our imaginations were set afire by the enormous tiger skins from our father's hunting expeditions spread across the floor. When we stood astride them or sat on their stuffed heads— stretched in a ferocious permanent snarl, complete with daunting incisors and raspy tongues—we became Mowgli, Tarzan, or the Phantom.

The weekends stretched out blissfully. A yoga teacher would arrive on Sunday mornings to give us boys a long session of convoluted poses, from *surya namaskar* to *kapalbhati* and *nauli kriya*. Few Indians did yoga in that era, but my parents had embraced it after Pratap's crippling bout of polio, as a means to strengthen his legs.

One of the high points of the holiday weekends was watching my father at his morning prayers, something I studiedly kept away from during the regular months of antagonism. This was a daily ritual but on weekends stretched on for an hour or more. After showering and completing his yoga, he would sit cross-legged—wearing only underwear, bare-chested, somehow exuding cleanliness of every kind—on the carpet in front of the home temple, brimming over with statues of Maa Durga and Maa Kali as well as Shiva, Ganesh, and Hanuman—his favorite goddesses and gods from Hinduism's infinite pantheon—as well as his worn copies of the *Bhagavad Gita* and *Hanuman Chalisa*, several gleaming *lingam*s and *yoni*s carved from black stone and photographs of his deceased father, grandfather, and grand-uncle.

He would smile at us if he saw that any of us was watching him, patting the ground to invite us to join him if we wished. The moment he turned his face toward the temple and closed his eyes, I saw that he had been transported to a place that I didn't know of, a magical spot somewhere inside himself where he always, almost instantly, found peace. We would be stilled into quiet and immobility by our father's single-minded concentration.

He would begin to chant, "Om, om, om . . . ," that sacred, mysterious sound becoming more resonant with each repetition, like a deepening series of bells. I could see how with each repetition he moved even further into a state of peace. I didn't understand the process that was under way, but I always felt happy for him.

A great joy of a very different kind came in the afternoons, with long swimming sessions at the Calcutta Club. Once in the cool embrace of water, we three consummate swimmers were like a pod of dolphins, flashing past the other kids, confident and joyous, always together.

Driving home as a family from the club, my father—after grueling sets of tennis, followed by drinks—would flirt with my mother. The attraction between them in those moments was evident even to us kids. He made mischievous sexual allusions while my mother pretended to be shocked. My parents' favorite music played once again at home: Connie Francis, Eartha Kitt, Frankie Lane, and Millie Small, interspersed with Tom Lehrer's wisecracks and the pathos of Begum Akhtar's *ghazals*. We sprawled out on our parents' bed with them, vying to rest our heads on our mother's stomach, wonderfully soft and cool to the touch.

Come bedtime, we would settle heavily into our single beds, with the dogs at someone's feet or on the floor, the air conditioner humming loudly, and the door to my parents' bedroom left reassuringly ajar. We would close our eyes and pray silently for a few minutes. Our parents didn't guide us about what we should pray for or how or why.

My prayers consisted of wishing good things for everyone in our family, including our dogs. For each individual, I had a set of wishes—for Pratap, that his polio-torn legs would be miraculously healed or at least would not handicap him; for my mother, that her choking asthma would be cured and that she and my father would live happily; and so on, an endless detailed list of things that I prayed fervently would come true. I prayed in Hindi—virtually the only time that I reverted to using my family's original language, replaced in Anglicized Calcutta by English, which for all practical matters was my mother tongue.

After we finished our prayers, Papa would settle down on a low chair to tell us riveting bedtime stories about our *zamindar* ancestors in the Uttar Pradesh badlands, more than seven hundred miles to the northwest.

In one of them, set in medieval times, a magical giant cobra lifted one of our ancestors onto its hood, thereby preventing our clan from being wiped out in a murderous late-night assault by rival *zamindars*. In another story, my widowed grandmother and teenaged father, armed with shotguns, rode off on horseback at dawn to a relative's *haveli* to wrest back jewelry that the latter had wrongly laid claim to.

A particularly dark story that our father rarely told, but of which we remembered every detail, was about how his own father—newly married and barely into his twenties—had been murdered by cousins trying to usurp his inheritance. Even here, good eventually won—our treacherous relatives had not known that our grandmother was pregnant with our father, her first and only child.

Despite the grim tenor of those stories, I felt safe and secure. Even at that age, I understood that the moral of Papa's stories, which he wished us to absorb, was that it was our family *dharma* to endure even the most terrible suffering without complaint or recourse to dishonorable actions. That was the core message of my father's favorite texts, the *Bhagavad Gita* and Rudyard Kipling's "If," copies of which he kept not only at home but also in his office. However shattering the blows faced in life, we boys—like our grandmother and the best of our ancestors—were to remain superhumanly brave. We were to do good for others without giving any thought to self-interest.

In such moments, my father seemed to embody the goodness his stories spoke of, revealed in the steadiness of his gaze even when his eyes were soft with affection. Despite the palpable awkwardness between us, persisting from the months of strain that had preceded the holidays, I knew for a fact that he loved me, too, and I was safe with him. Even when I faced hardships in school and later in life, the recollection of my father's absolute protectiveness and of our family history of fortitude gave me the strength to endure them.

✦

Looking back, I realize that neither of my parents ever admonished me for my feminine traits and behaviors. There were no rebukes, no hostility. As an adult, when comparing my childhood experiences with others who had also had gender-atypical traits as children, I realized how lucky I was. The majority of the people I spoke to, in India and elsewhere, told me that their parents had persecuted and shamed them. A friend in Delhi told me he had been beaten mercilessly, abusively called a *hijra*—the common term for India's traditional "third gender"—and locked up in isolation for hours by his parents, all because he insisted on shaving his legs and wearing dresses at home.

It made me think about why my parents handled that matter more kindly than did others from their era. I know that my mother had always half wished that I were a girl so that I could remain at home with her and be the loving confidante she desperately sought. That longing may have contributed to her setting aside any discomfort she felt about my behavior. In my father's case, despite his being a manly man in the colonial mode, it's likely that not having a father himself led him to follow his natural instincts as a parent rather than being hamstrung by tradition.

And though they looked like quintessential products of their class, my parents were more unconventional than many of their friends. They broke social rules, big and small. In an age of arranged marriages, theirs had been a love marriage. My mother spurned jewelry and makeup and was drawn to yoga rather than to parties. They also had a naturalness about both sexual matters and nudity—my father routinely wandered around the house in a jockstrap or briefs, and my mother in just a thin petticoat, bare-breasted—that I later realized was unheard-of in families like ours. They thought nothing of taking us children to striptease performances, flirting with each other in our presence, letting us read adult novels, or, in my father's case, teaching us raunchy British songs such as "Roll Me Over in the Clover." Perhaps that freethinking streak made them more capable of withstanding the fears that other parents felt about their children's gender-atypical behavior.

Their response was close to the best that could be expected, given the times. Even if they had been actively supportive and had sought to give positive direction to me as a gender-atypical child, child psychology services barely existed in India in that era—and very few parents of their generation anywhere in the world would have had better alternatives. Gender-atypical children were viewed by most psychological and medical professionals as deviant or sick individuals who would grow up to be homosexual. Given the oppressive stigma attached to homosexuality and the laws criminalizing it, their approach was to "cure" children through "aversion therapies," including electric shock

treatment to the genitals or other areas while the child looked at images of the "wrong" gender. The idea was that such images would
become frightening rather than arousing. Those so-called treatments
were not only ineffective but left children at high risk of depression,
anxiety, and self-destructive behaviors.

However, while my brothers and I remained very close, they, too,
began to see me as a girly-boy, like the students at my school. One day,
when some of my parents' friends were visiting, Bharat—to whom I
was particularly attached, as we were just fourteen months apart in
age—blurted out, "Siddharth reads Barbara Cartland and Mills and
Boon! And he plucks his eyebrows. Look at them!"

Everyone turned to look at me. I sat there in shock and then said in
a trembling voice, "I don't." (I was referring to plucking my eyebrows;
they are naturally arched and tidy by some twist of androgyny.)

"Yes, he does!" insisted Bharat in his most convincing voice. I
was close to tears. Forever after, throughout my childhood and teen
years, Bharat would repeat those announcements to adult audiences
at unexpected moments. I would sit speechless, at best mumbling in
protest. Though I knew that it was just Bharat's bull-in-a-china-shop
way momentarily getting the better of him, my sense of shame was so
intense that I could never speak about it to him. I thought bringing it
up would only confirm that I really was a girly-boy.

⌖

By the age of nine or ten, I began to be attracted to boys and men.
The first object of my attraction was one of our drivers. It was a vague
kind of desire, not the headlong sexual pull that I began to experience
a few years later. I'm not even sure why I found him attractive. He
wasn't handsome, and his skin exuded the rancid odor of cheap alcohol. My desire had something to do with his dissolute style as well as
a somewhat transparent, creamish nylon shirt that he often wore that
displayed his smooth, hairless flesh.

I'm not sure what I felt first, romantic desire or sexual desire. I know I first experienced romantic desire through the pulp novels I was reading. I longed for the heroes to love me obsessively, to sweep me away—preferably on a magnificent Arab stallion—to the land of happily-ever-after. It was an inexplicable yearning, a strange ache that made me feel as if I had been separated from an unknown someone for whom I continually pined.

Even though the books depicted romance only between men and women, I didn't really wonder if that implied that I would have to transform myself into a woman. I only concluded that I would have to be alluringly feminine, because it was feminine charm that drew the heroes to the heroines instead of the other women.

I first felt sexual desire through the Barbara Cartland and Jacqueline Susann books, but it was only in the Harold Robbins books that I found regular snatches of explicit sex. I fixated on the description of the men's bodies, their cocks, what they did, the pleasure they felt. I came across a thrilling section in *The Pirate*, several paragraphs long, where a gigolo about to have sex with a wealthy woman instead remembered the headlong pleasure he had recently experienced while being fucked by a handsome black man. That elevated my excitement to a degree that I had not known before, with those passages remaining forever alive in my mind.

Sexual desire became another yearning within me, and this one was a force located in my groin—single-minded, insistent, and attention-seeking. It led me to discover the joys of masturbation, an inexhaustible source of pleasure. And though I was furtive about the practice, locking myself up in my bathroom, the fact that my parents treated sexual matters openly and casually spared me the common trauma of thinking that the act itself was sinful or deviant.

At that early point, and for many years later, I did not wonder whether other boys—my brothers, for instance—fantasized about men or women or whether the nature of my newfound desires had any link to my feminine behavior. Such was the blissful ignorance of childhood, not knowing that my desires, like my femininity, made me disgracefully different from most other boys.

TWO

A BOY'S WORLD

My first great experiences of desire and romance occurred, ironically, in an atmosphere marked by brutal physical and sexual abuse. I left home at the age of eleven, in 1973, to go to the Doon School, India's Eton and Andover, a famed bastion of boys-only education where all the men in my family had gone since its founding in the last decades of the British Raj. I left behind a world in which I was despised for my femininity only to enter one where it made me an object of both desire and condemnation.

I had joined Doon desperately hoping that I could start over again as a regular boy in this new setting. From my very first day, I boasted, shoved, and strutted, mimicking the tough boys who had dominated La Martinière.

My aggressive behavior made an immediate impression, though not the kind I had been aiming for. Within the very first days, I ended up in fistfights with classmates as well as school seniors. Bharat, then in his middle years at Doon, sought me out to warn me that several boys—including his peers—had complained to him that I was insufferably aggressive. I must behave better, he said, clearly wondering why his gentle brother had suddenly turned rogue. I usually heeded

Bharat's advice, but because there was no other way to hide the fact that I was a girly-boy, I decided to persist.

As it happened, my disguise didn't take long to fall apart. It was too alien to me to be kept up for long. More to the point, I was quite simply not the strongest among my peers. A month into my stay at Doon, I was defeated in a fistfight. I still remember its course as if it had ended just minutes ago.

It was with a boy of my age, but taller and better built. We fought in our changing room, a small chamber adjacent to the bedroom that we shared with three other newbies. Every inch of wall space had uniforms and pajamas hanging from wall hooks, rows of shoes were lined up below, and a long towel rack occupied the window area. There was just enough space left for two brawling boys of our size. We boxed each other on the face and stomach. We tore at each other's hair. He knocked me to the ground. We wrestled. I fought as hard as I could—because I had everything to lose.

But I was outclassed. The fight ended with all my strength exhausted and him sitting astride me, scornfully saying that I wasn't half as tough as I acted. I didn't cry but, lying on the floor there, I felt the sinking dread from La Martinière coming over me again. Now that I had lost a fight, they were going to figure out that I was "girly" and despise me.

⚜

Doon displaced home. For the next seven years, I spent nine months of every year at its secluded campus in Dehra Dun, in the foothills of the Himalayas.

Home became a painful ache in my heart—a faraway place from which letters arrived. Almost all were from my mother, the envelopes bearing her fluid, elegant handwriting. Her letters were long and often were written not on letter paper but on the backs of Polaroid "instant" photographs that she had taken of our dogs, the potted plants, and the half-dozen pigeons that she had allowed to roost in the veranda.

Despite her resolutely cheerful tone, the pain of her loneliness bled through. It mirrored mine; I ached at every letter, treasuring them, reading them over and over again in quiet moments, holding back tears.

My father wrote every second week jointly to Bharat and me. His letters were brief, two or three short paragraphs, impeccably typed out by his secretary on his company letterhead. At the very end, he added a personal line or two by hand. When Bharat passed on our father's letters to me, I'd just glance through the letter or say I wasn't interested in reading it, to underscore that I faithfully sided with our mother over our father in their battle. That small act kept alive my enmity toward my father despite the distance of a thousand miles.

✤

Doon was a place out of time, a place out of place. An elite British school had been transposed to India to groom us, sons of privilege, into "a class of persons, Indian in blood and color, but English in taste, in opinions, in morals and in intellect," as Macaulay had so precisely described the goal of his imperial education policy, launched in 1830s British India. As the vanguard of "Macaulay's Children," we were expected to dutifully fulfill our roles as the rulers of modern India, like the countless politicians, administrators, generals, judges, and tycoons who had been schooled there over the decades.

In that world unto itself, our human interactions did not resemble anything we had experienced at home. Fear blanketed the school. It stemmed from the relationship between the school's senior class and the rest of its cohorts. Outside our hours in the classroom, the seniors governed our lives as prefects in a system that dated back to the founding of the school in 1935, when India was still a colony, replicating the prefectorial systems of Eton and Harrow—where Doon's first headmaster and his deputy, both British, had taught before moving here.

Our residential dorms were the prefects' fiefdom, places they ran with only minimal interference by the housemasters. The prefects supervised us through our tightly regimented days, every waking hour of which was governed by the clamor of massive brass bells ordering us from one activity to another. We sprinted from our dorms to the academic buildings, the playing fields, and the arts and crafts workshops, speedily getting into and out of unending sets of uniforms.

We obeyed the prefects because they enjoyed practically unrestricted powers when it came to administering punishments: levied if we were late in answering any bell through the day, if we did not execute every uniform to perfection—whether it concerned the knot of our ties, the sheen of our shoes, or the precise height of our knee-high socks—or, often, simply because the prefects arbitrarily disliked something about us.

Physical punishments included grueling sessions of extra PT, jack-knives and star jumps, crawling on all fours on gravel paths until we bled from scuffed knees and palms, and holding convoluted positions for an unbearably long time. The corporal punishments that they were allowed to administer included brutal practices such as "putting"—where they whacked our backsides with hockey sticks or cricket bats, often using the edge to inflict even more pain. All those punishments were carried out in the absence of teachers, allowing prefects to be as violent as they wished.

Their power and our oppression were multiplied by the tradition of "fagging," a practice that had also been adopted from elite British schools. Under that system, boys in junior grades worked as house slaves for the seniors by attending to every task put before them: making their beds, shining their shoes, lugging pails of hot water for their baths, even massaging them if required. So, from our perspective as juniors, the school administration seemed to have given the prefects life-and-death power over us, to manhandle and punish us as they pleased.

Inevitably, that scenario made abuses a certainty. The prefects were strapping, hirsute young men of sixteen to eighteen compared to the diminutive boys aged ten or eleven who had not even begun

the growth spurts of male adolescence. They were, however, still im-
mature, and their newfound sense of power over others often went to
their heads.

Endemic bullying was one consequence. The perpetrators included
not just the usual minority of cruel and psychopathic boys but also a
sizable number of innately decent ones whose sense of empathy and
of right and wrong went awry because of the savage atmosphere and
often from being victimized themselves.

The novelist Vikram Seth, a decade my senior at Doon, said during
a Founder's Day address at the school in 1992, years after he graduated, "For years after I left, I thought of school as a kind of jungle, and
looked back on it with a shudder. . . . I was teased and bullied by my
classmates and my seniors because of my interest in studies and reading, because of my lack of interest at that time in games, because of my
unwillingness to join gangs and groups."

The bullying regularly escalated to terrifying extremes. At that
young age, I was unable to comprehend the nature of these predations, and thought of them as bullying, though they were something
else altogether.

❖

One of my sharpest memories is of an afternoon in the summer months
of my third year at school. A prefect in my residential house had developed an inexplicable hatred for a roommate of mine, an awkward,
harmless boy. The prefect was a powerful young man, his face marked
by volcanic clumps of acne and a perennially enraged gaze. He started
persecuting my hapless roommate by subjecting him to unending punishments through the day, interspersed with blows and kicks.

One afternoon, a few weeks into this persecution, my roommate
had become so withdrawn and anxious that he looked visibly ill. The
four of us who shared the room with him were worried to see him like
that, but our awareness of being helpless ourselves kept us from trying

to comfort him. We knew, without having to ask, that matters with his persecutor had taken a turn for the worse. We were all half asleep in the summer heat when the prefect entered our room, yelling at us to get up, which the five of us did with alacrity, our hearts pounding.

He slapped our roommate hard across his face, then told him to remove his shorts and underwear and bend over his bed. Weeping, our roommate followed his orders. Then his persecutor yelled at us to take one of the long bamboo poles used to hold up the mosquito nets and push it up our roommate's rectum.

We were stunned. By now we had learned to obey the prefects un-questioningly. But we still retained enough sense of what was right and wrong from our homes to know that this was going too far. We hesi-tated. The prefect punched and slapped several of us, painfully hard.

With no choice but to obey, we all gripped the bamboo pole and placed its fist-thick end against our roommate's anus. He was weeping uncontrollably. We held the bamboo there, not applying any pressure.

The prefect hit us again, more violently this time. Terrified, we pushed the bamboo lightly. We were hit some more. The bamboo's gnarled end went in a bit. Our roommate screamed.

Afterward, we helped our roommate dress. None of us said a word. We were all too terrified to discuss whether we should collec-tively complain to our housemaster.

Astonishingly, none of us ever discussed that atrocity in our remain-ing years together at Doon. And that was one key reason why abuse continued to flourish there through the decades: both the victims and the witnesses learned to hide it behind silence, suppressing any knowl-edge or memory of the brutal things we underwent or witnessed.

✤

Sexual abuse flourished at Doon.

As a pretty boy, I became a favored target of this abuse. Nothing in my short life had prepared me for dealing with the terror I felt or the shock at realizing that desire—the glorious thing I had instinctively responded to in Barbara Cartland romances—could take on so vile a form.

In my second year at Doon, a huge prefect named Nutty began tormenting me. He had looked at me with unsettling intensity ever since I had joined school, but now that he was in the seniormost batch, he felt emboldened to act as he wished. Nutty was notoriously crazy, hence his nickname. Even his classmates gave him a wide berth.

Though I did my utmost to avoid him, there was no escaping in the second half of the day, after classes ended and we returned to our common residential house. Unfailingly, several nights a week, instead of studying after dinner like my other classmates, I would do an unending series of somersaults on Nutty's orders.

One after another, I did the somersaults virtually in the same spot of a study room I shared with a dozen other students, as there was just enough space for me to do two somersaults before I banged into the wall or furniture. Nutty stood right by me, staring down with a strange mix of lust and hatred writ large on his face.

Each time I paused out of exhaustion, half hoping that he'd relent, he yelled, "Who told you to stop, you pansy!" "He's insane," I'd tell myself angrily, and return to the somersaults, even though my head was burning from forehead to nape from chafing against the stone floor.

No one interceded. My classmates kept their eyes studiously trained on their homework, fearing that they would otherwise be made to share my predicament. The seniormost prefects charged with running our house would sometimes drop by to look at me somersaulting, crack a joke or two with Nutty, and then continue on their way. They did not intervene even when Nutty, a star hockey player, "putted" me repeatedly with all his strength—transferring his frustrated lust into agonizing blows of the hockey stick on my upturned buttocks. I never really expected any of the other prefects to intervene, as some of them occasionally partnered with Nutty in abusing me. They would together corner a terrified civet—a catlike animal often found on Doon's verdant grounds—in one of the study rooms and begin beating it to a pulp with hockey sticks and cricket bats, stopping only to fondle and slap me around as I angrily tried to stop them from killing the hapless beast.

Every so often, Nutty would make an offer: if I'd do just one naked somersault in the privacy of his dressing room, he'd stop punishing me. I asked Bharat, whose watchful presence had kept me from being subjected to even worse treatment, if I should comply with his wishes. But he yelled at me, his anxiety evident, that Nutty would rape me if he got such a chance. So I kept silent whenever my tormentor made his offer.

One night about a year later, I was sleeping in a long dormitory that I shared with about a dozen others. My bed was in a corner, by one of the windows. Gray-white mosquito nets covered each of the beds.

Suddenly I woke to find that I was lying on my back and somebody's hand was on my groin. Another hand was holding up the mosquito netting. There was a large face pressed against the netting, staring down at me. Through the netting, the face seemed to be a featureless apparition, something from a horror movie.

I shut my eyes quickly. I wanted to scream for help, but I was frozen with terror.

The hand fondled me, moving from my penis to my testicles and then toward my backside. Even as the hand continued to fondle me, I just lay there with my eyes shut in dread.

The boy in the bed on my left turned and muttered. The hand lifted off my groin, and I felt the netting fall. Lying there with my pajamas pulled down, I began to cry. I even peed, unable to control myself.

The lights came on. There was chaos. Someone said, "It's Dube. Let's call his brother."

Bharat came from his nearby room with two of his friends. I was still sobbing, eyes shut, lying where I was in a pool of pee. Comforting me, he led me to the bathroom to wash up.

When we got back to my dorm minutes later, Bharat was in a towering rage. He yelled, telling my roommates to get out of their beds, asking each of them if he had seen anyone enter the dormitory. Bharat struck one of my hapless peers who couldn't force himself awake at that early hour.

The next morning, Bharat took me to our housemaster, a genial man with an obedient Labrador. He sat behind his large desk in the study attached to his house. Bharat and I told him about the events from the evening before. I could sense that the housemaster was irritated. At some point, my fear from the night gripped me afresh and I started crying. The housemaster brusquely told me to stop crying. "These things happen," he said. "You need to become tougher."

⟡

The only reason I escaped even worse sexual assaults in my most vulnerable years was that Bharat was such a strapping jock that even boys several years older were reluctant to take him on if they went too far with harassing me. Even though Bharat and I had never explicitly discussed the matter, I knew he would fight anyone who tried to rape me, though he was helpless to protect me from being felt up or threatened, as those abuses were too ubiquitous to be challenged.

But the school administration played no discernible role in protecting me in those early years. Later, after Bharat graduated, I was protected to some degree by the mere fact that I was somewhat larger in size by then—I had attained the age of fourteen—and because I had gained a reputation of being a ferocious fighter if pushed.

Nonetheless, though the intensity waned over the years, I continued to face sexual abuse and assault until my final year at Doon. I came to think of it as an unavoidable part of life there, to be somehow taken in my stride. Even so, every incident was inevitably traumatic— whether it was the lewd comments and leering by the occasional gang of students or the nerve-racking experience of being cornered by particularly aggressive seniors who would feel me up and try to make me touch their penises, shoving me around and threatening to punish me for refusing.

I knew that many boys fared far worse than I, in great part because they did not have a protective elder brother as I did in Bharat. It was not just the markedly "pretty" ones. Virtually every prepubescent boy was androgynous and hairless, and consequently even those who later grew into masculine hulks often faced sexual abuse in their junior years.

But so overpowering was the atmosphere of fear and so complete the lack of redressal mechanisms that even though both physical and sexual abuse were widespread and flagrant, I can recall only three boys being even temporarily expelled for such atrocities in all my years there. Almost without exception, none of the victims, myself included, ever spoke of our traumas to even our friends or siblings. It was even rarer to turn to teachers, as the school environment valorized a boyish code of courage in which "sneaking" to teachers was the most unforgivable act. And, like victims of abuse universally, in our shame and self-doubt we blamed ourselves rather than the perpetrators, certain that we had been singled out for punishment for our own weaknesses and flaws.

In my worst years in school, I frequently had suicidal thoughts; killing myself seemed the only escape possible from this constant hell. Years later, I recognized that desperate wish in Vikram Seth's Founder's Day speech, when he said, "I had a terrible feeling of loneliness and isolation during my six years here. Sometimes at lights out I wished I would never wake up to hear the chhota hazri bell."

❖

Despite the continuing abuse, I found some kind of unhappy equilibrium by my middle years at Doon. A key element was to suspend thinking about what I was going through. I realized later that it was a common adaptive mechanism among us boys when faced with that bizarre world of regimentation and fear.

One of my favorite haunts was the swimming pool; I was happy every second of my time in the water, doing backstroke lengths effortlessly and incessantly, carving out an impenetrable cocoon. Another refuge was the library, where I pored over a vast number of the books and magazines over the years, investigating everything from atlases to bound back issues of *Life* and *Time* magazines. I took solitary walks around the sylvan campus, which had once been part of the colonial Forest Research Institute. My childhood habit of daydreaming about safe refuges inhabited by protective animals continued, providing me with an escapist sanctuary.

I also lost myself in songs about love and passion, which I listened to on a boxy cassette player, often breaking rules to climb up to the roof of my residential building so that I could listen in privacy. I loved Joan Baez, Neil Diamond, and Janis Ian, but the British diva Shirley Bassey was my obsession. Every lovelorn song of hers—from "I (Who Have Nothing)" to "Feelings"—seemed to echo my own deep yearning for romantic love.

I was too troubled to shine academically, barring in English and the social sciences, for which I had a natural aptitude. Nonetheless, to my surprise (because by now I had a deadeningly poor opinion of myself), I managed to pull in first-class grades. I was also too awkward among other boys to do well in team sports, but as I instinctively enjoyed exercise, I went riding at the nearby stables and was a star swimmer, eventually captaining the school swimming team.

In my later years, I was also sustained by close friendships. Those had been impossible to forge when we were juniors because the embattled terror most of us lived in aborted the potential for making real connections to others.

Invariably, my friends were also outcasts of one sort or another—for being bookish or artistic, for being frail, for being bad at sports, or simply for being too independent-minded to fit in. My three dearest friends, Gautam, Nimis, and Rahul, proved to be the handful who, like me, still actively sought out affection and close emotional connections. Those qualities had no place at Doon, where almost as if by osmosis we had rapidly learned that being affectionate was a despised girly trait. Our obvious need to be with one another set apart our friendships from the awkward jousting camaraderie of the other boys. We sat next to one another at meals, hung out at the end of the playing fields farthest from the action, defended one another as best we could from bullies, and went off together on midterm expeditions. During our long summer breaks, I unfailingly visited them in Bombay, which they all happened to be from.

With those friends, I felt a deep, almost instinctual bond, similar to my ties to my brothers. This closeness was practically a miracle. We all knew—sometimes just from the way we were looked at, even when there was no active jeering—that others sneered at the closeness of our bonds and any affection we displayed in public. Inevitably, that had a chilling effect on us. It was only away from school—on midterms or in the summer holidays—that we unreservedly expressed our affection toward one another. Then Gautam and I, who were especially close, would sleep every night cuddled like puppies in a shared sleeping bag or bed.

Yet in all our years in school none of us ever spoke to the others of our innermost thoughts—about what we prayed for, dreamed of, fantasized about, or feared most—the intimate disclosures that would be the lifeblood of my closest adult friendships. We were yet to develop into our full, independent personalities, where we would cease to be essentially our parents' children and become ourselves by the conscious choices that would come to define us as individuals. So in a real sense, we didn't *know* each other. Yet our friendships not only became singularly deep while in school but also proved to endure over our lifetimes. It was almost as if instinct had unerringly led us to find our soul mates.

❖

To avoid attracting trouble, I tried to keep a low profile. I gave seniors and my more thuggish peers as wide a berth as possible. But my efforts to be left alone were never successful. Not only could I not escape the unwanted sexual attention of seniors, but my feminine mannerisms made me a constant target.

The tenor of the mocking was markedly different from that of La Martinière. There, my tougher fellow students had told me clearly that I needed to behave like a boy, not a girl. At Doon, I was given the confusing message that I should be a boy even though many of my critics secretly wished me to remain girly.

As at La Martinière, the animosity against my femininity seemed to surface only when several boys were together, as if ignited by some kind of atavistic pack mentality.

One of my indelible memories of Doon is of an afternoon when I was fifteen or so. I'm in the changing room attached to our dorm with a group of my classmates. They are coaching me on how to be a man.

"Come on, Dube, you can walk without swaying your hips!" says one of my classmates.

"Try it like this . . . ," says another. "Keep your spine stiff. And move your arms like this . . ."

I walk the length of the changing room again. All eyes are on me. It's still girlish, they tell me. I try it again. And again. And again.

I still fall short of the masculine ideal, they tell me. Each has advice on how I can correct the way I walk, talk, sit, stand, behave. Nonetheless, they are all amiable. We have become friends of sorts and I'm a willing participant, even though I'm aware of the undercurrent of scorn in their tones. Over the years of being ostracized, I have lost some portion of my will to fight back. I now envy their camaraderie and long to share in it, even though it seems composed only of inane or weird things, including endless arguments over sporting competitions and a painful game called *thols* that has them bashing each other in the testicles.

"Dube, you should learn about Test cricket scores," one of them says. "Then we'll have something to talk about."

I agree.

We go off for afternoon tea. For once, to my elation, I'm included in their gang.

Ironically, it was at Doon that I first experienced intense, wondrous romances. They were the high point of my years there, hinting that the environment could have been a natural paradise for me if it had somehow been shorn of the abuse and violence.

My first romance began when I was twelve—ironically, in the same year as my sexual harassment by Nutty. I did not associate one with the other. While one was my first experience of mutual romantic love, the other was about violence—even hatred. Though both were driven by desire, they had nothing else in common.

That first love was a jock in my class, with sinewy muscles, a wide grin, and a thatch of silky hair. His relentless joking around and playing to the gallery hid an enormously affectionate nature. We'd sit next to each other in class so that we could secretly keep our legs pressed against each other's. During movie nights, in the dark of the crowded auditorium, our embrace was so tight—our legs entwined, his lips pressed to my neck, his arm encircling me—that we were almost sitting one on the other. We disguised our erotic intentions by pretending to tickle each other under our shirts. Eventually, the tickling would give way to lingering caresses on the chest, nipples, stomach, and back, expanses of my body that suddenly came alive with an almost unbearable sensitivity. In the Rose Bowl, a sprawling outdoor auditorium that allowed for great privacy during evening performances, we'd take turns resting our head on each other's lap. When I did so, I could feel the burning heat of his large penis through the flimsy fabric of his cotton *kurta-pajama*.

Every day, I could smell him on myself long after we parted at dinner, forced to return to our separate residential houses. He smelled clean, of Liril soap and sometimes of Old Spice cologne. I'd inhale his smell deeply and unfailingly feel comforted.

Though we were mad about each other for two years, we didn't go beyond kissing and caressing each other. He often tried to. I knew that he had had sex with other boys—he had the skillful assurance of the experienced in the way he kissed, caressed my buttocks, or tried to undo my pajamas. But at the brink, I always pulled myself back from acting on my desire. That, quite obviously, exasperated him.

After that first relationship faded out, I had several strong mutual attractions, all of them long-lasting and emotionally rich, too. They were with pleasant, good-hearted boys of my age or at most one grade senior or junior to me.

However, it was in my last years at school that the great romance of my youth finally happened. It was of such all-consuming intensity that I was to remember it all through my life.

That boy was idolized as much for his sportsmanship as his movie-star looks and physique. Though we had known each other for years, our mutual attraction sparked one summer evening. It was half an hour before dinner, when the sky was still bright. He walked over to where I was chatting with a friend at the corner of the main playing field, looking at me so intently—as if he had just recognized something about me—that my sentence trailed off.

Within a few days, our attraction turned into lovesick obsession. He meandered slowly past my classroom several times a day just to catch a glimpse of me, his eyes intently locking on mine. I began to spend too much time with my eyes on the corridor, waiting for him to appear. My studies suffered.

The morning assembly gave us precious time to be together. He would stand behind me in the choir section, our bodies pressed so tightly against each other's that we could hear the other's heart hammering.

After sports hours, I'd sit in his private study with him, listening to *Goodbye Yellow Brick Road* on his cassette player. We'd just stare at each other full of desire, rooted to our chairs and unable to make a move. In its entire span of two years, our relationship remained essentially a wordless one, everything expressed through looks and secret touch.

Inevitably, many of his classmates knew about our romance. To tease us, they'd call me across to his table in the dining hall. "Dube, are you his? Do you love each other? Why don't you love me instead? Come on, aren't I handsomer? Okay, now sit on his lap. Listen to me, do it!"

He never responded to their banter, but through it he'd smile at me in a steady, protective way that affirmed our feelings for each other. So, far from being an embarrassment, those episodes left me elated.

With the great love of mine, if he had pushed me even a little bit more, I would have had sex with him. We came close to it on several occasions. But my most cherished memory of that boy's character was the fact that he held back out of some kind of loving concern for me.

One night, to my surprise, he called me out of my study and began to pace awkwardly up and down the length of the adjacent playing field. I walked by his side, filled with foreboding at his silence, fearing that he wanted to break up our relationship. Then, abruptly, he said, "I don't want to spoil anything about you."

I was flooded with relief. I knew he was referring to my being a virgin. Despite being vilified as a "lender," everyone close to me knew that I'd not had sex with anyone in all those years, and the label had been attached to me by frustrated seniors bent on coercing me into sex.

But I ached so much to make love to him that I embarrassed myself by blurting out with transparent eagerness, "What if I want to be spoiled? What if I don't care?"

He stopped and turned to look directly at me. I was elated by the emotions I could see on his face—no different from what I felt for him, the overpowering, almost painful mix of physical desire and appreciation for the qualities we saw in each other. But even though I had given him the go-ahead and the perpetual awkwardness between us diminished greatly, we never had sex.

❖

There was nothing singular about my romances. In a boarding school with five hundred boys speeding through adolescence into manhood, they were inevitable, and very little effort, if any, was made to hide them from others.

In our common rooms, boys would pair off romantically to the Eagles' "One of These Nights" or Donna Summer's "Love to Love You Baby," holding each other around the waist or shoulders in transparent attraction. We routinely teased one another about the objects of our desire. No one insisted that he wasn't attracted to some boy or another.

How could we not desire one another? We were in the throes of becoming full-fledged sexual beings. Our physiological sexual pressures were so intense that even masturbating several times a day provided us only momentary relief. Not only was it a world without girls, but virtually every one of us was attractive—our bodies lean from exercise and good food, shorts scrunched around strong thighs, bulging crotches and muscular buttocks. How could the campus not course with desire?

And because many of us had never stopped aching for affection to fill the void of being away from our parents and home, our desire was often combined with emotional need, making those our first earth-shattering experiences of romantic love.

As in my case, the romances didn't always, or even usually, lead to sex. Doon's notoriety as a hothouse of homosexual love was exaggerated. (When AIDS hit India in the late 1980s, nearly a decade after I had graduated from Doon, a popular joke had it that the acronym stood for "Acquired In Doon School.")

Beyond the minor perils of jealousy, unrequited desire, and even battered hearts, these romances could do us good. Those experiences of eros were probably the only aspect of Doon that advanced our capacity for love and tenderness.

⊹

Despite Doon's homosocial environment, the school's ethos was rigidly heterosexual. There was no hint of homosexual desire in the novels and poems assigned to us in literature classes—everything was about women and men, whether as star-crossed lovers or as married couples. There was not even any mention in our biology textbooks about homosexual behavior among animals.

Given this institutionalized stress on heterosexuality, it was no surprise that our schoolboy views on same-sex desire were rife with contradiction. Thus, despite the ubiquity of romance and sex between us boys, the unspoken construct that governed our thinking was that once we left Doon we'd be attracted to women, marry, and then send our sons back to our alma mater.

Our views were also shot through with homophobia and misogyny, both stemming from the notion that anything feminine was inferior, even contemptible. There was the despised slur of "lender" for boys who gave blow jobs or were fucked, condemning them for playing the "passive" role that a woman was assumed to take in sexual intercourse. In contrast, no shame was attached to being the penetrative partner, or the "taker," seen as a masculine boy simply satisfying his sexual needs through a quasi-heterosexual act of penetration.

Strikingly, the harshly homophobic views were largely voiced by the abusers who forced themselves on other boys instead of having consensual relationships. In contrast, the students who didn't hide their romantic feelings for other boys rarely voiced homophobia or did so in only a halfhearted way, as if to keep up appearances. Nonetheless, the upshot was that homophobia dominated our views about homosexuality, even for many of us who had strong romantic feelings for other boys.

The homophobia solidified as we graduated from school. The prejudice that same-sex desire was disgraceful had been so deeply internalized by everyone that, with rare exceptions, there was now a blanket denial of the attraction and feelings they had previously held for their classmates. The denial was so extreme that graduates from Doon—or similar boys-only schools—rarely behaved any better or more understandingly toward gay men and lesbians later in life. It was as if we

had collectively vowed to keep our past strictly secret, an unmention-
able, collective folly of boyhood.

✤

About a year into my first romance, at age thirteen and in seventh class,
I wrote a short story for our weekly English essay assignment about
two boys falling in love with each other. The setting was not a boarding school but a neighborhood more European than Indian, with the
boys living next to each other in row houses. One was handsome, the
other more femininely beautiful. Both were loving and decent. The two
characters also remained staunchly virginal despite their desire for each
other.

Sadly, a few years into the boys' deepening love for each other, one
set of parents decided to move away, turning an uncomprehending ear
to the boys' protests that they could not bear to be separated. The boys
were heartbroken.

I remember I left the future of their relationship unstated, giving
no hint whether the boys met or renewed their relationship later in
life. The story had no Barbara Cartland–style happily-ever-after finale.
I may have somehow concluded, despite my inexperience of life, that
same-sex love was a doomed venture, certain to end in tragedy, or
perhaps my belief in happy endings had cracked from being too close
a witness to the dissolving of my parents' marriage.

While I was writing the story, my words flowed out effortlessly
onto the ruled pages of the essay book. But upon completing it,
I told myself that I should tear it up, feeling that I was crossing
a forbidden line. By writing it, I was breaking with all that I had
imbibed—from books, lyrics, movies, everything and everyone—
that love was always between men and women, between boys and
girls. Yet, in the impulsiveness of my youth, I handed in the essay to
Krishna Kumar, a young teacher who was idolized in the few years
he taught at Doon.

A few days later, I was gripped afresh with trepidation as Kumar began returning our essays to us, calling out the grades we had scored and, in his characteristically acerbic manner, adding a comment or two of stinging criticism or (far more rarely) faint praise. Though I was sitting in the front row of the class, my turn never seemed to come. I took that as proof that I had erred badly in submitting the essay. I burned with apprehension at the prospect of Kumar mocking me in front of all my classmates over that freakish story.

Kumar had just two or three essay books left when he turned to hand me my book, announcing "Seven on ten! That's the highest I've ever given anyone. Well done!"

Weak with relief, I barely registered my classmates calling out "Wow! Well done, Dube!"

I spent that class in a haze of delight. As I was leaving class, Kumar called me back to say that he wanted to publish my story in the *Doon School Weekly*, a campus paper largely featuring works by students. I was overjoyed. It would be my first article in the *Weekly*, an honor at that young age.

A few days later, Kumar asked me to stay after class and, looking distinctly awkward for once, told me that the teachers overseeing the *Weekly* had decided against running the essay. He didn't elaborate. I didn't have the gumption to ask why or even express my disappointment, though my dejection was no doubt evident.

In my remaining years at school, I went on to have several articles published in the *Weekly*. Even so, I never quite forgot that rejected short story of gay love. I felt it surpassed all my published articles in authenticity of personal feeling. It was only later in life that I realized what the story actually was: the first public statement of my orientation, despite its fictional form.

Two decades after I graduated from Doon, Krishna Kumar and I became close friends in New York City. When I asked him about the essay and why the *Weekly* had turned it down, I was surprised that he remembered it readily. Kumar told me that he had been impressed with how it handled a difficult matter and even more by my courage in submitting it. He had shared it with the teachers on the *Weekly*'s editorial staff, and he had no doubt that although it had opened their eyes, they had probably justified their decision to not publish it on the grounds that it would hurt the sensibilities of parents as well as the younger children. And so I came to learn that I had been a young schoolboy when I first suffered censorship for daring to mention homosexual love.

❖

Nowhere in the India of this time, either in my years at Doon or later, during a year of college at Delhi's elite St. Stephen's College, was there anything to help a young man or woman deal with his or her homosexuality. There were no openly gay men or women to validate the way I felt or for me to emulate or turn to for advice and help. Indian newspapers and magazines were silent on the subject of homosexuality, which did not feature even in popular "agony aunt" columns. So were films and television. In that pre-internet age, there was no way for me to learn about the nascent movements for gay rights in the United States and other industrialized countries.

The nullifying silence was punctuated only by incidents that revealed a widespread, intense hatred of homosexuals. When out with my parents, whether in Calcutta or Delhi, I found that the conversation often turned to prominent men who were rumored to be homosexual: the unmarried editor of a Calcutta newspaper, an unmarried business magnate who reputedly had a young male lover on his staff, and a former *nawab* in Delhi who was married and had children. I don't recall a single mention of women rumored to be lesbian; the conversations were all about men. Those men were spoken about in disparaging, hate-filled tones that I never heard in any other context, even when talking about the most vile politician or corporate swindler. Inevitably, someone would call them pansies, the insult triggering unpleasant memories of being taunted at Doon. Someone would pronounce that they should be sent off to England or Pakistan, as homosexuality was a vice peculiar to English and Muslim men.

Far from contesting those comments, everyone seemed to be whole-heartedly amused. I shrank at seeing that my father was often an active participant in those discussions, adding prejudiced comments about the men, even though he knew several of them well. I was too unsure of myself then to dwell on the peculiarity that the class of Indians who were most sexually liberated—what with the striptease shows, affairs, and divorces—reviled just one kind of sexuality so intensely, and that, too, a sexuality that was invisible in that era, in which there was not even a single avowed homosexual in the country. Those repeated displays of homophobia convinced me that I would never get succor from anyone, not even my parents, if they discovered I was homosexual. So I kept my dark secret to myself, a subterranean source of anguish.

My despair might eventually have mounted into some kind of breakdown, but I was spared that predicament because of my father's loving attentiveness.

He and I had become steadily closer since my penultimate year at Doon. I never forgot the exact moment that the toxic hatred I harbored toward him as a soldier for my mother's side of their marital battle dissolved. Sick with hepatitis A from a schoolwide epidemic, I had been transferred from the school infirmary to my parents' Delhi home and woke at a predawn hour to find my father seated beside my bed in the darkness, caressing my head, in the exact spot where he had been when I had fallen asleep hours earlier. He had spent the entire night watching over me. I remember that my first feeling was not joy but shame and embarrassment at being the object of such love. In that moment of self-awareness, my hatred fell away forever.

Once I graduated from school, sensing that I was deeply troubled, my father urged me to move to the United States for college, ideally close to Bharat, who was an undergraduate at Harvard. He said the new setting would do me good. He looked intently at me while saying that, obviously hoping that the overture would give me the confidence to open up to him. I looked away evasively; uppermost in my mind was the terror that he would despise and disown me if he came to know the truth.

THREE

IN AMERICA

Heeding my father's suggestion, after three semesters at St. Stephen's College I headed to Tufts University in suburban Boston, joining there as a second-semester sophomore. It was January 1982, two years into Ronald Reagan's first term as US president. I was twenty years old and, for the first time in my life, anonymous. No one on the campus knew a thing about the secrets I carried from my past. Even Bharat, at Harvard, was a twenty-minute bus ride away. It was a completely new start.

At St. Stephen's, which was coed and hence a less warped place than the boys-only worlds of Doon and La Martinière, my spirits had been rejuvenated by the deep, caring friendships I had made with several women and by rediscovering a prankish side to my personality that had irritated my teachers but won me popularity with other students. But now I embraced the atomistic Tufts environment: the single-minded focus on studies, solitary hours alone in the library, and the acute competition at swimming team practice. Despite intense pangs of loneliness, I found peace in the silent library stacks and the ethereal snow-blanketed campus. In every way, it was the opposite of India—and that difference was exactly what I needed at that point.

In those first months, I had little time to think about my homosexuality, which had become a tortured preoccupation for me in Delhi. It was a blessed relief not to be endlessly burdened with those dark thoughts, to instead be engrossed in constructive things. I began to hope that my anxieties had been magically solved or had faded into irrelevance now that I had reached the liberal West. I also harbored a Mills & Boon–style fantasy that an American hunk—a Warren Beatty look-alike or one of my sexy swim-team mates—would be enthralled by my exotic beauty and that we would live happily ever after.

But those proved to be fantastical hopes. The worries and self-loathing about my sexuality reemerged once I settled down— and they were magnified by soon discovering that in the United States the hatred for homosexuality was many magnitudes greater than in India.

At the sprawling university library, praying with a pounding heart that no student I knew should chance upon me, I began to read the occasional articles in the *New York Times* and *Boston Globe* about homosexual issues. I would hold the newspaper so that people sitting nearby could not see what I was reading, or I would pretend to be engrossed in an unrelated article on a facing page. It was in this illicit, conflicted way that I first came to read and learn about homosexuality and thus my homosexual self, the self of my intense yearnings, as well as of self-loathing and despair.

So absolute was my lack of theoretical knowledge of the subject that everything I read came as a revelation. Despite having studied at India's leading school and college, I had never come across any scientific information on homosexuality, not even in biology textbooks. The sum total of my reading had been the mild allusions in Jacqueline Susann's books, a handful of sexual passages in Harold Robbins's potboilers, and Gore Vidal's oddball *Myra Breckinridge*.

The articles that I read most attentively, almost greedily, were those reporting on the roots of individual sexual orientation, a matter of obvious personal relevance. I knew nothing at all about it. Indeed, until I read those articles, I had had no way of knowing that the study of sexuality, including same-sex attraction, was an established field of research. As it happened, the early 1980s saw major advances in research on sexual orientation, led not just by mental health specialists but also by a diverse range of sex therapists and researchers, and I was faced with a bewildering onslaught of information to digest. Old, crude notions were giving way to a more sensible understanding among scholars and specialists. The research had begun to show that sexual orientation, including homosexuality, had complex origins that included genetics and hormones as well as psychological dynamics within the family and society.

I felt enormous relief at seeing that homosexual attraction was discussed in reasoned, matter-of-fact terms, as part of a scientific effort to understand a complex human issue. I also remember my relief at realizing from these articles that the consensus among American psychotherapists and sexuality researchers was that same-sex attraction was not an abnormality or a mental illness. That had been one of my strongest dreads—that my homosexual desires meant I was crazy or deviant. I read that nearly a decade earlier, in 1973, the American Psychiatric Association had removed homosexuality from its list of mental disorders. I was equally relieved to find that most American mental health experts now felt that the goal of therapy should not be to convert homosexuals to heterosexuality but to help them become happier with their orientation.

But my main recollection of these readings is that, with a few exceptions, they were grim, both in subject matter and tenor. I read with disbelief numerous articles about the hate and persecution faced by gay Americans. Everything I had absorbed in my teens from books, from James Bond movies and *The Graduate*, and not just the purring of Donna Summer and Barry White but even Joan Baez's "Love Song to a Stranger" and Bob Dylan's "Love Is Just a Four-Letter Word," had made me imagine that Westerners had wonderfully free sex lives, unburdened by shame or censure, let alone persecution by their police and governments.

Prominent in the news at that time were legal battles over US "sodomy" laws, and that was where I learned that homosexuality remained a serious criminal offense in over half of the fifty American states, including Massachusetts. Astonishingly, men were being arrested even in the privacy of their homes for having sex with their boyfriends or other men. (It was to be several years more before I knew for a fact that a similar law criminalized homosexuality in India, with equally harsh punishments, and that, like the US laws, it was a legacy of British colonial rule.)

Other articles reported that homosexual men and women lived in terror of being thrown out of their jobs and homes and being socially destroyed if their sexual orientation was discovered. They were also disproportionately the targets of violence—often what the young, bored, and drunk male perpetrators thought of as "recreational" violence—ranging from being beaten, assaulted with a weapon, spat on, and chased to having objects thrown at them. Even in cases involving extreme violence and murder, US courts were unconscionably biased against gays, with judges often accepting killers' pleas that their violence had been spontaneously triggered by their revulsion against homosexuality.

I read that US immigration law explicitly barred "suspected or self-declared" foreign homosexuals from entering the country because they were "afflicted with sexual deviation." That meant that I would be unable to immigrate if my sexual orientation were discovered, and I would have to return to India. In the naiveté of a young man from a distant developing country, I had assumed that the United States—as a rich Western democracy and beacon of freedom—would surely have long since guaranteed equality for every citizen, even those who were homosexual.

Another set of disturbing articles described a mysterious killing disease among homosexual men that had been discovered in the summer of 1981, just six months before I had arrived in the United States.

The facts were still trickling in. Doctors in Los Angeles, San Francisco, and New York City—and subsequently elsewhere—were finding that young and middle-aged homosexual men, ranging from twenty-five to forty-five years of age, were developing harrowingly aggressive forms of diseases that affected only people whose immune systems had been devastated, including extremely rare cancers, pneumonias, and parasitic conditions. Many of them died rapidly, failing to respond to even the most powerful drugs.

As early as mid-1982, experts feared that this deadly disease had reached epidemic proportions among America's homosexual men, with tens of thousands thought to be infected and certain to develop life-threatening ailments in a few years. Fear turned into panic among homosexual men because, at that early point, scientists still didn't know the cause or means of transmission of this never-before-seen disease. Theories abounded—some thought that the disease was caused by "poppers" and other inhaled party drugs, while others opined that it could be transmitted by casual contact or by mosquito bites, or could spread through the air like the flu or tuberculosis. It was as late as September 1983 before the US Centers for Disease Control and Prevention concluded that the cause of the disorder was an infectious agent that was spread not through air, water, food, or casual contact but through sexual intercourse (whether homosexual or heterosexual), as well as by exposure to contaminated needles and blood.

No one even knew what to call the terrifying new disease. Some derisively called it "the gay plague." Others called it "gay cancer." Health experts first called it GRID, for "gay-related immune deficiency." In late 1982, over a year after the first scientific reports describing the condition, the disorder was given the name by which it is now known: acquired immune deficiency syndrome, or AIDS. Whatever its name, the stigma against homosexual men in the West worsened because of their association with this frightening, runaway epidemic.

Those bleak articles made me realize how unwelcoming the Tufts campus was to gay students. Rather like St. Stephen's back in Delhi, the college felt entirely heterosexual, a universe of men and women attracted only to the opposite sex. That reality was more evident here because amorous desire was so visible everywhere in public, as men and women flirted, touched, and kissed unabashedly. In contrast, gay men and women were invisible. Out of the eight thousand students at Tufts, even by the time I graduated in 1984, I knew definitely of just two other gay men and not even one avowedly lesbian woman.

The overwhelming majority of gay students at Tufts in my time, whether American or foreign, did not join the Tufts Lesbian and Gay Community (TLGC), the student-run lesbian and gay group. Though the group had been established several years before I joined Tufts, it was not a visible presence on campus, and in my years there, I did not even know of its existence. Even in the mid-1980s, in their annual group photos, most TLGC members wore bags over their heads to hide their identity.

There were compelling reasons for not revealing one's sexual orientation at Tufts. A year before I joined, homophobic graffiti—"Fags Must Die"—had been spray painted across the Memorial Steps. In the dorms, men and women discovered to be gay were often ostracized. Sensing that, I soon moved to an off-campus apartment, despite the twenty-minute commute by bicycle through a grim neighborhood.

Matters were not helped by the university administration's policies. The TLGC's application for official recognition as a student group—so it could receive funding from the university like other student groups—was rejected year after year. Despite many reported incidents of homophobia on campus, the university neglected to add sexual orientation to its nondiscrimination policy. By not handing out AIDS prevention information, the university failed to help its students protect themselves against AIDS, even though the disease was by then known to be cutting a swath through young gay men, many of whom were infected in their college-going years.

At that time, especially on days when I was feeling low for one reason or another, I would often feel dirty for poring surreptitiously through those news articles, as well as the gay sex ads and personals in the *Village Voice* or the steamy gay romances that I later chanced upon in Harvard Square bookstores. However, I realized later that even that furtive exposure to gay issues aided in my emancipation in a haphazard, piecemeal manner.

The regular mention of homosexuality was profoundly affirmative in itself. The realization that there were countless other men and women facing the same challenges and fears gradually helped break my apprehension that there was no one else in the world with my shameful affliction. That psychological isolation, the invisibility even to each other, was among the most crippling aspects of being gay. A gay psychiatrist had commented, in one of the earliest articles I read, that it was "a miracle" if any homosexual could become a stable and happy individual, since "unlike women and blacks who can at least identify with one another, gays have no one to counteract the negative societal assault on their egos." I was so struck by the insight that I purchased that issue of the *New York Times* from the newsstand, storing it in a suitcase out of risk of discovery.

And at least in the liberal papers that I read, despite the primarily grim context of the articles, I found that the reportage was largely respectful of homosexual men and women. They were portrayed as normal people engaged in the universal search for fulfillment in life, seeking romantic love, family and community, acceptance and self-respect.

The usage of the word "gay" instead of "homosexual" in the *Village Voice* and by gay people themselves reinforced this sense of respect. Both the *New York Times* and the *Boston Globe* used "homosexual," though the individuals they quoted often used "gay." Even in those early days, when my politics were yet to take root, I was intrigued by the word. I didn't know why it had become a synonym for "homosexual men" (it being many years before the internet made information readily available), but I loved the joyous association and also the fact that it left us beguilingly undefined and, consequently, wholly human—rather than defining us reductively in sexual terms, as in "homo*sexual*" or in "*sexual* orientation."

And some of what I read proved inspiring. In the spring of 1982, I read that Wisconsin had outlawed discrimination based on sexual orientation, becoming the first state to do so. I was moved by the courage of Congressman Gerry Studds, a Massachusetts Democrat, who fought back after his homosexuality was revealed in 1983; his constituents reelected him the following year, affirming that his political ability mattered in public office, not his orientation. I read about a handful of other openly gay men and women being elected to public office. There were frequent reports on campaigns by gay and lesbian rights organizations to pressure politicians to get rid of sodomy laws and prevent discrimination in employment, housing, and other aspects of life. Several men arrested under sodomy laws had taken the police to court. Many individuals and groups came to their help—not just gay activists but also elected officials and civic, labor, and religious groups and leaders—because they believed that everyone should be treated justly as a core principle of human rights. I read about the annual "pride" marches in Boston and other major cities. It was a huge affirmation compared to what I had known in India.

❖

While I was dealing excruciatingly slowly with my sexuality, I found I was being rapidly transformed in other ways by being at Tufts and in the United States.

I relished the demanding academics. It would have been difficult for all but truly indifferent students not to be infected by the industrious mood and the celebration of learning, so in contrast to the lassitude of undergraduate studies in India (where barely anyone studied during term, instead cramming madly right before the annual exams). I had done decently in India, apart from my year at St. Stephen's, where, relishing my newfound popularity, I had played the class joker, but here I excelled as a result of my genuine interest in the subjects I was studying as well as the resulting diligence.

I realized that without conscious design on my part I was drawn to learning about injustice and marginalization. I spent my time studying everything from India's political economy and Latin American history to communism and radical politics in developing countries, to the global political economy of hunger. (I soon chose a double major in international relations and literature.)

Those courses helped me make sense of my own situation of exclusion. My reading about homosexuality had already made me realize that I was not entirely alone, that there were scores of men and women who were dealing with the very same anguish as I of their vilified same-sex desires. But the books about poverty, racism, and other kinds of subjugation made me understand that the predicament of gay men and women was no different from that of countless other outcasts.

One of the most moving works I read at the time was Mulk Raj Anand's *Untouchable*. This novel, written in the 1930s, portrayed a day in the life of Bakha, a young Indian man from an "untouchable" caste. Like generations of his ancestors, he had no choice but to follow the caste occupation of cleaning latrines in the village of his birth— these being pit latrines from which feces—lumps of which inevitably spilled onto him—had to be scraped off with a broom and then hauled away in a basket.

The injustice was made even worse by Anand's account of how the better-off reviled Bakha for his work, paid him a pittance, and recoiled from his touch even though all of them depended on him for maintaining hygiene. *Untouchable* depicted realities that persisted even fifty years from the time Anand had written it. I recalled how the men and women employed as "sweepers"—whether in homes, including my own family's, or in public places—were always visibly shrunken from generations of deprivation. Everybody shrank from them as if they carried a fearsome contagious disease—and they themselves avoided touching or even looking at anyone.

I was never to forget the chilling opening lines of Richard Wright's *Native Son*, set in a tiny, dark ghetto room: "A huge black rat squealed and leaped at Bigger's trouser-leg and snagged in his teeth, hanging on." Those first pages of violence set the tone for the rest of the book. The naked anger of Wright's writing was such that it made everything I had ever read so far seem censored. His rage at the dehumanizing racism black Americans faced through their lives also shook me into realizing just how unjust a country even the United States was.

Whatever lingering rose-tinted notions I had about the United States as a superior society were exploded by Howard Zinn's *A People's History of the United States*. Zinn exposed the rapaciousness of the United States' past and present, at home and then abroad as an imperial power: the merciless genocide of Native Americans; the unimaginably brutal chattel slavery of abducted Africans; the unending failure to tackle its domestic burdens of poverty, ill health, racism, violence, and drug use; the reprehensible use of nuclear bombs and chemical weapons in its modern-day wars; the subversion of democracy in independent-minded countries in favor of biddable despots.

What a chasm there was between the glorified notion of America that I had grown up with as a beacon of freedom and liberty and its blood-soaked reality. As it was many years before globalized television news and the internet made viewers intimately familiar with the problems of every part of the world, those of us from developing countries still naively harbored the colonial-era belief, dinned into us by our "Macaulay's Children" education, that the Western world was perfect in every sense while our own societies were congenitally backward and needed to emulate our former colonial masters. It came as an enormous shock to begin to be disabused of those notions—and consequently to begin to understand how completely I had swallowed and internalized that self-serving propaganda.

I had never before read history like Zinn's—accounts based on the views of oppressed women and men, rather than the elite. It was through Zinn's book that I first began to understand that, although human societies are invariably unjust and cruel in their treatment of vast numbers of people, the excluded always fight back and it is the efforts of countless ordinary, wronged people—and the leaders who emerge from their ranks—that overwhelmingly fuel social progress, not the altruism of elites.

And then there was Frances Moore Lappé's *Diet for a Small Planet*. That simply written book jolted me awake to the world's staggering material inequities. More than a billion people went hungry every day, and millions starved outright every year. Lappé showed that the massive scale of global hunger was caused not by laziness on the part of the poor, overpopulation, or even an overall shortage of food but by exploitative inequality both within and between countries. These facts were graphically evident every day at the Tufts campus cafeterias. Not only was there a smorgasbord of food, drink, and desserts—so unlike the unremittingly Spartan fare of Doon and St. Stephen's—but it was invariably left half eaten or discarded by many students.

I had never before seen anything like that wastefulness—and I was appalled by it. Everywhere in India, even in my family's privileged circles, the Gandhian and socialist aspirations that India had begun with at independence still largely inspired people, and greed and waste were scorned. I was stunned, too, to see the plethora of possessions owned by many of my peers at Tufts, from countless clothes to expensive sports cars; no one I knew in India, not even our equivalents of the Rockefellers, spoiled their children like that; the excesses of the maharajas were by now a fading memory. That thoughtless feeling of entitlement and embrace of consumerist excess struck me as a uniquely American trait, as I had not seen it even while vacationing in Europe with my parents' wealthy friends.

Following Lappé's advice about the small steps each of us could take, I turned vegetarian, so as to free up for others the many pounds of grain that would otherwise have gone into producing the meat I would consume. I took part-time jobs, wanting to contribute as much as possible toward paying for my education, rather than letting my parents cover everything. I was suddenly keenly aware that, in this era decades before India's economy boomed, it was a strain for even families like mine to cover the high costs of private American colleges. I was also impressed by the conscientiousness of some of my American peers who juggled studies and part-time jobs while putting themselves through college. I felt that model was inherently more responsible than the custom among well-off families in India and Great Britain, where college-going children were not expected to take part-time work.

In the fall of 1982, I began working two afternoons a week in a small university office that dealt with foreign students, located in the basement of a quaint old house. My responsibilities consisted of sorting and distributing the mass of incoming mail and handling the equally large volume of outgoing mail. I handled the routine work with such enthusiasm—even licking the stamps and labels with my tongue instead of wasting time on using the wet sponge—that the full-time clerical staff began to look at me with some distaste, perhaps because my naive embracing of the work just heightened their awareness of its drudgery. And though I was paid the minimum wage, roughly three dollars per hour, I was thrilled to receive my modest bimonthly checks.

Buoyed by that first experience of the dignity of labor, I decided to spend the winter of 1982 working full-time, rather than flying back to Calcutta for the one-month break as my parents had indulgently urged me to. In addition to Anand's *Untouchable*, I had been reading Mahatma Gandhi's autobiography, *The Story of My Experiments with Truth*. Inspired by the Mahatma's insistence on cleaning toilets himself, I decided to seek work as a janitor. I was hired almost instantly, because very few people wished to work over the Christmas holidays.

I was assigned to cleaning the cavernous main gym, including the showers and toilets. To my shame, my dedication vanished in my very first hours on the job. After scrubbing row after row of stained, dirty toilets, I was nearly overpowered with repulsion—it took all my willpower to keep from quitting the very first day. Early every weekday morning, I forced myself awake in the grim near darkness, reported for work, pulled on thick gloves, and somehow spent the entire day cleaning. Though I worked diligently at mopping and cleaning the sports areas, I cheated with the bathrooms, splashing pails of water over the toilets instead of scrubbing the bowls with the toilet brush as I was duty-bound to do.

Rather than being a period of revelatory personal growth in the tradition of the Mahatma, it turned out to be just a depressing year ending. When the new term began, I hastily refused an offer to stay on as a part-time janitor and left, shamefaced but relieved. I had begun to realize the finite limits to which I could follow my ideals. However sincere my empathy, I was not made of the stuff of Gandhi or his true followers.

✤

It was back in India, when I was home for the long summer breaks, that my engagement with matters of exclusion and injustice set down real roots.

In the summer of 1984, just after graduating from Tufts, I volunteered with a charitable organization, the Lutheran World Service, that worked in Calcutta's shantytowns. I had no practical skills to offer, no knowledge of poverty beyond what I had read in the courses at Tufts, and not even a working grasp of Bengali because of my Anglicized upbringing. But the head of the charity's Calcutta office generously found a task for me, asking me to document and write about its grassroots efforts, explaining that it had been struggling to report on its work.

I began to visit parts of Calcutta that I had not even heard of before: Ultadanga, Khudirampalli, Rajarhat, and beyond. Calcutta, despite its legendary poverty, was actually a refuge for those fleeing even harsher deprivation, and its "squatter" settlements housed countless rural migrants, often from states with even more intense poverty than West Bengal (where poverty rates were falling at record speed because of a pro-poor land reform campaign undertaken by the Marxist government), as well as Bangladeshi refugees, millions of whom had fled during the bloody war of independence a decade back. Around the ubiquitous ponds and canals on the city's outskirts, in areas that still seemed semirural and far from the city's chaos, they had pieced together shacks from mud, broken bricks, and scraps of thatch, plastic, and tarpaulin. It didn't require any expertise to realize that Bengal's ferocious monsoon rains, just two months away, would beat through those skeletal structures.

Inside the huts were bare mud floors, inevitably a paper calendar on one wall, a handful of cheap cooking vessels and an earthen *chula* stove in a corner, a few bedraggled clothes hanging on a nylon line, a stainless-steel trunk for storage. There was no furniture—not even beds. The entire family, often spanning several generations, would spread out on wafer-thin reed mats at night.

There were no bathrooms, so everyone defecated in the open. Drinking water came from a few creaky hand pumps. Everyone bathed in the ponds and canals—though they seemed relatively clean by the standards of Indian cities, they were increasingly contaminated with feces and other pollutants. There were no schools in the vicinity and no municipal services, not even electricity connections. Medical clinics and hospitals were miles away. In that context of utter want, anything that the Lutheran World Service did—whether it was the crèches and schools it built and ran or its adult literacy sessions, basic health programs, and training classes for "cottage" industries—provided a lifeline, possibly even a way to climb out of poverty.

Everything I saw and learned over several weeks of visits to a bewildering number of programs, I turned into a report for the charity organization as well as an article published in Bengal's venerable English-language newspaper *The Statesman*. My article was painfully earnest in its portrayal of the charity's work—which was probably why the subeditors gave it the maudlin title of "Light at Least a Candle." But the staff of the Lutheran World Service was delighted by the public attention it got for their work.

Later that summer, I volunteered at a grassroots organization working in rural Bihar. It had been recommended by the Lutheran World Service, which provided some of its funding. The three-day journey by train, bus, and cycle rickshaw took me from the sooty industrial expanse of Calcutta to the sleepy provincial towns of Patna and Muzaffarpur and then on to villages, which gave way to scattered hamlets, consisting of a few mud huts grouped together.

Eventually I arrived at the Paroo Prakhand Samagra Vikas Pariyojna, which in Hindi literally means "project for the comprehensive development of Paroo." All in all, its premises consisted of a tiny brick office, about a dozen mud-and-thatch huts, and a makeshift acacia hedge circling the compound. As a visitor, I had been allotted an independent hut, consisting of a tiny room furnished with just a *newar* cot. There were no lights or fans, because there was no electricity connection. Water came from communal hand pumps for bathing and drinking. The dry pit toilets were functional and clean, placed near the residential huts. A kitchen housed in one of the larger huts was where the group's dozen staff were served simple vegetarian meals, all of us sitting in rows on the ground.

The atmosphere was consciously that of an ashram, a traditional Hindu hermitage. It reflected the asceticism of the group's founder, a middle-aged American named William Christensen. I knew from the Lutheran World Service that William-ji—as he was known locally, *ji* being an honorific—was a Christian priest from the Marianist order that dedicates itself to working with the poor. But William-ji did not proselytize. For all purposes—barring his looks—he was an Indian villager, fluent in Hindi and the local Maithili dialect, always dressed in a *lungi*, *banyan*, and rubber slippers. The staff, all men, were of diverse faiths, including Hindu, Muslim, and Christian.

I threw myself into the work. Education was one of the pillars of the group's efforts—chosen precisely because the Dalits, the former "untouchables," had for eons been barred by the dominant castes from being educated. (*Dalit*, meaning "oppressed" in Marathi, was adopted by the former "untouchable" castes in the years following India's independence as a self-description expressing pride and assertiveness, much like the term "black" was adopted by African Americans.) Harsh caste strictures also forbade them to own any land, the key source of wealth and productivity in rural India. Because the group could not get public schools to take in the Dalit children—the teachers and students were exclusively from the dominant castes—they established small schools near the Dalit hamlets in the area.

Those were schools in name only—held under shady trees, in a cattle shed, or in a large hut. But they were overflowing with children, from toddlers to teens, grouped together in a mass, as each school had just one teacher. The children were unfailingly attentive, repeating the Hindi alphabet and words that the teacher was writing on the blackboard or singing songs with gusto. When the midmorning meal of *daal*, rice, and bananas was served, they ate it hungrily but even then maintaining the politeness and order that are expected of Indian children.

Dalit families were initially wary of sending their children to the schools, terrified that it would excite the wrath of the dominant-caste landlords. When those fears eased—in great part because of William-ji's mediation with the landlords—the pent-up demand for schooling was so overwhelming that the charity was soon forced to limit enrollment to just one child from each family, typically the eldest girl, in an attempt to correct the pervasive cultural bias against women. It was heartbreaking to see the younger siblings standing wistfully near the schools every morning, sometimes repeating aloud what they could hear the teacher saying. William-ji readily agreed when I asked him if it would be possible to start afternoon classes for the children not going to the day schools. When the afternoon schools opened soon after, the classes were, from the very first day, flooded with eager children. I felt prouder of that development than anything else I had ever achieved in my life.

By dusk, I'd return to the vicinity of the ashram, given the risk of encountering one of the many poisonous snakes in the dark. I'd stop outside to watch the cattle wending their way home without coaxing or herding. I could almost hear my mother exclaiming that the Hindi word for this precise time was so accurate and lovely—*godhuli*, "cow dust," literally the haze of dust kicked up by their hooves.

I returned to Calcutta changed forever by that summer of 1984. My own suffering seemed less random and unfair now that I could see so many other people who had also been wrongfully cast out by society, many of them suffering immeasurably more than I had. The passion I felt for social justice was genuine; it also made me feel that I was being an upright and good person, that I was living up to the very best aspects of the *dharma* my family held dear. That gradually bolstered my nascent feelings of self-respect and self-worth.

I had braced myself for the worst but received, instead, an outpouring of affection. At some point, as my tears subsided, I heard him say how proud he was to have me as a friend, that I was strong and brave to have faced all this on my own. From the tone of his voice alone, there was no doubting his care for me, as well as no doubting that the secret I had revealed to him had not lessened his affection for me.

For the first time ever, we talked about our Doon years. Despite his evident heterosexuality now, he told me about his romances at Doon, ribbing me for having forgone my chance of having sex with our attractive classmates. Toward the end of my stay with him, he, too, disclosed the secrets that had been weighing him down: that in his early years at Doon he had been routinely sexually abused and that he had been beaten viciously during a terrible witch hunt launched by the school's prefects to weed out homosexuals, in which they hypocritically thrashed the young boys they were themselves abusing. Our friendship became immeasurably stronger from that day, cemented by the trust we had placed in each other.

Buoyed by his support, I resolved to confide in Bharat, to whom I remained deeply attached and from whom I had never in my life hidden anything, except my gay identity. Some months later, in the spring of 1983, Bharat developed pneumonia, and I went to Duke University, where he was studying law, to look after him. On the evening I arrived, he had a high fever and looked visibly ill. But I forced myself not to latch onto that as an excuse to delay telling him. We had just turned off the lights in his bedroom—I was sleeping on a sofa bed—when I said I had something important to tell him, something that would explain why I sometimes appeared sad. He sat up in bed and said he had wondered about that.

At that point, I lost every shred of self-control and began to shiver uncontrollably, faced afresh with the terror of being rejected by someone I loved dearly. I began to cry. Bharat, no doubt shocked by that, began to rise painfully out of bed. So I forced myself to say, barely audibly and choked with sobs, "Bharat, I like men, I'm gay." Even at that anguished moment, I felt a twinge of pride that I had identified myself

FOUR

COMING OUT

After about ten months in the United States, I couldn't keep myself from telling the truth to one of my friends from Doon and later St. Stephen's, now studying at the Wharton School in Philadelphia. I was visiting him over the Thanksgiving break and had hoped that the joy of seeing him would ease the dispirited mood that I had been in for several days, my torments intensified by the bleak November skies and the weeklong break from studies. But to my embarrassment—as our friendship had so far always been uncomplicated and fun—my spirits had not lifted.

In early evening, we found ourselves sitting face-to-face in his tiny apartment, him lounging on the sofa bed and me sitting rigidly upright on the chair. He was looking at me expectantly, with an expression of concern that I had not seen before in our decade of friendship. It made me break down. My confession erupted—haphazard and unformed, told through sobs. The only thing I recall is blurting out, at some point, "I like men, I like men."

I'm not sure how long it was before I stopped crying. But it was clear that he had been comforting me for a while before the sound of his voice broke into my consciousness.

as gay and gone beyond the euphemism about "liking men" that I had used with my friend in Philadelphia.

To my utter surprise, Bharat burst out laughing, saying that he had guessed this several years before. And then, obviously to put my mind at ease, he proceeded to tell me about all the pretty boys he had been attracted to while at Doon.

That was a great leap forward. With my fears of rejection diminished, I gradually began to tell my closest friends. I realized that the intensity of my fears diminished with each successive confession, though I still remained tense and apprehensive.

I wrote to tell my dearest friends from my year of college in Delhi, Alka and Rosie, in a letter addressed to them together. Several weeks passed before I heard from them—such was the speed of even airmail to India—but my ties to them were so special that I surmised, correctly, that all I would find in their letters would be an outpouring of love and affection for me. I told Pratap, my eldest brother, when we next met.

My greatest surprise was when, on successive weekends while at Tufts, I confided in two dear friends, Sankar Sen and Siddhartha Gautam, who were studying at nearby East Coast colleges. (Sankar and I had been friends at Doon; Siddhartha and I had become close friends a few years earlier, when on holiday in Calcutta.) Both promptly told me that they were also gay and had been struggling to decide whether they could safely tell me about it! Those were life-changing developments—I now knew other gay people in flesh and blood. And they were wonderful individuals whom I loved and who were patently not abnormal or sick. I now had company in charting my life as a gay man.

❖

A year after joining Tufts, I decided to confide in one of the handful of American friends I had made there, from the swim team. For no clear reason, I felt he might be gay, too. It was impossible to tell—he was a jock with a thick Mark Spitz mustache. Though I had never felt that he was attracted to me, I had the inkling that he was smitten with a mutual friend.

One evening, walking back to the main campus from the swimming pool, I told him that I was gay. He merely glanced at me and said, evenly, that he was honored that I had taken him into confidence, his expression remaining as controlled as ever. He then started to talk about our Latin American history class.

Our friendship carried on as earlier, our discussions involving swimming practice, classes, and other everyday matters. Though I wondered why he never asked me anything about my being gay—my other friends and Bharat always seemed to have new questions to ask of me—I was grateful that there was no strain evident in our friendship and let the matter rest there.

But then, some months later, over dinner at his off-campus apartment—he often cooked Kraft instant macaroni and cheese for me, amused that I found it irresistible—he suddenly began to weep, covering his face with his hands. I sat frozen with shock, unable to get up to comfort him. He blubbered that he was gay, that he was obsessed with our common friend, and was tortured as he didn't dare confess his feelings to him.

That evening marked my first turn at helping another gay man confront the traumas of our condemned desires. It was strange to be in that position so soon after I had myself first confided in anyone.

Just as surprising, witnessing my friend's anguish, was realizing that even though he was American, his burdens of fear and self-loathing were as terrible as mine. Like me, he had never had a relationship or even sex with a man; to keep up the pretense that he was straight, he had forced himself, for years, to date and have sex with women. His Catholic family expected him to get married, preferably to another Italian American, and to have a large family. He feared that he would lose them if he told them he was gay. He had never confided in anyone till now, harboring his tortured anxiety just as I had for years.

❖

Even though my fears and sense of isolation began to ease now that I knew that I had the support of my friends and brothers, my self-hatred about being gay persisted. I continued to deny my desires in practice, my subconscious goal being to avoid the fact that being gay ultimately means having sex with men. In effect, I had broken free from solitary confinement only to wind up under house arrest: a more salubrious setting but a prison nonetheless.

My internalized homophobia was one factor in my embrace of the enduring current of Hindu philosophy that emphasizes the blanket repudiation of desire—material, sexual, and even psychological—in the individual's search for wisdom and spiritual progress. This subjugation of all desire was spotlighted in the *Bhagavad Gita*—my father had gifted me a copy when I was first leaving for the United States—as well as vividly in Mahatma Gandhi's autobiography, *The Story of My Experiments with Truth*.

Gandhi seemed just as tortured as I was, even when writing about heterosexual desires. His torment dated back to age sixteen, the precipitating incident being that he had failed to be with his father at the moment of his death because he was having sex in the adjoining bedroom with his wife, already some months pregnant. "This shame of my carnal desire even at the critical hour of my father's death" was a source of such anguish for Gandhi that he believed it had directly led to the infant's death within a few days of its birth. At the age of thirty-seven, Gandhi decided to forever abstain from sex, but he was to remain tormented by his sexual desires to the last years of his life.

Following those precepts, by my second year at Tufts, I led a markedly monastic lifestyle. I moved off campus to a tiny studio apartment, a bleak clapboard place buffeted by passing traffic. I had never yet smoked or drunk, and I remained strictly vegetarian. I gave up the expensive Fiorucci jeans I had worn in India for Levi's, which I often teamed with Gandhian *khaddar kurtas*, the most visible assertion that I was now an aspiring follower of the Mahatma. Mornings and evenings, alone in my apartment, I practiced yoga and meditated. I read reams of poetry, having developed a passion for Emily Dickinson, Langston Hughes, and Federico García Lorca. Every night came to a close like the one before, with me sitting in the *vajrasana* pose on the floor near my bed, reading the *Gita* or Jiddu Krishnamurti's philosophical works, facing a framed photograph of my yoga teacher in India, Ma Chaitnashakti, her face exuding a peace I longed for myself.

The solitude and reflection were helpful, even healing. I was particularly consoled by Jiddu Krishnamurti's insistence on confronting fear—not particular fears, but *fear* itself, which, he said, was the crucial "first and last step" in any individual setting themselves "absolutely, unconditionally free." So many of my youthful life experiences had been terrifying. More than anything else, I wished to live without the constant, overpowering feelings of threat and anxiety that had taken root in my Doon years.

I was also emboldened by Krishnamurti's insistence that "truth is a pathless land" and every individual should think through every single matter independently and break with their dependence on the views of the herd or even of spiritual leaders, including Krishnamurti himself. He wrote, "To deny all morality is to be moral, for the accepted morality is the morality of . . . good citizens in a rotten society." It was the very opposite of the conformity that had been drilled into me in my regimented school years.

And on homosexuality, in words that were music to my soul, he said bluntly, "Why do we make it into such an enormous problem? Apparently we don't make heterosexuality a problem at all, but we make this into a problem, why?" All those insights, so impatiently critical of the dogmas of mainstream religions and standard morality, I mulled over hungrily, and they were liberating.

For the first time since I was a young child, I noticed, I was now often filled with joy—rising unexpectedly when I was biking home or looking at trees or reading poetry or listening to music; exactly the cartwheeling, ecstatic joy that I had known as a child. I felt an immense relief to know it again. One afternoon on the Boston Common, I spotted a young woman doing cartwheels effortlessly, endlessly, down a path and was struck with wonder, thinking, "Ah, that is precisely how my soul feels when I'm joyous."

For all that, the unstated goal of my ascetic lifestyle was, I knew even then, an unhappy, unhealthy one. By being a celibate do-gooder, I could lay claim to being moral despite my sinful desires. In contrast, my subconscious reasoning ran, if I allowed myself to be actively gay by having sex, it would mean that I had embraced a sexuality that I still thought of as depraved and sinful.

Consequently, my romantic and sex life at Tufts was even more barren than at Doon, amounting to not even a single kiss or holding hands, even though thoughts of sex remained uppermost in my mind, consumed with desire as I was at the sight of all the attractive men on campus. I sometimes feared that I would lose all self-control if I saw another set of muscular golden thighs or a taut male stomach or firm pectoral muscles or the hint of armpit hair.

Two of my college mates cautiously showed that they were attracted to me—but I fled from both. With my panicked rebuffs, I inadvertently ruined those friendships.

Several women made obvious passes at me, too. Not wishing to hurt their feelings but afraid to tell them that I was gay, I played the innocent Third World student, pretending that I didn't understand.

✤

Eventually, in the summer of 1984, after graduating from Tufts, a few months short of my twenty-third birthday, I resolved to tell my father that I was gay, for very personal reasons that overcame my knowledge that he abhorred homosexuality.

I didn't feel the need to tell my mother, because though we remained emotionally close, our relationship had not made the transition to an evolving, adult understanding, in great part because of her worsening mental illness. But over my years abroad, my father and I had become ever closer. I was moved by his encouragement of my passion for social justice. With my growing maturity, I had come to realize that he cared profoundly about poverty and injustice and was deeply ambivalent about our family's privileged position, despite being a businessman with an appreciation of the finer things in life. Indeed, I understood that my growing sense of social justice was owed most to him, to what he had taught us brothers and to the personal example he set. I had come to admire his ability to cope uncomplainingly with whatever difficulties he faced, whether it was his mounting business problems or the inexorable unraveling of his marriage. I marveled that he remained cheerful as well as generous to others, regardless of his own stress.

More than anything else, there was the old imperative to be truthful with him because he had always put the highest stock on honesty, telling us children that anything could be forgiven if individuals remained unfailingly honest and trustworthy. If anything, I believed that I had lived up to the letter and spirit of my father's dictum.

Though I was determined to tell him the truth, I became anxious about doing so once I reached Calcutta for the summer holidays. I kept imagining that he would be so consumed by anger that he would disown me. I should have had more faith in my father's decency and love, but I lacked, at that young age, the capacity to think it through calmly. In a feverish, half-fantastical way, I made plans about which friend I could stay with if my father threw me out and how I would find the money for my flight back to the United States. (My tuition and other expenses were covered, as I had won a fellowship for graduate studies at the University of Minnesota.)

The right time to tell him never seemed to come. Two weeks of my vacation ticked away. And then one evening, on the way to our regular game of badminton at the club, my father asked in a tone that was distinctly purposeful, "Why didn't you bring Anita along today?" My heart began to thud anxiously. This was not how I had wanted to start my confession, by discussing women.

I said, "I don't want her to get the wrong notion—to think that she is my girlfriend."

He was driving, but even so he turned momentarily to look at me.

After a few moments of silence, he asked, "Son, is there something you want to tell me?"

Now that I had been given a clear opportunity, all I wanted to do was to avoid it, to delay, to pull back from this precipice. I said, "Dad, there's really no point, because your knowing won't make either of us any happier."

He pulled the car over to one side of the road, outside the luminescent marble expanse of the Victoria Memorial. I was frozen with fear. He looked at me with an expression of somberness and gentleness that I remember distinctly even today, and said, "Don't worry. You can tell me anything."

I buried my head in my arms, began to cry, and said, "Papa, I like men. I like men, not women!" My courage had failed me, and I couldn't utter the word "gay."

I waited, terrified, for the anger and the blows.

Instead, through my disorienting anxiety, I could feel my father hugging me tight, kissing me on my bowed head, saying over and over again that I was a special child, that he loved me enormously, that everything would be fine. I could not have dreamed up a happier response.

But I also heard him repeat, almost as if trying to convince himself with a mantra, "Don't worry, son, we can fight this together. We can solve this." Despite my gratitude for his loving response, I bristled inwardly. I knew he meant that I should go to a psychiatrist to change my orientation. My father was never the kind to give up on trying to fashion the life of his loved ones into exactly what he thought best. But, for that moment, I just gave myself over to the joy of being comforted by him and of hearing such deep love in his voice.

Of course, that discussion left a lot unresolved. Over the next few days, I could tell from my father's unusual quietness and the intent way in which he looked at me that he was thinking about the discussion we had had. Not knowing what to do, I kept silent and wished the matter away.

But then, a week or so later, over breakfast, my father suddenly erupted with uncharacteristic rudeness, calling me "an unrealistic fool," and left the table, food barely eaten, slamming the dining room door on his way out. At first I thought his comment had something to do with my plans to spend the summer working in violence-torn rural Bihar, which we had just been discussing and which he was opposed to because of the likely risks. By the time it dawned on me that he was actually referring to my homosexuality and my anger surged, he had already left for work.

Commandeering my mother's car, I headed straight to his office on Shakespeare Sarani, incensed. He gave me a chilling look as I barged into his room without even knocking, but after seeing the anger on my face, he asked his staff to leave us.

I yelled, "Dad, I've never lied to you or done anything wrong, so if you're ever rude to me again about my being gay, I'm going to walk out and you won't see me again!"

My father parried the threat consummately. "How can you even be sure you're homosexual if you've never had sex with either a man or a woman?"

I said, "Dad, trust me, I've always known that I'm attracted to men, not to women."

True to his forceful nature, he continued to redirect the conversation. I began to feel foolish, standing there like an angry child opposite his imposing table, my back pressed against the wall to keep my knees from giving way.

He asked me not to tell anyone else, that I could at least agree to that wish of his. I said I would consider it but then immediately became angry at my acquiescence, certain that he wanted me to keep the matter under wraps more because of the social shame of having a homosexual son than out of concern for me.

To my surprise, I also felt a surge of satisfaction that my father was now paying the price for his own homophobia. "This will teach him a lesson," I thought to myself. He would learn never to hate and condemn needlessly. This was sweet, ironic revenge.

He pushed further, saying I should get married, that that was what all homosexual men did in India and even in England.

"There's no way I'll get married, Dad." I was relieved to find some firmness in my voice once again.

Not one to quit, he said, "You must promise to go to a good psychiatrist when you get back to America."

I said "No" firmly, adding that I didn't see how a psychiatrist could be of any use. My confidence began to return.

I went back to the point that I had been making at the beginning of our conversation, the point that was most important to me. This time, I spoke with a sense of maturity that I had never known I possessed. "Dad, you have to treat me with respect. I've never lied to you, so don't I deserve your respect?"

My comment must have hit at a nerve, because he lost control, shouting, "I feel sick at the thought of a man giving you a—blow job!"

"Well, if it makes you feel any better, just think of me giving *him* a blow job!" I said without any forethought, equally out of control.

He looked stunned. I had won.

FIVE

FIRST STEPS

Now I felt I could allow myself to open up to relationships and sex, rather than constantly denying myself these needs. I began a new life at the University of Minnesota to study journalism, which I had now decided on as a career. It all felt unimaginably different from the desperation I had been sinking under just thirty months earlier at St. Stephen's, before I left for the United States.

Just a few months after moving to Minneapolis, I summoned up the courage to go to a gay bar—something I had never yet done. In the back pages of the local weekly magazine, the Twin Cities' equivalent of the *Village Voice*, I had spotted ads for two gay bars. I picked the Saloon, which conjured up images of rugged cowboys in sexy leather chaps.

On a Saturday night, I dressed myself in a white *kurta-pajama* (which I had washed, starched, and ironed to crisp perfection), certain that its stark Indian minimalism highlighted my exotic good looks. I put on an alluring dash of Dior's Eau Sauvage and set off downtown by bus. I knew where the Saloon was housed because I had figured out the directions earlier that week, so that I would be able to find it at night without having to ask for directions. The neighborhood was deserted and looked even seedier than it did in the day.

I finally found myself outside the Saloon. It was a dangerous-looking windowless expanse, the walls pulsating with loud music. There was only a dark door leading in, with a small neon sign on top. I was riven with contradictory emotions—sexual excitement mixed with intense apprehension. I had a raging hard-on despite the fact that my entire body shook with nervousness.

When I walked in, I was sure I would find countless virile men locked in copulation and blow jobs, the handsomest of whom would immediately turn their amorous attentions to me. That was the plea-surable fate that had befallen all the virginal young men in the few gay porn movies I had seen. What would I do? How should I respond? What about AIDS?

I walked into a large, dimly lit room, rancid with trapped cig-arette smoke, a long bar on one side and a wooden dance floor on the other. There were certainly men everywhere, but barring one or two who were kissing or hugging each other, the others were merely talking, dancing, or standing alone along the walls. This was no bac-chanal.

My spirits plummeted upon realizing that no one had paid the slightest attention to my entrance. They sank further still when I no-ticed that the dress code was blue jeans, plaid shirts, and boots, a uniform worn by almost every man there, whatever his age, size, or looks. In my *kurta-pajama* and delicate Kolhapuri slippers, I looked like a Hare Krishna monk who had stumbled into a lumberjack camp.

I edged my way to the bar and asked the bartender for a beer. Even that was a first for me, my first alcoholic drink. But rather than feeling happy about my brave foray into gay life, I felt crestfallen, faced with the incontrovertible fact that my attire was odd beyond belief in this setting and not a single man had shown the slightest interest in me so far. I was too dispirited to even savor the novel experience of watching men dancing freely together and sometimes kissing and fondling, or the campy histrionics of others.

It must have been at least half an hour later that, summoning up all my courage, I pushed myself away from the bar toward a man leaning all by himself against a nearby wall. He was not attractive, so I reasoned that my overture was a safe bet. He glanced at me as I came up, but as I said "Hi" and proffered my hand, he turned away deliberately and walked off, not saying a word. Face aflame with embarrassment, I quickly took his place against the wall, praying that no one had witnessed my humiliating rejection.

An hour passed. It was either my courage returning or the unaccustomed effects of the beer, but I finally decided I would dance and try to enjoy myself, even if it meant dancing alone in my odd garb. So that's what I did. As much as possible, I kept my eyes shut tight as a way to reduce the indignity of knowing that everyone else on the dance floor had a partner. After a while, I succeeded in relaxing somewhat, losing myself in the music. Madonna's voice seeped into my mind, singing "You must be my lucky star" in her devil-may-care twang. Forever after, I thought of "Lucky Star" as a gay anthem.

I skulked out of the Saloon later, my mood very different from the one I had entered with. On the bus back to my apartment, it took every ounce of my strength to prevent myself from bursting into tears. What an awful evening it had been, and I had made such an ass of myself!

Though it was nearly midnight when I reached home, I was so upset that I couldn't keep myself from phoning my friend Sankar in Boston. Sankar was leagues ahead of me as far as integrating into gay life was concerned, so I was sure he could help me make sense of what had gone wrong. Despite the late hour, he tut-tutted sympathetically as he heard me out, sounding appropriately outraged upon learning that the one man I had approached had turned away so rudely.

In Minneapolis, 1986: Sankar had gone American, I quasi-Gandhian

And then a note of suspicion evident in his voice, Sankar asked, "Siddharth, what were you wearing?" (By now I was infamous among my friends for the *kurta*s.) On hearing my shame-faced admission that I had worn my best *kurta-pajama* to the Saloon, his mirth drove all the sympathy out of his tone!

❖

In Minneapolis, I took huge steps forward in actually leading the life of a gay man. Toward the end of 1984, some months after my disastrous first visit to the gay bar, I went to a meeting of a gay students' group, the University Gay Community. The meeting was being held late in the week after the late-afternoon classes were over, at the Coffman Memorial Union, one of the main buildings near the river.

While searching for the room through its labyrinthine corridors, I realized, to my surprise, that I felt furtive and anxious. Becoming part of this group would be an irrevocable statement on coming out—from now on, it would be difficult for me to control and limit just who knew that I was gay. I hated the feeling that I still had those worries.

My doubts faded when, upon entering, I saw a group of twenty or so men, most, like me, graduate students. The meeting proved to be unexciting, with seemingly no agenda and purpose beyond that of getting together, but I relished it. Barring the visit to the gay bar, it was my first time in a group of other avowedly gay men.

I became a regular participant at the meetings as my feelings of furtiveness lifted. The meetings were never particularly interesting, always remaining somehow stiff and lifeless, but I still enjoyed the interaction.

I hoped, too, that being part of that group would lead to a relationship, which I ached for intensely. But though I was attracted to several among them, nothing concrete came of it. That was my introduction to the discordant laws of adult attraction: those to whom you are attracted are not attracted back; those you're not attracted to inevitably desire you; and only rarely is attraction both mutual and simultaneous.

It was no surprise that I was not really sought after. I was awkward and shy in large groups and by now also relentlessly serious, while the rest of the men in the group were far more mainstream, interested in the standard, fun things about college life. My personality was writ large in my semi-Gandhian dressing style, which, even in the ferocious cold of the Minnesota winters, inevitably included a *kurta* and *khadi* jacket topped off by the bulky sweaters from South America that were all the rage with US activists back then. Only someone with a taste for peculiarly dressed foreigners would have fallen for me.

Despite the lack of romance, a great outcome of being a part of this group was that, through some of its more bookish members, I was introduced to the pioneering works of Western gay and lesbian writing, many of them published in the previous few years. I read them, one after another, in rapt succession: James Baldwin's *Giovanni's Room*, John Boswell's *Christianity and Homosexuality*, Rita Mae Brown's *Rubyfruit Jungle*, John D'Emilio's *Sexual Politics, Sexual Communities*, E. M. Forster's *Maurice*, Michel Foucault's *The History of Sexuality*, Jean Genet's *Querelle of Brest*, Christopher Isherwood's

A Single Man, John Rechy's *The Sexual Outlaw*, Mary Renault's *The Persian Boy*, and Edmund White's *Nocturnes for the King of Naples*.

What a welcome relief it was to discover that vast history of men and women who were like me. It was a relief to know that many others had felt and struggled with the same things I did: the unstoppable urge for love, intimacy, and sex; the terrible shame and self-loathing generated by the prejudice we saw all around us; and the courage it took to act on what we felt, even if we did so in secret. However tortured that history, however tragic the outcome for individual after individual because of the intolerance he or she faced, it was still validation that I belonged to a community that had heroically endured across eons despite terrible persecution.

More than anything else, I hungrily latched onto the evidence that many famous historical figures had been attracted to the same sex, whether exclusively or in part. Knowing that so many thinkers I admired—from Oscar Wilde, Marcel Proust, and Leo Tolstoy to García Lorca, John Maynard Keynes, Virginia Woolf, and Constantine Cavafy and then on to Baldwin, Foucault, and Marguerite Yourcenar—felt the same desires as I did was the most powerful affirmation possible. There was also a fantasy thrill to knowing that such iconic macho men as Alexander the Great, Emperor Hadrian, and the warriors in Thebes' Sacred Band had all been smitten with other men.

My joy at discovering that history was dwarfed by outrage at learning just how cruelly men and women with same-sex desires had been persecuted over the centuries. Since my days at St. Stephen's, when I had confronted my own orientation and become fully aware of pathological homophobia, I had assumed that men and women like me had faced persecution everywhere and always. But even so, what I read now, a chronology of brutality and injustice throughout almost the entire course of Western history, far outstripped my worst imaginings.

The most heinous of the outrages became indelibly etched into my memory like bloodstained milestones: the countless "effeminate" men and "sodomites" who were blinded, mutilated, castrated, hung, drowned, and burnt at the stake across most of Europe from the thirteenth to the mid-nineteenth centuries; the homosexual men who were killed, and the lesbians who were raped, in Nazi Germany; the postwar persecution across the English-speaking world—stretching from the United States and Canada to Great Britain to Australia—of gay men and women who were imprisoned (often after mass raids in bars and parks), listed as dangerous sex offenders, incarcerated in mental hospitals, sterilized, and lobotomized; all the way to the present, when hysteria about AIDS was driving a resurgence of sodomy-law arrests and violence against gay men and the US Supreme Court would rule, in 1986, that state sodomy laws could remain in place on the basis of "millennia of moral teaching."

Reading all that, I often felt that there was no safe place in the world for gay individuals. And though I searched hard to understand the root cause for gays' being singled out across the centuries, there was of course no rational, legitimate answer. The truth was simply the depressing one that in society after society the powerful men—and often women, too—who dominated religion or politics maliciously targeted homosexuals as scapegoats, just as they targeted those they demonized as being whores, witches, heretics, congenital criminals, or subhuman because of their race or color. That hatred was then transmitted from generation to generation so that it became an unexamined truth, bred into the bone, making them the constant targets of disgust and violence.

✤

Fortunately, as I was a graduate student on the University of Minnesota campus, such threats usually seemed worlds away. That was in great part because the University of Minnesota was a progressive place and the several gay students' groups that had sprung up over the years had already secured remarkable gains, far in advance of Tufts and other elite East Coast colleges.

The Twin Cities campus was home to one of the country's earliest gay student groups, founded in 1969, a few weeks before the Stonewall Revolution. It was known as FREE, for Fight Repression of Erotic Expression, a name redolent of the Flower Power era. Its evocative goal was to win for gay men and women the "freedom to walk hand in hand down the street, to embrace in public, to dance together, to live in peace with [their] lovers without feeling the guilt and shame that this straight, sick society [has] forced upon [them]." In 1972, two officers of the group had the distinction of becoming the first same-sex couple to receive a marriage license in the United States, a decision speedily overturned by a court.

The university administration had also been admirably support-ive, recognizing FREE as an official campus organization within a year of its founding. In 1986, the year I graduated, the university amended its antidiscrimination statement to include sexual orientation. That was, in large part, because of the efforts of the gay students' group and the University Lesbians. (By 1993, far ahead of its compeers, the university had established the Gay, Lesbian, Bisexual, and Transgender Programs Office to implement antidiscriminatory policies and inte-grate gay and queer studies into the curriculum.)

Most striking was how largely unafraid we were, those of us who had crossed the harrowing first hurdles of coming out. With Sankar, who had also moved to the university for graduate studies, as well as several men from the gay students' group, I went out for dinner and to the two gay bars in town. At the bars the atmosphere was relaxed, men enjoying themselves with no apparent sense of threat. None of us, Americans or foreigners, seemed to care about the existence of Minne-sota's sodomy law, which might result in police raids or other forms of persecution I had read about in various US states. (Inexplicably, given the state's long history of liberal politics, its sodomy law remained in force until 2001, eventually being struck down by the courts.) In my off-campus apartment building, I cared little about discrimination.

Of course, I realized that as a graduate student at a progressive university, I was enjoying a fleeting moment of peace; homophobic dis-crimination would surely reemerge when I entered the job market, even in media organizations or academia. (My craving to be open overcame my awareness that I was imperiling my chances of being allowed to set-tle in the US, given the immigration ban on gays.) The homophobia was evident the moment I strayed far from the university or the gay bars; at the blues bars that I loved for the live music, men would stare hostilely at Sankar and me whenever we danced together. Our gay American friends told us that we escaped being beaten probably because we were foreigners, our dancing together being excused as an alien peculiarity.

Encouraged by the blessed feeling of safety on campus, I became increasingly open about being gay. By the winter of 1985, I had revealed the truth about my orientation to dozens of people since my first terrified confession three years earlier.

Thus, within a month or so of striking up a new friendship, I would inevitably broach a discussion about my being gay. Though I was no longer worried that my confession would provoke an adverse reaction, it was still highly stressful for me to initiate the discussion. Consequently, each and every telling became a formal, portentous event in which I would tell the friend that I had something to discuss with him or her and we would then go for a walk or a coffee where I would state the matter seriously, saying "I wanted to tell you that I'm gay."

Everyone reacted differently but fortunately always well. I was struck that almost all the male friends I confided in, whether Americans or foreigners, told me that I was the first openly gay person they knew. This was a telling commentary about how guarded gay men and women were even at that progressive university and how even those of us who had come out largely kept to the company of other gay people or to a select group of friends.

In contrast, many of my new women friends said they already knew lesbian women and gay men. Even more strikingly, several told me that they'd had romantic relationships with other women, beginning in their teens and continuing up till now, even though sexually they were more strongly attracted to men and hence did not categorize themselves as lesbian. That opened up a world of fluid possibilities in romance and sex, though it was a realm I was incapable of making much sense of at that time. I was intrigued by their honesty. Very few of the men I knew had ever admitted to being attracted to other men, even as teenagers or youthful experimenters.

My openness began to seep into the work environment. At some point, the two teaching assistants with whom I shared our large office room were talking about their girlfriends. One of them, a rather macho midwesterner, who looked like a sports reporter but in reality was specializing in mass communication theory, was getting married soon. When they turned their attention to me and there was a distinctly interrogative pause, I said, as naturally as I could manage, that I was gay and single.

There was a long silence. One of them then made a polite but meaningless comment that had nothing to do with my disclosure. We all turned to our work, an awkwardness settling over us. I had felt a pang of apprehension in being candid, especially as I hadn't thought this through at all. I remained tense and nervous through the rest of the day. But later, on my bicycle ride home, the discomfort was replaced by a sense of enormous relief when I realized that I no longer had to ceaselessly evade or lie as before.

⬧

Unexpectedly, and with a romantic start worthy of the Mills & Boon novels I had devoured as a child, my first adult relationship began. It was the fall of 1985, shortly after my twenty-fourth birthday.

While waiting for a play to begin at the Walker Art Center in downtown Minneapolis, I noticed a man looking at me, half smiling. A black turtleneck accentuated big muscles, fine features, and blond hair. I smiled back. The man came over, said that he'd noticed me several times on the university campus, where he worked, and upon waking that morning had inexplicably felt that we would meet.

And so it began, love and romance—the things I had craved since I was a young child.

I saw Eric every day after he finished work. I longed for my first daily glimpse of him, the delight of once again feeling my affection for him as well as the thrill of erotic attraction.

We'd embrace on the street, even sneaking in a kiss on the cheek once in a while. I would draw in his faint body smell, so mild and scrubbed that it almost seemed disinfected.

We spent most of our evenings at my apartment, as it was nearby. Within seconds of closing the door behind us, we'd be kissing wildly. Dinner would be forgotten. Darkness would fall. Hours would be spent on the carpet of my living room or on my bed.

But despite being tremendously turned on by Eric, it took me a long time to start overcoming my hang-ups about sex, which had intensified over the many years from Doon to now. So I insisted, to Eric's frustration, that we keep our jeans on even while kissing, to ensure that we didn't end up having sex.

When we finally progressed beyond kissing and Eric stripped completely for the first time, I was awed by the beauty of his musculature, the heavy pectorals, the curving, thick thighs, and the full buttocks, all so different from the light-boned physique of the Indian men I knew. Out of his marble-white, hairless body jutted a hefty penis.

But almost immediately after we crossed that frontier, our relationship began to fall apart. Now my intense fears about contracting AIDS were to blame.

From what I had read about the AIDS epidemic among gay American men, Eric fitted the profile: he was already in his mid-thirties and had previous sexual experience. My fears were so intense that I held myself back even from oral sex, let alone sexual intercourse. Everything about AIDS caused a blind fog of confusion and terror. I was left too nervous to have sex that could have satisfied Eric.

My apprehensions could easily have been solved had there been accessible resources—such as counseling services to provide advice on safe sex—at hand. I don't recall any such service on the campus at that point; the university health services certainly did not make a noticeable effort to provide the gay students (or straight students, for that matter) with such information. Nor was there any guidance provided by the gay students' group. I had never even come across a guide to safe gay sex.

With no source of expert advice, I gleaned whatever I could from articles in the *Village Voice*, gay magazines, and—to a lesser extent—the *New York Times*. Despite reading all that with great attention, I never felt confident that my understanding was correct and foolproof, in large part because even that information was not explicit enough to be practicable and was also hedged with ifs and buts. The most exasperating of the qualifications was, one, that there was a risk that condoms could break or fail, and two, that the advice amounted not to "safe sex" but only to "safer sex," a critical qualification that implied that there was still an untold risk of contracting HIV.

Thus, correctly or incorrectly, my conclusions at that time were the following: Always assume that your partner is infected. Hence, always and unfailingly have safe sex. Fucking even with a condom might be unsafe, because of a risk of the condom tearing. So might giving a blow job without using a condom. The only safe sex acts were nonpenetrative, notably kissing (but even deep kissing possibly carried a slight risk), mutual masturbation, getting a blow job (possibly a slight risk there, too), and giving a blow job only along the penis shaft.

Was it any wonder, then, that all that I ever allowed myself to do with Eric was an unsatisfying sort of canoodling that allowed me to scrupulously avoid putting his penis head into my mouth?

The high point of our sex together, spread over those months, amounted to oh-so-pleasurable blow jobs by Eric. Mine were obviously nowhere on a par with his, not just because I lacked expertise but also owing to my fears. They just could not satisfy Eric. Consequently, I would simply masturbate him to ejaculation.

Never having discussed those issues before and also feeling awkward because only Eric was the object of worry about AIDS (given that I had been a virgin till now), I lacked the skills to open up to him about these fears. I castigated myself for that inability at that time. It was only much later in life that I realized that our problem of being ill equipped to handle sensitive discussions was a common one among gay men almost everywhere, reflecting our late start and crippling inexperience with romantic relationships as well as the many psychological burdens we had invariably developed due to the hostility we faced.

Our awkwardness was so severe that Eric and I never talked

about his putting my fears to rest by getting tested. A commercial test for the antibodies to the AIDS virus—the term "HIV" was yet to be adopted—had became available some months earlier in 1985. People were encouraged to be tested. But there were enormous fears about testing, given the life-destroying hopelessness that would follow a positive result. By now the coverage of Rock Hudson's desperate struggle against AIDS had made the disease known everywhere and American gay men lived in terror of contracting it. The desperation was such that many gay men sought out the Hemlock Society, which provided advice about home euthanasia and physician-assisted suicide, or convinced friends or sympathetic doctors to agree to help them commit suicide if they fell direly ill as the only sure way of cutting short the endless horrors caused by AIDS.

I knew instinctively that my relationship with Eric would have worked and lasted happily under better circumstances, free of the dread of AIDS. Eric and I were strongly attracted to each other, and we were both serious-minded people looking for a lasting relationship. But despite Eric's patience, my worries were so crippling that our relationship ground to a halt in a matter of months. I felt paralyzed, unable to make sense of what had happened to so quickly destroy something that had seemed an answer to my fervent prayers for love.

❖

A few months after my relationship with Eric ended, I began to rapidly lose weight—from my already skinny 140 pounds—and was constantly tired. The fear and shame that I might somehow have contracted AIDS from Eric kept me from seeking medical advice or even mentioning my anxiety to Bharat. But eventually, finding it difficult to attend classes or cope with everyday chores, I had no choice but to go to the university medical services.

After describing my symptoms to the attending doctor, I said I was from a high-risk group for AIDS. It was the first time I had ever made the admission, and I burned with embarrassment at saying it.

I was very fortunate, because the doctor was thoroughly professional. He simply asked me which high-risk group I came under. I said
I was gay. I hastily added, almost involuntarily, that I had barely ever
had sex, as if that qualification would reduce the opprobrium attached
to being homosexual.

My blood was drawn for testing for the AIDS virus and several
other possible causes. The results would take three days to come in,
the doctor told me. However, given that my lymph glands were not
swollen and I didn't have night sweats, it seemed unlikely that I had
AIDS, he added. I was weak with relief.

Three days later, I was back in his office. It took a superhuman
effort on my part to control my shivering: What if his confidence had
been misplaced? The doctor walked in, instantly picked up the report—no doubt aware how nervous I was—and told me that the AIDS
test had come back negative. He kept up his clinical demeanor, but
even so, I could sense that he was pleased to be able to give good news.
All I had was a severe case of hypothyroidism, which could easily be
solved. That was my first encounter with the terror of testing for AIDS.

⌖

I spent another year in the United States, but there were no more romantic developments in my life in spite of desperately wanting a steady
and loving relationship, I felt incapable of negotiating one, given the
mess I had made with Eric.

I slipped back into a dead-end pattern of burying myself in my
work and my ascetic lifestyle. I also pined for several unquestionably
heterosexual men, a subconscious ploy to avoid sex or romance. I was
attracted not to some especial masculinity but to their comfort with
themselves, their ease in the world, the fact that they didn't carry the
scars of exclusion that we gays always did. Though I wrote lovelorn
poems for those men, I had the good sense to never give them to them.

I was such a mess that I once again bolted from men who showed
any signs of being attracted to me. In New York City, where I spent the

latter half of 1986 as an intern with a leftist magazine, I met a glorious Brazilian man at a literary party—velvety skin set off by a shirt of cream-colored linen, with curly locks and an immense mouth—who, ignoring my protests, dragged me onto the makeshift dance floor, gyrating with his crotch flush against mine. He bit me on the neck and kissed me on the mouth. His exuberance was infectious. I forgot my shyness and self-consciousness for some hours—as I didn't drink alcohol or take drugs, those means of unwinding were not open to me—dancing wildly and kissing him with passion. But I refused his invitation to spend the night at his nearby apartment. And when he called the next morning and for several days after that, leaving messages on my answering machine in a plaintive voice, I didn't return his calls.

Beyond that one evening, the sum total of my gay adventures in New York consisted of walking furtively a few times down Christopher Street, lacking the courage to enter the smoke-filled bars or the porn stores. I quickly glanced away if anyone looked at me with interest. In that violent, drug-ridden city, an epicenter of AIDS, I was not going to have sex.

⌘

In the winter of 1986, a few months after my twenty-fifth birthday, I left New York City and moved back to India. In one of those odd twists of life, I felt that to fulfill myself at that juncture I needed to return to India, the place I had been so desperate to escape from just a few years earlier. I was aching to work on the issues of poverty and social justice back in my own country. I thought that I could be of real use in impoverished India, whereas wealthy America had no real need for me.

But, in considerable part, my decision was also an effort to stave off my fears about the bleak likely course of my love life, which stretched out ahead terrifyingly bare and alone. My relationship with Eric had been a short-lived disaster, but none of my handful of gay Indian friends there was in a relationship or even dating seriously. Of all the gay or lesbian Americans I knew, only one was in a live-in, long-term relationship. The few men I had met through personal ads, some a generation or more older than I, seemed to have searched fruitlessly for love year after year. Gay men and women everywhere seemed doomed to lives without lasting romantic love.

The one compelling reason to stay on in the United States was the knowledge that living in India as an openly gay man was sure to be even more difficult and possibly dangerous. I knew by now that homosexuality was a serious criminal offense in India, proscribed under Section 377 of the Penal Code, which had come into force 101 years before my birth, when India was a British colony. I had not yet read the text of the Indian law but knew that it was similar to the US sodomy laws—with a common origin in medieval England's "buggery" law—and entailed equally harsh jail terms that could extend to imprisonment for life.

My awareness of the possible dangers ahead was magnified by my father's vehement opposition to my returning. He told me he feared I would be ostracized and persecuted for being gay. He urged me to settle in the United States and to forget about India.

Yet I eventually set aside my own anxieties as well as my father's warnings. As it turned out, I had utterly underestimated India's potential for both happiness and trauma.

SIX

INDIA

Within months of moving to Delhi, where I began to cover economic development and social justice issues for *Business India*, an influential weekly magazine, I realized that there had been no discernible progress in how Indian society treated gay issues since my days at St. Stephen's. Neither the homophobia nor the nullifying public silence on gay matters had eased; indeed, in some ways, they were even more entrenched than I had imagined as a college student. Five years was an epoch in my short life then, and although I had changed profoundly in how I dealt with my orientation in these matters of the heart and body, India seemed frozen in time.

At *Business India*, several of the senior staff openly used homophobic slurs. Their target, because of some festering office intrigue, was a senior editor, a mild-mannered man from Calcutta who spoke with a British accent and habitually chugged on an unlit pipe. When he was out of earshot, they called him "pansy" and, bizarrely, an "effete Bengali homosexual."

The comments cut especially deep because they were so similar to the ones I had heard from my father and his friends in years past. And just as before, no one challenged them, either. Consequently, from my very first months of employment in India, I retreated from the candor about my orientation that I had so come to relish in my last few years in the United States. I rebuffed efforts by my colleagues at *Business India*—and then at the *Washington Post*'s South Asia bureau, which I joined in 1988—to discover anything about my personal life.

But I was no longer used to evasion. All the hiding also contradicted my openness around friends and family. I soon realized that I was once again living a double life, constantly wary, just as in the years before I had come out of the closet. My frustration at being forced back into that unpleasant state would have been sharper still if I had not realized that it was not the solitary imprisonment of the past, where I had hid my secret fearfully from everyone, but a halfway house that I could tolerate.

There still proved to be no way to escape the pervasive prejudices against gays in Delhi, everywhere, at every level of class. I witnessed that hostility in the company of my beloved friend Siddhartha Gautam—one of the two friends who had confessed that he, too, was gay when I had come out to him several years back—who had also moved to Delhi in 1986 to do a law degree at Delhi University after a BA at Yale and an MPhil in development studies at Cambridge.

There was a palpable intensity to our friendship, evident in the amount of time we spent alone with each other, how we constantly touched and embraced, and how protective I was of him in my unaccustomed role of responsible elder brother protecting a madcap, vulnerable younger sibling. We proudly called ourselves "Tiddarth and Tiddartha," à la the indistinguishable detectives Thomson and Thompson in the Tintin comic books. It didn't matter to either of us that we didn't look alike. We had everything else in common: our first names, our Calcutta childhoods on neighboring streets, and our shared calling for social justice.

My protectiveness had to do with the fact that Siddhartha had been diagnosed with Hodgkin's lymphoma at age fifteen. Though extended treatment had brought the cancer into remission, the threat remained, never spoken about but ever present and ever dangerous.

Perhaps because he sensed that he had only a short lease on life,

Siddhartha lived it at breakneck speed and with the most exceptional intensity. Being in his vicinity was a sure recipe for getting entangled in adventures and scrapes.

Siddhartha Gautam

As both he and I loved to dance, we overcame our shared dislike for swanky hotels and decided to go to the discotheque at the Taj Mansingh, given pride of place just below the hotel's ornate marble staircase. The manager greeted us effusively, no doubt because we looked affluent. Though the disco music was largely unmemorable, Siddhartha and I had a wonderful time dancing together for hours. We always felt invincible when we were together, and so we laughed off the alarmed stares from several couples and the way they edged away from us. At some point, I noticed the manager staring at us from behind the bar, a hostile look on his face, but I ignored that, too.

By our third visit, some weeks later, the manager's warmth was nowhere in sight. He was polite but didn't seem happy to see us back. Siddhartha and I had just started dancing when one of the staff interrupted us and said that men weren't allowed to dance together. Siddhartha and I retorted that we had danced there together before and that we weren't touching each other or doing anything inappropriate. I looked around to speak to the manager, but he had mysteriously disappeared. Eventually, because so many people were staring at us, we decided to dance separately. We left after a while, offended and fuming.

Siddhartha and I decided to go back the following weekend, having resolved that we wouldn't stop dancing with each other. So when a similar request was made of us again, we said no. This time the manager appeared and told us grimly that we would have to leave the dance floor. Over the din of the music, Siddhartha and I took pains to politely explain that it was only fair to let us dance together, given that we were not hurting anyone. When it was clear that he was not going to agree, we went back to dancing—leaving the manager standing stone-faced in the crowd.

A few minutes later, the music went dead, the lights came on, and the loudspeaker announced that "stag dancing" was forbidden. Near the entrance, I saw that the manager had been joined by another officious-looking man, probably a more senior colleague, who was also staring at us. Quite a few of the couples, giving us baleful looks, went and sat down by the bar. Siddhartha and I stood our ground. Many minutes later, finding that we were the only people left on the dance floor—everyone else was sitting down in a semicircle, staring at us with hostility—we left the discotheque, ignoring the managers as we passed them.

Siddhartha and I should have been distraught at this public humiliation. But we were indomitable when together, even possessing the alchemy to turn our humiliation into victory. On the drive to my brother's home in Panchsheel Park, our bleak mood vanished, replaced with fits of laughter as we regaled each other with our best moments of the evening—how we had bravely stood up to the manager's silly homophobia and the idiocy of people who were offended by seeing men dancing together. We yelled out to the empty streets, "Beware! We're the leaders of a tribe of homos! We'll soon conquer all of Delhi! No one is safe!"

When we were together, Siddhartha and I could cope with whatever homophobia we encountered in the well-off neighborhoods to

night, matters would deteriorate. On one occasion, I came to b.
with a landlord and his adult sons. Luckily, my years at Doon h
made me a tough opponent, and they backed off after we traded a fev
punches.

Very often, Siddhartha and I—and occasionally some of our other
friends—would arrive at the local police station to file a complaint
against the landlord. There, facing a bunch of dismissive, rough-
mannered policemen, we took pains to present ourselves as unimpeachably respectable, upper-class young men, not the bohemians that
the landlords insisted we were.

At those times, both Siddhartha and I felt intensely fearful of being
identified as homosexuals. Though we never came to discuss the particulars of our fears, his were doubtless very similar to mine. My fear
sprang from knowing that the police would automatically brand me a
low-life criminal because of Section 377. And because my criminality
was defined by sex, the police would view me in the same way as they
viewed prostitutes: as a sex-crazed person who deserved scorn and
abuse.

⟡

Given that pervasive hostility, it was not surprising that the overwhelming majority of gay men and women, irrespective of their class,
were closeted. In Delhi, through Siddhartha, I met a small group of gay
men and women, all middle- to upper-income professionals and most
a decade or more older than I. Numbering about two dozen, with the
men in a majority, we were drawn together into friendship because of
our shared secret orientation. Many of those men and women were
candid about the matter only with their close friends and select relatives and had not come out in their workplaces or broadly in society.

In fact, the bulk of them were not out in any real sense at all;
only their partners and that small group of people knew about their
orientation. The most flamboyant man among our group of friends,
a senior bureaucrat then in his forties, was married and had teenage

which we were accustomed. But we soon came to realize that outside those settings any disclosure of our being gay could have far more harmful consequences.

After moving to Delhi, Siddhartha had lived in a series of rented apartments in the cheaper sections of Defence Colony, Lajpat Nagar, and Jangpura. Siddhartha's flawless Hindi and his angelic looks always enchanted his landlords initially. But in just a few weeks they would inevitably turn hostile.

They disapproved of the unending stream of bohemians visiting Siddhartha—men of feminine appearance (some with tweezed eyebrows and a hint of kohl), rough and macho men, obviously single women (based on their arriving and leaving without male companions), and even one flagrant cross-dresser who sometimes arrived decked out in the shiny slips he favored. Singly or in a group, they all disappeared into Siddhartha's apartment.

The curtains were then pulled tight. Whatever the hour, there was music and loud laughter, sometimes broken by suspiciously long silences. Impromptu parties took place at odd times, occasionally even in the afternoon. The sound of *ghungroos* and male voices seductively singing "*In ankhon ki masti ke, mastaane hazaron hain*"—"Countless men are intoxicated by my bewitching eyes," a courtesan's siren song from a classic movie—would drift down. Siddhartha's voice, excited and giggling at a peculiarly high, feminine pitch, would float above the din.

Soon enough, the landlords would insist that Siddhartha move out, saying that his lifestyle was unacceptable in a respectable neighborhood. Though they strongly suspected that he was gay, it was never brought up. They had no firm proof, and the large number of women visitors must also have confused them. But, Delhi being lawless in such matters, the landlords either refused to return Siddhartha's rental deposit or, without giving him due notice, insisted that he leave immediately or be thrown out forcibly.

Because I had long taken on the role of being Siddhartha's responsible older brother, I inevitably got involved in the crises. Try as we might, matters would deteriorate. On one occasion, I came to blows with a landlord and his adult sons. Luckily, my years at Doon had made me a tough opponent, and they backed off after we traded a few punches.

Very often, Siddhartha and I—and occasionally some of our other friends—would arrive at the local police station to file a complaint against the landlord. There, facing a bunch of dismissive, rough-mannered policemen, we took pains to present ourselves as unimpeachably respectable, upper-class young men, not the bohemians that the landlords insisted we were.

At those times, both Siddhartha and I felt intensely fearful of being identified as homosexuals. Though we never came to discuss the particulars of our fears, his were doubtless very similar to mine. My fear sprang from knowing that the police would automatically brand me a low-life criminal because of Section 377. And because my criminality was defined by sex, the police would view me in the same way as they viewed prostitutes: as a sex-crazed person who deserved scorn and abuse.

❖

Given that pervasive hostility, it was not surprising that the overwhelming majority of gay men and women, irrespective of their class, were closeted. In Delhi, through Siddhartha, I met a small group of gay men and women, all middle- to upper-income professionals and most a decade or more older than I. Numbering about two dozen, with the men in a majority, we were drawn together into friendship because of our shared secret orientation. Many of those men and women were candid about the matter only with their close friends and select relatives and had not come out in their workplaces or broadly in society.

In fact, the bulk of them were not out in any real sense at all; only their partners and that small group of people knew about their orientation. The most flamboyant man among our group of friends, a senior bureaucrat then in his forties, was married and had teenage children—a pretense that allowed him to lead an active sexual life with other men despite the visibility of being a bureaucrat.

I came to find that most gay men entered such sham marriages in a desperate attempt to keep their orientation from becoming known. The threat of blackmail and violence was an everyday reality, because most gay men had no place to meet, socialize, or have sex beyond public areas such as parks and toilets. That was many years before gay support groups and gay-friendly bars opened in Delhi, let alone in smaller towns and cities.

It was no doubt because of the stress and obstacles raised by secrecy and fear that so few among them were in relationships. There were only two or three long-term couples, all lesbian, among our group of friends. But even those women were guarded about their relationships outside the circle of family and friends. They passed themselves off simply as close friends sharing a flat. None of the gay men in our group was in a long-standing or live-in relationship. In all of Delhi, I knew of only two gay male couples, both part of the sequestered world of design and fashion but, even so, painstakingly discreet about their relationships and orientation.

The only time everyone let down their guard was when we hosted parties at one of our homes. Invitation was strictly through a network of friends. In those evenings together, there was an unfailing feeling of security, of having a safe space where the world's hatred could not intrude.

They were often standing room only, because the parties were fun and inclusive. They were the only ones I knew of in Delhi where everyone was welcome, irrespective of orientation or class. The city's one cross-dresser and a handful of working-class *kothis*—*kothi* is the Hindi term for a feminine man who cross-dresses and adopts women's behaviors when he wishes—some of whom sold sex to men, would join us. So would three gay men from Western European embassies, two gay fashion designers, and some of the party boys who always hung around them.

Someone would begin to sing a Hindi film song, accompanied by someone inventively using a tin can as a *dholak*. Siddhartha or some other flamboyant character would swan into the center of the room, copying a Bollywood dance or a traditional *mujra*. The more camp the performance, the greater the praise.

Apart from such unguarded moments, the extent of fear that even the most privileged of gay men lived in was evident from the fact that not one of us, anywhere in India, allowed his real name to be used in the first major article in the Indian press on gay men, published in 1988. It was a cover story in the then widely read but now defunct *Sunday*, a liberal weekly for which I often wrote at the time. Titled "The Love That Dare Not Speak Its Name," the article described us as "the country's most silent and secretive minority." It was an accurate description. The only gay man who spoke on the record, using his full name, was the British theater director Barry John, a foreigner settled in Delhi. There was still no prominent gay Indian man or woman in the public eye who could start rolling back homophobic stereotypes and assumptions and become a role model for others like them.

⟡

The first year of my return to India also marked my first adult sexual experience there. It happened on a visit to Bombay in early 1987, where I was staying with a close friend—the very one I had come out to a half decade earlier in Philadelphia—and his wife. One of their favorite pastimes was to tease me about my ascetic life: my yoga, my lack of interest in alcohol or cigarettes, and, most glaringly, my monklike sexual abstinence. One evening, they energetically ganged up on me, insisting that I get out of their house and not return until I got laid.

I gave in to their bullying, relieved to be forced to do what I ached to do anyway. I was more open to the possibilities here, in a place where HIV was not raging as it was in the United States—the first domestically transmitted cases, contracted and spread within India rather than from abroad, had been recorded just a few months earlier.

Of course, neither they nor I knew even one avowedly gay man in Bombay, so going out on a date was ruled out. There were no gay bars in the city in 1987. The possibility of finding dates through the internet was still many years away. But I had heard from Siddhartha, always a reliable guide on matters of the flesh, that men cruised for sex near Flora Fountain. So I walked the short distance there from my friends' Colaba home.

As the ornate fountain came into sight, my heart began to hammer so uncontrollably that I stopped for a few minutes, worried that I'd be incoherent even if I met someone. On entering the small park circling the fountain, I detected several men's forms in the poor light. I noticed a handsome man, Nepali in appearance, staring at me, dressed simply but neatly in a light shirt and dark pants. He came up and spoke to me in Hindi. We must have exchanged names, but my wits deserted me in a rush of nerves, and the next thing I remember, I was following him into a run-down office building on a side street.

We climbed three flights of creaking wooden stairs, tiptoeing past sleeping forms on the landings. He stopped on the top landing, lit by a weak bare bulb and street light filtering in through the grimy windows, and—to my shock—started unbuttoning his shirt. I realized then that that small space was his home. I was about to balk at having sex in that open space, but then desire overcame my fears.

He laid out a thin mattress and turned off the light. Casually, with his back to me, he peeled off his clothes. I watched breathlessly, my heart hammering. He turned to face me. He was beautiful naked—a David-like figure gleaming in the smoggy light, small penis jutting out high. He grinned upon seeing my admiration, came up to me, caught my hand, and placed it squarely over his penis, making me envelop it in my palm. His confidence was aphrodisiacal.

He kissed me. His lips felt thin and foreign, and his mouth tasted unpleasantly of onion and fried food. Naked and so close, I also smelled a rank odor from his armpits. But my aversion lasted just for a second; lust took over.

I began to kiss him back. Then, pulling him tight against me, I

groped at his body and instinctively reached down to caress his testicles and the silky skin of his inner thighs.

He drew away and began to undress me, tugging at my T-shirt and
pants. I realized, feeling gauche, that I was still fully dressed—I had
not undone even a button in all this while. Touchingly, he folded my
clothes with care, placing them with his own on a suitcase under the
stairwell.

He pulled me down on the mattress, immediately laying himself
atop me. For a moment, it felt odd to have a body and a cock rubbing
so wildly against mine, someone's lips suctioning at my mouth and
neck, hands touching every part of my body. But I soon lost control
again, kissing him back feverishly, biting his neck and small erect nipples with such force that I worried I would draw blood, running my
hands without restraint over every part of his body.

At some point, he asked me in a whisper to take his cock in my
mouth—or did I want him below, in my ass? In my state of desire, I
wanted everything: to blow him, to be fucked by him. I whispered
back, suddenly aware again of the people sleeping on the landing just
below, to ask if he had a Nirodh. As Nirodh was the only condom
brand available in India for decades, the word had become synonymous with condoms.

"Nirodh? Why a Nirodh?" He was clearly perplexed. I realized he
had no concerns about AIDS; for him, condoms were solely a contra-
ceptive barrier. Cursing myself for forgetting to bring a condom along,
I told him that I couldn't do anything much without one.

I didn't explain to him why. He doubtless found my behavior
highly peculiar—after all, why would a man insist on a condom being
used when he didn't have to worry about getting pregnant? Neverthe-
less, he said nothing.

He just spat in his hand and, reaching down, slathered the saliva
generously over our cocks, the cool liquid a welcome comfort. Then he
went back to kissing and rubbing against me, his body excitingly hard
against mine, the pleasure making me forget about everything from
condoms to the people sleeping nearby.

He came very soon, his semen bursting all the way to my chest. Then he lay still on me, his face buried in my shoulder, his breath coming fast. Lying there, despite suddenly becoming aware of the sweat and sticky mess all over my body, I felt a rush of satisfaction from giving him such pleasure.

After a while, he roused himself and began to masturbate me. I stopped him, whispering that I didn't want to come. He kissed me on the mouth gently, again and again. I was astonished by how affectionate he was. Like me, he was aching for love and companionship just as much as for sex.

When I said I had to get home, he wiped his semen off me carefully with a towel and handed my clothes to me one by one. Once I had dressed, he embraced me for a long while, caressing my hair and whispering that I was extraordinarily beautiful. I could tell that he didn't want me to leave.

And so it was that I had my first adult experience of sex in India, encapsulating all the paradoxes of gay life there. It was a country in which the only connections possible were brief sexual encounters with complete strangers—furtive and fearful yet offering pleasure and even the possibility of real tenderness.

SEVEN

LOVE—AND FEAR

But then, one morning in February 1988, over a year after my return, I finished an early walk through Delhi's Lodhi Gardens— its pearl-like tombs and great trees ethereally beautiful in the mist—and exited onto Lodhi Road, where my car was parked. There I ran into a man who became one of the greatest loves of my adult life. It was a lucky accident, so fortuitous that it would not have happened if either of us had taken a few seconds more in reaching that pavement where our paths crossed, where we looked at each other, where we struck up that first conversation.

He was a mystery man: a Frenchman from Paris, though of Tamil and Vietnamese ancestry. He was a Bharatanatyam dancer. I had never heard of a name like his: Tandavan. (He told me that Tandavan was the manifestation of the god Shiva associated with the eternal cycle of renewal brought about by perpetual creation and destruction.) I had never seen anyone who looked like him, either—a dark Nureyev, breathtakingly sexy, incredibly gentle.

Tandavan was a decade older than I, but he looked ageless. I fell in love with him instantly, not bothered by the fact that we hardly even knew each other. He fell instantly in love with me, too. This was not the fantasy of a love-starved twenty-six-year-old—I knew it as a certainty, in an unfathomable way that I've never known since. A month later, Tandavan gave up his Paris apartment and returned to Delhi to stay with me in a small rented flat in Jor Bagh, a minute's walk from the spot where we had met. We weren't strangers anymore.

Had I been with a partner less loving and less self-assured, my accumulated burdens and fears would have rapidly wrecked any relationship, as had happened with Eric in Minneapolis. But Tandavan brushed aside all my problems as if they were trivialities. Often, through the years of our relationship, I thought to myself that he was like a loving parent who was patiently teaching a child the skills of life.

With my romantic life practically barren since my school days at Doon, I needed to love and be loved without restraint. That I did with Tandavan. We gave ourselves almost desperately to each other, as if we couldn't believe we had found each other and wanted to make the most of this blessed good fortune before life snatched it away again.

Tandavan already had experience of life's vagaries: his boyfriend of thirteen years had committed suicide after a long struggle with depression back in Paris, and though more than two years had passed, he was still drifting along, unable to wholly live in Paris or to leave it. My desperation sprang from years of yearning for romantic love as well as from fearing that I was doomed to a life without it. We promised to be with each other forever.

Tandavan had a gift for making everything sensually intense. Overnight, my world turned into a feast of color, smells, tastes, and senses that I hadn't even known about until then. He fed me, by hand, from small turquoise blue bowls as iridescent, fragile, and perfectly formed as birds' eggs. He called me *nai-kutti*—the Tamil diminutive for "puppy"—his tone making it a synonym for all the love he felt for me.

He dressed me in his chalk-white cotton *lungi*s, with thin borders of gold, red, and blue. He bought handwoven papers to draw and paint on, making me stroke them with my eyes closed to feel their concentrated mix of nubby grain and silk. He brought me music: I fell under the thrall of Maharajapuram Santhanam and M. S. Subbulakshmi, as well as Maria Callas and Édith Piaf.

Of all those pleasures, the most sublime was watching Tandavan practice Bharatanatyam every morning on the small patio outside our flat. There was the rhythmic, syllabic Carnatic music, the vocals punctuated by the beats of a *mridangam* and the plaintive notes of a violin. There was the geometric precision of his arm movements. There was the strength with which he sprang and whirled from the demi-plié position. There was the resounding force with which his bare feet hit the ground. There was his beauty—his antelopelike musculature, neither distinctly male nor female, the expressiveness of his dark eyes, the sheen of sweat on his velvety brown skin, the single line of hair that rose to his navel, the areolas that ringed his nipples. Shiva must indeed look like this in his ecstatic, dancing form as the creator of life.

Tandavan, at Delhi's Jantar Mantar

Then there was the physical everyday intimacy. I couldn't get enough of that. My Brahmanical obsession with personal hygiene fell away. On waking, I kissed Tandavan passionately without waiting for either of us to brush our teeth. I wore his shirts to work and his *kurta*s at home, inhaling his distinctive chocolaty smell from them. I showered with him, and we soaped every part of each other's bodies—parts that I had never yet touched in another person, let alone caressed. I licked, kissed, and mouthed every single inch of him—deep into his mouth, his ears, his eyelids, his nipples, his armpits, his almost womanly buttocks, his anus, his balls and dark cock, his toes, and the soles of his feet, cracked and leathery from dancing. The tastes of the most intimate parts of his body were the richest nourishment to me.

And then there was the sex, lovemaking beyond anything I had ever imagined. Every inch of Tandavan's body seemed to be an erogenous zone, alive to pleasure, so much in contrast to mine, which had till then been deadened by denial. His nipples—as large and sensitive as I imagined a woman's to be—became my obsessions, and I tongued and sucked at them as if I were an infant suckling his mother.

Tandavan taught me to forget myself and surrender to pleasure. A giant dam of desire, pent up since my adolescence at Doon, broke inside me. We had sex all the time, many times a day. There were hour-long sessions as well as quickies. Sex when I was burning with fever; sex when he was unwell. We were insatiable.

Tandavan was the first person to fuck me. It was agonizingly painful. Not only was I a virgin, but he was rough with desire and his cock was large. I remember flailing angrily at him to stop, to go slower, to ease the burning pain. But ultimately he was all inside me, and despite the continuing discomfort and pain, there was soon more unmanageable pleasure than I had ever known before, driving me to the most uncontrolled, wild orgasm. (I thought to myself that heterosexual men—knowing only how to fuck—were missing out on a realm of fantastic erotic pleasure.)

And soon, to my astonishment, through Tandavan I discovered an insatiable pleasure in fucking. My fantasy role-playing from my childhood had always been to be fucked by the men I was attracted to—but now, with Tandavan, I found I loved to fuck even more than being fucked, though being fucked gave me the most all-consuming orgasms.

There was physical pleasure beyond my comprehension in the sex—and there was communion. We had to possess each other and ejaculate inside each other for our union to strengthen, to be fertilized.

I turned my back on celibacy without any regrets. There had been nothing enlightening about it, that destructive struggle against an integral human longing, that twisted obsession with excising a need as natural and essential as breath.

✧

In the first month or so, Tandavan and I used condoms. But I soon threw caution to the winds and began to have unprotected sex.

I knew well that I was placing myself at risk. Tandavan had come of age at a point when AIDS was exploding unnoticed in Paris, as in other major Western cities, and the odds were high that he might have contracted HIV. We didn't know either way, because he had never taken an HIV test. Though there was no place to test for the virus in India back then without the risk of the results being leaked, I could have asked Tandavan to have himself tested on one of his frequent visits to France. But I didn't. My acceptance of the risks, after years of protecting myself worriedly, was an unspoken affirmation that our lives and futures were bound together forever.

✧

Over the months, our life settled into a full, happy routine. Tandavan taught dance and art at the nearby Lycée Français on Aurangzeb Road, going off on his bicycle every morning. He then went on to dance practice at his music accompanist's home. Even after the honeymoon period had long expired, we ached to see each other. I would leave work as early as I could, driving my little Fiat home as fast as possible.

Delhi was still verdant and orderly, and we lived in its most idyllic part. In the adjacent Lodhi Gardens, there were glorious trees and bird life—frangipani, laburnum, silk-cotton, Indian rosewood, and *gulmohar*; mynahs, kites, parakeets, owls, hornbills, sunbirds, and even the occasional cormorant. In the evenings, between the India International Centre and the embassies, there was a constant supply of films, dance recitals, and talks.

At home, Tandavan made inventive fresh salads, casseroles that were a fusion of France and Pondicherry, and bananas flambées. We inevitably had company. Many of my closest friends had moved back to Delhi after university abroad. Tandavan, free-spirited and exotically beautiful, was a magnet. Perhaps too often for my taste, our one-bedroom flat would be bursting at the seams with an assortment of guests—Indian, French, and innumerable other nationalities—for impromptu dinner parties.

Tandavan and I often went to my brother Pratap's home, where he and his family treated us warmly. I found even an greater warmth and naturalness at the home of my only other relative in Delhi, my aunt Nandini, the very youngest of my mother's five siblings and hence of my generation rather than my mother's. We had been close since our childhood. I had not discussed with her my being gay, so I was surprised and deeply touched to see that from the moment that Tandavan and I started living together she made it a point to specify that he was always invited with me to her in-laws' home, where she lived in a traditional joint family. From every one of her family, Tandavan and I only felt love and warmth. They may have privately discussed my being gay among them, but not once in their company did I ever feel that my choice of romantic partner was remarkable or made me different.

I was struck that my other favorite aunt, Usha, who lived in the small town of Jabalpur in Madhya Pradesh, also treated my relationship with Tandavan with complete ease, insisting that we visit her often, giving us a bedroom with a double bed, and taking care to give us privacy. I thought of telling her and Nandini categorically about Tandavan and my being a couple, but decided against it on realizing that they were certainly already aware of it yet had not asked for any explanation on my part. All the evidence began to convince me that traditional Indians were immeasurably more accepting of same-sex desire than Anglicized Indians like my father. Siddhartha, with whom I had been debating the matter, insisted that that was true, judging from his personal experience of being raised in a more Indian setting than I, a sprawling extended family that shared a large Calcutta house.

In contrast, my father—though unfailingly courteous to Tanda-van—did not display the same kind of warmth. I didn't raise the matter with him, as all I wanted him to do was what he was doing already, treating Tandavan politely. But the unfortunate downside was that I stopped joining my parents and brothers on family holidays, to which my brothers' girlfriends were invited. It created something of a hiatus in my relationship with my father after a decade in which we had drawn closer and closer.

✧

One outcome of that turning point in my life was that I now longed to taste everything that I had denied myself so far—and so, a few months after we got together, Tandavan and I began having a sexually open relationship.

It began as thrilling threesomes with some of the attractive young Frenchmen posted in Delhi for their mandatory year of military service. We then branched out on our own. Beyond bouts of acute jealousy—mostly on my part because Tandavan had had experience with navigating the matter in his previous relationship—none of it caused real stress. Our hearts belonged to each other. The casual sex amounted to just extra heapings of sensate pleasures. Those trysts, I was to later realize, also proved to be milestones in my developing a rational, uncomplicated attitude toward sexuality.

I started off by rediscovering the myriad cruising areas in Delhi that Siddhartha had shown me in my days of abstinence. At the vast Nehru Park, as the sun began to set, the atmosphere would crackle with lust as scores of men would eye one another hotly, strike up flirtations, and then—as darkness fell—disappear into the park's numerous groves and rock outcrops to have sex. At the busy Dhaula Kuan bus stop, where the nearby expanses of unlit open land and parks provided ample privacy for sex, the numerous cruisers included fit young *jawan*s from the adjacent army base. Even in the congested, brightly lit Connaught Circle in downtown Delhi, I could see dozens of men cruising one another, usually going off to cheap hotels or homes for sex but sometimes furtively enjoying hand jobs or blow jobs in the small neighborhood park.

Everywhere in India that I traveled as a journalist, I came to find that there was a rip-roaring same-sex life among men. They were desperately seeking one another out for sex in parks, public toilets, railway sidings, any secluded spot. Many would travel for hours to get to those cruising spots. In some of the areas, it often felt like a frenzied sex party, entire crowds of men dissolving into pairs or even small groups. It was thrilling to witness and participate in all of it.

Even more astonishing than the massive scale of nighttime cruising was finding, once I grew attuned to it, that men were picking other men up almost everywhere and at every hour—during any routine interaction in the day, in shops, while walking down a street, or waiting at the bus stop. The flirtation had its own secret lingo. It worked through gestures and innuendos known only to those already initiated into the sexual network but invisible to all others: a deep stare and an inviting smile, a handshake held for far too long, a hand dropping suggestively to the crotch, or the otherwise inexplicable offer of "*Aur kuch sewa kar saktha hoon?*" ("Can I serve you in any other way?").

Given the lack of privacy in India, those connections usually led to assignations at night. But sometimes the goal was immediate sex, and ardent men would try to beguile me into a quickie in the corner of a shop or a by-lane, which somehow proved to be magically shielded from the pressing crowds in a way that was fully in sight yet invisible for the moment. I was left profoundly impressed with Indian ingenuity when it came to finding places for sex.

Participating in that sexual network was a vast range of men, almost anyone who mixed in public spaces rather than stayed in the isolation of elite privacy. They ranged from college students to policemen and soldiers to the myriad laborers, shopkeepers, and taxi drivers working in the vast informal sector, besides a smattering of white-collar professionals and a handful of foreigners.

I soon came to agree with what Siddhartha had long been telling me from his own experiences: virtually every youngish Indian male, barring those with westernized backgrounds like ours, burdened with a Victorian paranoia about homosexuality, was up for having sex with other men. As to whether they were gay or bisexual by orientation, or were having sex with men only as a fallback because women would almost never have sex outside of marriage or prostitution, was a conundrum that Siddhartha and I often argued over. The matter was complicated by the fact that though most of the men were married— or would eventually be married, per the social norm—they saw their wives infrequently, often after gaps of many months or even a year or more. The women stayed back in their native villages and towns, while the men moved to cities to find work. Obviously, there was no doubt that all those men were strongly attracted to other men, experiencing sexual pleasure with male partners, after which they continued seeking them out for more. Just what that meant in terms of primary or preferred sexual orientation was less clear.

Even less clear was the related matter that Siddhartha and I often also argued over—whether traditional Indian men and women were qualitatively more accepting of same-sex desire than those of us who were "Macaulay's Children." Siddhartha took the view that traditional Indians were far more accepting of same-sex desire than Anglicized Indians, whether it concerned men or women, saying that it sprang from tolerant religious and cultural traditions as well as from the limitless physical intimacy allowed only between those of the same sex, both as children and as adults.

I had mixed views on the matter. I saw that my aunts and other less Anglicized relatives had handled the fact that Tandavan and I were in a committed relationship in the most natural, constructive way I could have imagined, drawing him into the family fold with no questions asked. Moreover, from what I saw and experienced firsthand, many nonelite Indian men treated same-sex desire as routine and acceptable to an astonishing degree, qualitatively different from the overt prejudice displayed by Anglicized Indians or the kind of violent homophobia that erupted so regularly in the United States and United Kingdom as to be a defining cultural trait, such as gay bashing or the barbaric schoolyard tradition of "smear the queer."

I found that was true in both urban and rural settings. The naturalness with which the men expressed their desire was such that I was often taken aback.

The handsome man in Bombay with whom I had that unforgettable experience of making love on a staircase landing, just months after my returning to India, had displayed no discomfort at all with our bodies or what we did together. In a village not far from Delhi, where I was reporting an article on agriculture, two young brothers—barely out of their teens, their *kurta-pajama*s brown with dust from the fields—pleaded with me to spend the night at their family home rather than drive back to Delhi, their voices thick with desire, each gripping one of my hands, ardent coconspirators and bitter rivals at the same time.

In rural Bihar, where I was volunteering with a grassroots organization, one smitten man would serenade me with amorous Hindi film songs as we bathed at the communal hand pump every evening. That was the zenith of his ceaseless daylong advances. Our coworkers, all male, egged him on as if they were family members trying to facilitate a suitable marriage.

Outside Benares's Ramnagar Fort, I was ogled by two handsome young policemen sprawled out on a *charpai*, their limbs intertwined in a loose embrace. Winking, they patted their bed invitingly and called out to me in Hindi to join them, paying no heed to the crowds of Indian tourists passing by. The head of security at a Madras hotel, a man with a Tarzan-like physique and torn underwear that resembled that hero's loincloth, spent hours through one night making tender love to me.

Innumerable incidents such as those left me feeling that same-sex desire was both individually and culturally acceptable among quintessentially Indian Indians, even if it almost unfailingly ignited Victorian antigay bigotry among its Anglicized population. Not just on matters of same-sex desire, but on other counts, too, I was now finding that traditional Indian culture—which I had once shunned as retrograde—

often compared favorably to Anglicized India, whose norms seemed to combine the most patriarchal and oppressive aspects of elite British and Indian society.

Indeed, when we swapped tales of our adventures, Siddhartha and I often hypothesized, in amazement, that average Indian men were actually indiscriminately polysexual—either simply because they were desperate for sexual release and didn't care who provided it or possibly because they were genuinely attracted to the spectrum of genders. That omnisexuality was vividly evident in cruising areas that were frequented not just by gay men but also by small numbers of *hijra*s and women sex workers. (*Hijra* is a widely used term for a range of "third gender" traditions found across the Indian subcontinent of men who dress in women's attire but consider themselves neither strictly male nor female but an advanced amalgam of genders, with no exact match in the Western taxonomy of gender and sexual orientation. Many, though far from all, voluntarily choose ritualized castration.) Many of the men who were cruising would flirt with whichever of the women sex workers, *hijra*s, and men they were attracted to. Their decision about whom they eventually had sex with seemed to be determined by sexual attraction to the individuals available, as well as whether the *hijra* or woman sex worker was so attractive that it justified paying for sex rather than having it for free with one of the many available men.

So it was ironic that even many men who routinely came to the cruising areas seeking sex with other men had ambivalent and even homophobic feelings. While having sex, the men would vociferously insist on playing only the penetrating "male" role. They would avoid touching my genitals, sometimes even asking me to hide them from sight. They would reject any intimacy or gentleness such as kissing. They would show no reciprocity in terms of sexual acts. Their aim was literally *paani girana*—to "drop water," semen, as speedily as possible.

Those boorish men displayed all the depressing, warped twists of Indian male sexuality that I was coming to learn about. They were fixated on sex, talking about it incessantly in the most adolescent, prurient way. Yet they were torn by visceral disgust at actually having it, convinced that not only their own but particularly their partner's genitals were not merely dirty but also "polluting," in the foundational Hindu metaphysical sense of being one of the endless list of things considered so defiling as to imperil an individual's purity and caste status. That intense conflict was no doubt the reason why sex with those men was inevitably brutish and short, bereft of the headlong eroticism I had learned from Tandavan.

I had little patience with those men, even if they were physically attractive, and began to cut off flirtations as soon as I spotted telltale signs. Friends told me that some of the men would even get threatening or violent once they had ejaculated—demanding money, hitting them, or directing other men to their homes for forced sex. I snuffed out any threats with the authoritative, upper-class manner I put on.

Strikingly, in my experience, a disproportionate number of the homophobic and abusive men were policemen, with a smaller number comprised of swaggering young thugs. (In contrast, men from the army or other armed forces almost never displayed homophobia, just enjoying sex wholeheartedly.) The police made many of the cruising sites dangerously unsafe for the men there, to the point that apprehensiveness was almost as palpable an emotion as lust. Even off duty or out of uniform, they would use police IDs and force to extort sex and money. The hapless victim would beg and plead but eventually give in to their demands, faced with the even more terrifying threat of being hauled off to the police station to face worse torments and the risk of blackmail. Tellingly, the worst violence was directed at the men whom they had seen servicing others, especially if they were at all feminine in appearance.

I unfailingly intervened if I saw any harassment or abuse taking place, drawing out my government-issued press card and barking at the offenders in my most commanding manner. It invariably had the desired effect. After some grumbling, the policemen would leave, having reached some face-saving compromise for themselves, such as mumbling that I would be held responsible if they misbehaved again.

In time, after my travels across India, I decided that both macho behavior and the concomitant homophobia were strongest in the north, getting steadily milder as one headed toward its southern or eastern parts. I was not sure if that had something to do with the greater dominance of elite or land-owning castes in the northern region or the extreme misogyny of these areas, or if there were other factors at play. But there was no doubt of the harsh, poisoned notions of masculinity that northern men—especially those who were from well-off, dominant castes and groups—were raised with.

And though I eventually began to agree with Siddhartha's argument that traditional Indian culture was significantly more tolerant of same-sex desire than British or American culture, I also felt that India had been changed too much due to British rule, particularly because of its virulently homophobic laws and policing systems, for that legacy to have a significant impact any longer on the level of lived realities, with the vestiges of the traditional acceptance now outweighed by prejudice and violence. Consequently, I came to feel that despite the widespread homosociability, the limitless opportunities for male-on-male sex, and even the vivid examples of ease with same-sex desire among average Indians, the outcome was, in the balance, not a happy one. It did not make a haven—it provided only a dark space for us criminalized people to hide in, afraid and ashamed, and to have nothing more than furtive, hidden sex.

⸭

Despite the joy that I had found in India with Tandavan, there was no escaping the burdens of secrecy and fear that came with being gay in the India of that era. Once I began to live with him in a rented flat, rather than at my brother's home, those myriad apprehensions intensified into a constant low-level fear, much like a chronic fever. This was so even though Jor Bagh is one of the few areas of Delhi inhabited by numerous foreigners, where Tandavan and I did not stick out as sorely as we would have elsewhere.

By being together constantly—in our car, on the veranda of our flat, walking and biking together, going shopping—we drew the attention of some of our neighbors as well as of the domestic help and private guards in the area. From their comments and stares, I realized that Tandavan and I were the subject of much discussion, some of it patently suspicious and unfriendly. Tandavan remained relaxed and unguarded, but that was not surprising, as he was—for all intents and purposes—a foreigner to India and oblivious to many of its realities.

My tensions would cross into fear whenever we were being intimate with each other—whether it was kissing, having sex, or just cuddling together. I was aware that we were violating India's criminal laws, even in the privacy of our flat, and we could be arrested and imprisoned in consequence.

And then, one terrible evening, less than a year after I started living with Tandavan, my worst fears became a reality.

EIGHT

PRISONS

On that dreadful night in the winter of 1988, I had infinite time to castigate myself for my folly in moving back to India, my folly in not heeding my father's warnings.

Earlier that day, at the *Washington Post*'s Delhi office, I had received a call from the officer in charge of the Jor Bagh police station, who said that some neighbors had complained about me, although he refused to say what the complaints were. Casually, he suggested I drop by for a talk.

It was about 7:00 p.m. when Tandavan and I entered the police station, an unremarkable single-story building, its yellow paint faded and peeling, located at a quiet crossroads near our home. A few policemen sat in the hallway, desultorily talking to one another. They glanced at us but didn't stir. Bare bulbs emitted a faint, depressing light. The place felt like one more outpost of India's apathetic and callous bureaucracy, instead of a station serving one of India's most elite neighborhoods.

One of the policemen guided us to the officer's room, and after he had checked with the officer, we were told to enter. I walked through and immediately realized that I had made a terrible mistake going there.

The man sitting behind the desk in the muddy-brown uniform of the Delhi police looked at me with such aggressive loathing that I thought, momentarily, that he had mistaken me for someone else. He was short and powerfully built, with a clipped mustache, possibly a decade older than I. Looking only at me, not at Tandavan, he burst out angrily, almost as if in a rage, "Mr. Dube, I know all about you. I have received enough complaints about you. You are a homo! You have naked men dancing at your house, exposing themselves. Go back to America! If you want to live here, you will live as an Indian, not like an American!"

Breathless with shock, I just stood there.

The officer must have misinterpreted my silence. Or perhaps he lost whatever self-control he possessed. Banging his fist on the table, he shouted, "Watch it, I will come and arrest you! I will arrest you tonight! I will arrest you wherever I like, from the street or even from your house!"

My heart pounded, in a mix of rage and apprehension. I looked at that obnoxious man, who hated me simply because I was gay, and suppressed an urge to punch him really hard. Instead I collected myself and said, steadily but with anger in my voice, "Just try and arrest me, and see what happens."

All hell broke loose. The officer sprang up from his chair and charged around his desk toward us, his fists clenched as if he meant to hit me. Changing his mind abruptly, he pressed a bell on his desk. "Lock up these *gaandu*s!" he yelled in Hindi—calling us sodomites— at the two policemen who came rushing in. Then he approached me and stood practically nose to nose with me, his face apoplectic. I didn't budge. From the way he pushed back his shoulders, then locked his hands behind his back, I could see the effort it was taking for him to keep from hitting me.

Tandavan had been shocked and silent through all that. He was clearly finding it difficult to keep up with the Hindi and even with the officer's heavily accented English. Now he grabbed my arm, no doubt worried that I would hit back if the officer struck me.

The next thing we knew, Tandavan and I were being marched toward the back of the station. I presumed that was where the cells were, but the officer came to the door of his office and yelled that we should be locked up in the constables' duty room. The sole constable working there was taken aback when his colleagues told him that we were to be locked up here; clearly that was not normal procedure. I felt a slight relief; the officer was obviously restraining himself because he feared that I was well connected.

The policemen left. We heard the door being bolted. Through a large window near the door, I saw that one of the policemen had seated himself on a nearby stool to keep guard.

Tandavan and I sat down on the benches in the corner of the room. We were too shaken to speak. Everything had escalated too fast.

I forced myself to breathe deeply, so that my heartbeat would slow down and I could think more clearly. I put my hand on Tandavan's and tried to comfort him. Everything would be fine, I said. The officer knew better than to hit or jail us. The guy had held himself back because he realized that he would eventually get into trouble with his superiors for threatening me needlessly.

While I comforted Tandavan, my head swirled with angry recriminations. I had been foolish to listen to the officer on the phone that morning, I thought. I should have realized from his dismissive tone and his refusal to specify what the complaints were about that there was trouble in the offing.

Why had I assumed that being a government-accredited foreign correspondent would give me the leverage to handle anything? Why hadn't I had the basic common sense to tell Pratap, my brother, before coming here? He knew how to deal with India sensibly.

Or should I have left a note for Siddhartha, who was staying with us that weekend, saying that we had gone to the police station? He would have been able to do something. Why, why, why hadn't I behaved like a competent adult?

I wondered about the hate-filled threats the officer had spewed at us. How did he know I was a "homo"? Where had he gotten those ideas about naked men dancing in our apartment? Who on earth could have brought the fact that Tandavan and I lived together to his notice?

An hour passed. I knocked on the door, and when the guard opened it, I told him politely that I was entitled to speak to a lawyer and wanted to exercise that right. He said he would ask the officer. He came back to say that the station's public phone wasn't working. I told him I'd spotted a policeman chatting on it on our way to the lockup, but he ignored me.

It was now 9:00 p.m. I realized, to my alarm, that it was well past the time for Tandavan to have his evening dose of insulin. He had juvenile-onset diabetes and needed shots of insulin morning and night along with an adequate meal. My heart sank as I noticed telltale beads of cold sweat on Tandavan's face and the nervousness indicating that his sugar levels were dangerously out of balance. Though I knew he had kept quiet so as not to add to my worries, I couldn't keep from worriedly scolding him.

I knocked urgently on the door and asked the guard to check if they could free Tandavan. He was blameless, I pointed out, because the neighbors' complaints were against me and Tandavan had not talked back to the officer. In any case, he was a French citizen, not an Indian, and this was a medical emergency.

The guard returned a while later to say that the officer wanted to see Tandavan. It was 10:00 p.m. by now. Tandavan was sweating profusely, even though I had turned the ceiling fan on to its highest speed. He was clearly in medical distress, but before he followed the guard out, he tousled my hair and told me not to worry. It was impossible; he was all I worried about for now.

He looked ashen when he returned twenty minutes later. The officer had said that he would be released only if he signed a statement saying that he had witnessed me insulting and threatening him. Tandavan had refused to sign though the officer had badgered him relentlessly. He was utterly drunk, Tandavan said, so much so that he wasn't even trying to hide the bottle of alcohol he was drinking straight from.

The next hour was the very worst of my life—even my most fearful moments at Doon paled in comparison to this. I pleaded with the guard to get a doctor for Tandavan. He was clearly sympathetic, because it had now become obvious even to the untrained eye that Tandavan was ill. He went off once again but returned in a bit to say that the doctor would be called only if Tandavan signed the statement exonerating the officer.

Helplessly, I sat there watching my boyfriend, my love, tossing restlessly on the bench. It was nearly midnight when the door opened and four policemen came in, all carrying their wooden *laathi*s. They said they would take Tandavan to our house to have his injection and then bring him back here. By that time, Tandavan was pallid and shivering uncontrollably. As he couldn't walk, the policemen said they would take him pillion on one of their bicycles. Just as he left, I told him to quickly phone Pratap to tell him what had happened.

About half an hour later, the policeman guarding the room unbolted the door and said in a deferential tone that I was free to go. Looking at me with awe, he said that one of the city's seniormost police officials had just phoned the station officer.

I had to keep myself from running out of the police station to my car.

It was past midnight by the time I reached home. Siddhartha was waiting up for me, his face gray with worry. He didn't ask me to explain the events of the evening—and I said nothing, desperate to put them as far behind me as possible. Tandavan was fine, Siddhartha reassured me, and had fallen asleep within minutes of getting a meal and medication. But I was so filled with foreboding still that I couldn't keep myself from going straight to our bedroom to check on Tandavan, even if I woke him. Looking at his familiar, beloved frame in our familiar bed, I was filled with love and regret, blaming myself harshly for having put him in harm's way.

I tore myself away to call Pratap, to let him know that I'd reached safely. I could tell that the only thing holding him back from scolding me was concern. Minutes later, the phone rang. It was my father, calling from Calcutta. His voice was grim; his worst fears about my returning to India had come true.

The next morning, I resolved that Tandavan and I must leave India. The worst of my fears—that of being imprisoned, of being deprived of my freedom, of my ability to fight back or even to flee—had become a reality. It left me with a terrifying new awareness of what it meant to be criminalized—it meant I could be summarily imprisoned to suffer the corruption and capriciousness of India's rotten policing and judicial systems.

The only reason things hadn't taken a disastrous turn at the police station was that the homophobic officer had taken cognizance of my social status and held himself back from doing worse. From all that I had seen during my years in India, I knew that if I had been just an average gay man, Tandavan and I could have been beaten, raped, held indefinitely, and then blackmailed—our lives ruined, with no hope for recourse because we were criminals under the law.

❖

Just some months after our traumatic night at the police station, Tandavan and I learned from Siddhartha of a young gay man in Goa who had been arrested and was being held in isolation because the police and health authorities had found out that he had HIV. Siddhartha, I, and other friends in our group feared that that was the first salvo in a campaign against gays triggered by the AIDS scare, which was intensifying as a growing number of Indians came to be diagnosed with HIV.

We had long dreaded that hysteria about the disease would further demonize us. "AIDS is the last thing the Indian homosexual needed," the *Sunday* cover story on gay men had sympathetically noted in 1988. "Proscribed by law, ostracized by society, he now faces the prospect of being held responsible for a scourge that is not of his making."

My own recent experience sharpened my horror at the ordeal of Dominic D'Souza, a young man in Goa. On February 14, 1989, in Parra, a rural parish of northern Goa, Dominic had breakfast with his widowed mother and aunt, as he usually did. They left home before him and so missed meeting the lone policeman who arrived a short while later, telling Dominic that he needed to come to the police station in Mapusa, northern Goa's major town, as soon as possible. The policeman offered no explanation for why he was wanted.

Dominic was surprised, but Goa was a tranquil place then and his was a respectable Catholic family. Having phoned his boss at the Panjim branch of the World Wildlife Fund to say that he had been delayed unexpectedly, he started off for the police station on his motorbike. It didn't cross his mind to leave an explanatory note for his family.

From the moment Dominic arrived at the police station—a series of innocuous buildings dating back to Goa's Portuguese colonial rule—his life changed irrevocably. Without being told why, he was driven in a police van to the nearby Asilo Hospital, a place to which he went regularly to donate blood. Several doctors appeared and began to look closely at him, as if to conduct a medical examination without touching him. They badgered him with questions—asking if he frequented prostitutes, was homosexual, injected drugs, or had had sex on his recent holiday in Germany—but not one answered his increasingly anxious questions.

Dominic's fears turned to terror when he spotted one of the doctors entering his name into a register with "AIDS" printed across its cover. Traumatized, he did not protest when he was handcuffed and driven to an unused tuberculosis sanatorium a short distance from Mapusa. There, with the handcuffs removed, Dominic was locked, alone, in a vast room littered with rat and pigeon droppings, bare but for broken-down metal beds. Armed policemen guarded every exit. "[I] was left all alone with my helplessness and fright," Dominic wrote later of that moment. "[M]y arrest and isolation were the most traumatic and terrifying experiences of my life . . . [They] seem almost like the acts of a sadist."

Dominic D'Souza

Dominic's family and friends—led by Lucy D'Souza, his mother and a retired nurse, and Isabel de Santa Rita Vaz, a well-known professor of literature, whose amateur theater company Dominic was a part of—came to his defense. D'Souza and Vaz pleaded with Goa's administrators to release Dominic. They cited World Health Organization guidelines, which specified that people with HIV should not be incarcerated or quarantined. They emphasized that Dominic posed no threat to anyone and said they would guarantee that he would stay at home.

Dominic remained incarcerated. Officials and politicians, however sympathetic their tone, said they were constrained by the law. In 1987, Goa's legislators, concerned that their state was particularly vulnerable to an HIV epidemic because of the thousands of foreigners who were attracted to its unspoiled beaches and its fame as a drug-and-sex hippie haven, had approved punitive anti-AIDS measures that effectively turned HIV-affected people into criminals.

The state's health officials were empowered to demand HIV tests of anyone they suspected of being infected. Those who refused could be arrested even without a court warrant. Doctors were required to notify the authorities if they learned that someone had HIV, rather than protect the patient's confidentiality. Infected foreigners were to be deported, while Indians were to be imprisoned indefinitely in isolation.

In late March, Lucy D'Souza filed a case in the High Court, challenging her son's imprisonment on the grounds that it violated the Indian constitution as well as the WHO guidelines on HIV that the government had endorsed. She and Vaz also rallied public support for Dominic's cause. The Parra *panchayat* passed a resolution demanding that the authorities release Dominic and let him return home to his village.

On the day before D'Souza's suit was entered in court, she and Vaz led a massive demonstration through Panjim, the state capital, to seek Dominic's release as well as the repeal of Goa's draconian anti-AIDS law. They were joined by neighbors, women's groups, and local activist organizations. D'Souza carried a placard saying "I have AIDS, please hug me," to underscore that her HIV-positive son warranted love and support, not imprisonment and ostracism.

The support for Dominic was so strong that the *Times of India* commented, "It appears that the government [of Goa] has been taken aback at the barrage of protests and outrage from citizens, organizations and the medical community from within and outside the state over Dominic's incarceration." At least in Goa, the overreaction to AIDS could not be blamed on public sentiment. Rather, it sprang from the paranoia of government officials and the judiciary.

Eventually, on April 18, 1989, more than two months after Dominic's ordeal had begun, the court passed an interim order freeing him from his solitary confinement and placed him under house arrest. A police constable would be posted to ensure that he didn't leave his home. The court gratuitously instructed Dominic to "refrain from having sexual intercourse with any person" and not donate blood or act in "any manner so that the dreaded disease is communicated to others," yet again displaying its prejudice that HIV-positive individuals could not be trusted to behave responsibly. It was the first, harrowing chapter in Dominic's life as a figure of national notoriety.

✦

Yet, to our surprise, even after Dominic's widely reported saga, there was no punitive campaign by the government against homosexuals as part of AIDS-control measures. The government, as well as the media, treated his case without making a single reference to what Siddhartha, I, and some of our other friends knew for a fact: that Dominic was gay. His assertion that he had contracted HIV while donating blood, via contaminated equipment, was accepted unquestioningly, even though such a scenario was highly improbable. Infections from medical sources would have led to a telltale outbreak of cases, rather than just a single one. A tailor-made escape had been provided by the Indian peculiarity—stemming from our cultural diet of extravagant religious myths—of accepting even the impossible when packaged as a melodramatic tale of noble intentions going tragically awry.

When I look back at that time, it is fascinating to see what saved us. Here we were, gay men who felt nakedly visible and threatened, certain that the hostile government—probably some department of the police or Ministry of Home Affairs—was keeping close tabs on us. We didn't realize then that we had done such a good job of hiding ourselves that we truly were invisible, both individually and as a group.

Consequently, homophobic policy makers could easily deny our existence and assert that India had no homosexuals or very few of them, that homosexuality was a Western import with no real roots in India. Thus, in an interview with Siddhartha in 1989, the director general of the Indian Council of Medical Research, Dr. A. S. Paintal, insisted that homosexuality simply didn't exist in India because it was banned and subject to a harsh criminal penalty. However absurd that argument was, Dr. Paintal and other policy makers seemed to genuinely believe it.

And so it happened that, in those early years of the epidemic, the spread of AIDS was not blamed on gay men. Those of us who could see that gay and bisexual Indian men were indeed contracting HIV in large numbers kept quiet about the trend, knowing that drawing attention would only harm us.

But there was also a second, pivotal reason why we were spared the blame. As panic about AIDS continued to spread, it was another criminalized and reviled set of outlaws who were made the scapegoat for it: women sex workers.

❖

In April 1986, a few months before I had returned to India from New York, I read Indian news reports about six prostitutes in a Madras reformatory who had been diagnosed with HIV. That marked the first scientific confirmation that the virus was spreading between individuals who had contracted the virus within India, rather than abroad.

I was not surprised to learn that the epidemic had spread to India—it was, after all, five years since the first known cases of AIDS had come to light in the United States and two years since Asia's first cases had been confirmed, in Thailand. I thought with dread that India's abysmal public health system, its largely illiterate population of 750 million, and the cultural prohibitions against discussing sexual matters would make it impossible to contain the epidemic, especially given the example of India's scant progress in coping even with age-old infectious diseases, such as tuberculosis and cholera.

By the time I began to research the lives of those women, many years later, there was only one about whom anything much was known: Selvi. The other five women had vanished without a record, their lives and history obliterated by the fact that they were mere specks among the masses of India's poor. Selvi, who, like many Indians, used only her given name, was the only one with a traceable history, photographs, and even surviving friends and family.

Yet only a little is known of her early years, the period that ended with her imprisonment. She came from a destitute Tamil family of landless laborers, and was educated through class five. She had left an abusive husband and was providing for her toddler son through sex work on the streets. Sometime in March 1986, this small, dark-complexioned woman, aged twenty-three or so, was arrested for prostitution in or near Madras.

The police took her to the Madras Vigilance Home, a government-run, women-only reformatory in the city's Mylapore neighborhood. Selvi should have been produced in a local court within a day or two. This being her first arrest for prostitution, she should have been released after paying a fine of about fifty rupees. The whole saga, however harrowing, should have lasted no more than a week or so.

But the morning after Selvi's arrest, a young medical researcher named S. Nirmala drew a syringeful of her blood—and did the same with the other women rounded up the night before. None of them dared to question or refuse her, given both the trauma of their imprisonment and the enormous chasms of class and caste that separated her from them.

The next day, Nirmala carried vials of their blood, along with those drawn from more than a hundred other prostitutes over the previous two months, to the Christian Medical College in Vellore, a three-hour journey by bus. That evening, she called her senior collaborator in Madras, the microbiologist Suniti Solomon, to say that six of the samples had tested positive for HIV.

Those results had disastrous consequences for Selvi. While the other prostitutes at the home were produced in court and subsequently either released or sentenced to long terms in the reformatory, the six who tested positive were not taken to court. The warden did not give them any explanation.

A day or two later, Dr. Solomon and Dr. Nirmala arrived at the reformatory to interview them. The director general of the Indian Council of Medical Research had instructed Dr. Solomon to find out if the prostitutes were having sex with foreigners or Indians, to learn if HIV was beginning to spread domestically. All the six said that every one of their clients had been Indian.

Only a handful of top officials in the government's health-care system were informed about the results. The six blood samples were secretly flown to the United States for confirmatory testing at the National Institutes of Health in Maryland, a process that would take several weeks. Selvi and the other women were told nothing of that, and the reformatory authorities did not seek permission from the courts to keep them in custody.

Selvi's parents, who knew that their daughter had been working as a prostitute after leaving her husband, somehow tracked her to the reformatory from their home in Ulundurpettai, a nondescript town thirty miles away. Though they were allowed to meet Selvi, the warden curtly told them that she could not be released because she had a "blood infection" that required treatment. They did not argue. They were impoverished and illiterate and lived in a hovel, while the warden—the ruler of the jail, with its imposing buildings and high walls—embodied the might of the Indian government.

At the end of April, the US National Institutes of Health informed the Indian Council of Medical Research that the women were definitely HIV-positive. On the morning of April 29, India's minister of health and family welfare, Mohsina Kidwai, announced the news in Parliament, saying that six women with "promiscuous heterosexual behavior"—an elliptical but unmistakable reference to prostitutes—had been found to be infected with HIV in Tamil Nadu. There was pandemonium in the vast hall of the Parliament. The health minister reassured her colleagues that officials were monitoring the situation closely. But press reports—which inaccurately suggested that the women were suffering from AIDS (they were still asymptomatic)—fed a public frenzy.

The panic was most intense in Madras, after a leading newspaper, *The Hindu*, ran a front-page article on April 30, having tracked the "AIDS cases" to the reformatory. Selvi and the other five women paid the price for the panic.

They were immediately separated from the others at the reformatory and imprisoned in a barred room at a distance from the main building. Food was pushed in through a small window. The women were forced to do everything in that small room—eat, sleep, go to the toilet, wash their clothes. It was "like an isolation cell for the condemned," Selvi later told a friend. Of their fearsome, unknown affliction, they knew only that it was so deadly that no one would come near them or speak to them with compassion.

But within weeks, as the focus of the panic shifted to the scores of other prostitutes and individuals across India now being discovered to be HIV-positive, Selvi and the five other HIV-positive women in the reformatory were entirely forgotten, left imprisoned in those terrible conditions. Neither Indian nor international women's groups, human rights organizations, or the medical establishment, including Dr. Solomon and Dr. Nirmala, challenged their imprisonment or its punitive conditions. Indeed, the state government continued to summarily imprison every prostitute found to be HIV-positive, often in the same Mylapore reformatory. It showed that the outcast and downtrodden, even in a democracy that prided itself on its enlightened judiciary, could be locked away even indefinitely, without due process.

Forever after in India, AIDS was thought of as a disease of women prostitutes, merely because the first indigenous cases were detected among them. They were accused of spreading the sexual infection to hapless men, who then spread it to their innocent wives and babies. They had always faced persecution, but now—as the epidemic worsened across India—it intensified to an unprecedented scale.

Unlike us gay men, they were often easy to locate—in brothels or on particular street corners. They were impoverished. And they were "sexual" women, which singled them out for vindictive scorn and abuse in India, where misogyny is at its most brutal in crushing women who do not adhere to the cultural diktat that they be chaste virgins until marriage and then devout wives until death. The trauma Tandavan and I faced at the police station was nothing compared to the ordeals that Dominic had to go through. His suffering, in turn, paled in comparison with the calamities heaped on Selvi and countless others like her.

NINE

A PERFECT STORM

L ate in the summer of 1990, a few months before my twenty-ninth birthday, Tandavan and I left Delhi. I had been awarded a scholarship by the Harvard School of Public Health to study global health policy. Tandavan was moving back to Paris for the nine months that my course work would take. We then hoped to figure out some way of living together in the United States or France, however improbable it seemed, since the immigration laws of neither nation recognized gay relationships. We avoided any mention of the eventuality that we wouldn't be able to live together somewhere in the West and that moving back together to India might be our only option for staying together.

⊕

At Harvard, it was a joy to study again. I had researched such diverse things as a journalist in India that I longed to make sense of how they fitted together and what they said about India's prospects. My years as a journalist reporting on everything from automobile pollution to rural hunger had also led me to decide to specialize in public policy. Journalism was not an ideal fit for me, given the strength of my interests in social justice issues. The profession's unrelenting focus on breaking news kept me from digging deeply into the issues of deprivation and justice that I cared about. But with graduate-level training in an aspect of public policy, I could work as a researcher and policy maker as well as use my journalism experience to be an insightful commentator.

I was drawn to public health as it was one of the few aspects of deprivation in which it was realistically possible to achieve remarkable gains fairly quickly, the recent examples ranging from the global eradication of smallpox achieved in 1980 to the across-the-board gains made in Sri Lanka and the Communist-ruled Indian state of Kerala despite their relative poverty. In contrast, I had already seen that the process of realizing progress in other vital aspects of human well-being such as incomes, ownership of productive assets, education, and sociopolitical emancipation often took decades of effort and battles against groups that opposed equitable progress. Though I realized that progress was needed on every front of well-being if people were to move out of poverty and that providing better health in isolation could be helpful only to a finite degree, I needed a promising front to keep alive my hope that the burden of poverty in India and globally was not insurmountable. At a personal level, too, health was the aspect of human well-being I had felt most deeply about ever since I could remember, from watching my brother Pratap struggle to cope with the lifelong impact of the polio that had ravaged his legs.

I cared about everything I studied in those nine months of intensive course work at Harvard, whether it was infectious diseases, malnutrition, or epidemiology. But from the outset, one issue was my special focus: AIDS.

In every way, this was a disease about me—this virus that was intertwined with our essential human longing for sex and love, and with being outlawed, shamed, and persecuted because societies invariably seemed unable to address sexual matters rationally or humanely. For all I knew, I could have been infected with HIV by now. And the unhinged hatred of gay men spotlighted by our association with

AIDS—the Reverend Jerry Falwell claiming that our deaths were "God's punishment for homosexuals" and Senator Jesse Helms attempting to slash AIDS funding on the grounds that we contracted the disease through "deliberate, disgusting, revolting conduct"—triggered my fighting spirit.

I was immensely fortunate that Jonathan Mann, the architect of the international response to the pandemic, who had resigned just a few months earlier from leading the World Health Organization's Global Programme on AIDS in Geneva, had joined the faculty of the public health school. Mann had taken a disease that political leaders and officials invariably sought to ignore because of its sordid association with sex and turned it into an international health priority in just the four years between 1986 and 1990 that he led the global AIDS program.

Mann agreed to be one of my two academic advisers. In my second semester, I enrolled in his seminar course on AIDS.

His course was held in a small room in a modern high-rise in the busy downtown portion of Boston that housed Harvard's medical campus, including the public health school. Mann—an odd, compelling figure, frizzy hair standing atop an unending forehead, nattily dressed in a sports coat and bow tie—never sat at his desk. Instead, he would launch into his lectures as soon as he entered, almost as if he couldn't hold himself back, pacing the breadth of the room and stopping only when he wanted to challenge one of his two dozen students, drawn from every corner of the world, in debate.

He gave us students unforgettable insights into the pandemic. Mann was an epidemiologist by training, and one of his first efforts at the Global Programme on AIDS was to collate more accurate worldwide data on the epidemic. The results showed that AIDS was spreading exponentially—12 million people around the globe had contracted HIV by 1991, WHO estimated, of whom 2.5 million had died. In the United States alone, the worst-hit rich nation, one million people were estimated to be HIV-positive, and more than 150,000 had died.

Strikingly, the data now showed that the epidemic was spreading even more fiercely in developing countries than in the wealthy Western nations where it had first drawn attention a decade earlier. Eighteen of the world's twenty most severe national AIDS epidemics were in poor countries, mainly in Africa and the Caribbean. The "gay plague" was also the poor man's plague.

It was astounding: a disease that had come to scientific attention as a killer of five gay men in California had—by its tenth anniversary—morphed into a pandemic of millions of men and women around the globe, a vast majority of them heterosexual. Those millions were going to suffer unimaginably and die essentially because their leaders had inexcusably ignored this killer disease, out of discomfort with the sexual matters it raised or the hate-filled prejudice that these immoral people were reaping the wages of their own sin.

Even worse lay ahead, WHO warned. The number of people cumulatively infected worldwide was likely to soar to 30 million to 40 million by the year 2000. Though those estimates were disparaged at the time for being alarmist, they eventually proved to fall many millions short of the reality.

The epidemic was taking its greatest toll in sub-Saharan Africa. African leaders had so far dismissed AIDS as a Western affliction caused by promiscuity, saying that their traditional societies were immune to such a disease. But by now, in some parts of central Africa, as many as one in three of all urban adults were estimated to be HIV-positive, in comparison to an estimated one in thirty-five adults in New York City, the worst-affected American city. (Retroactive studies showed that HIV had probably begun to spread unnoticed in Africa since the 1970s or even earlier; by the time AIDS was "discovered" in the United States in 1981, more than 100,000 people in sub-Saharan Africa were probably already infected.) Deaths and funerals had become a daily occurrence, with countless men and women dying in the prime of their lives, leaving behind orphans and aging parents, ghost towns and untended fields.

The crisis was a warning of things to come in other developing regions. Asia, with more than half the world's population, was emerging as a new epicenter of HIV, Mann told us, because of a similarly incendiary mix of poverty and illiteracy, youthful populations, the barriers women faced in negotiating as equals in sexual relations, and high rates of the ulcerative sexually transmitted infections that enhance the spread of HIV.

That painstakingly gathered evidence belatedly convinced government leaders that the world faced an "unprecedented global crisis." By the time Mann resigned from WHO in early 1990—after clashes with the body's autocratic new director general, Hiroshi Nakajima—almost every developing country had begun national AIDS programs, nearly a billion dollars had been mobilized to finance their efforts, and the UN General Assembly had discussed the epidemic several times, the first instances of a disease being taken up for consideration by that body.

Of course, however crucial, those were just the preparatory first steps. Whether they would be translated into the right kind of action, and at the massive scale required, was another matter altogether. The history of public health was a depressing record of epidemics that could have been far more easily tackled than AIDS and yet weren't. AIDS had all the elements of a perfect storm—and that, too, a worldwide storm.

Policy makers, including conventional public health experts, had little understanding of sex and balked at grappling with the role of sexual behaviors in the spread of the disease. The role that public health efforts could play was also unclear, given that there was no treatment, cure, or vaccine in sight. It seemed plausible that more could be achieved by urgent societywide efforts to tackle inequality between the sexes, illiteracy, the lack of knowledge about how to negotiate condom use, the near-universal ignorance and discomfort about sexual matters, those being the basic factors that left so many millions ill equipped to keep from contracting HIV.

Given those unique challenges, Mann's other achievement at WHO was arguably even more historic. That was to push governments into agreeing to AIDS control strategies that respected human rights rather than relied on compulsion. The odds were heavily against him.

So far, health officials the world over had sought to control the spread of AIDS by using the punitive measures traditionally employed with other sexually transmitted infections such as syphilis and gonorrhea. They hinged on compulsory examination and testing, "contact" tracing (of the sexual partners of infected individuals), and enforced treatment, hospitalization, or quarantine for any length of time. Their reliance on such repressive measures was even stronger with AIDS because the hysteria about the disease made it seem to many to be an implacable demonic force rather than a challenging viral epidemic.

Mann's usual passion intensified visibly when he started explaining why a diametrically different approach was needed to control AIDS, one that protected every individual's human rights.

Basic civil liberties had to be explicitly protected because, virtually everywhere, the disease epidemic was followed by an epidemic of human rights abuses—with everybody from families, neighbors, and employers to government authorities turning on people with AIDS or whole sections of society blamed for spreading the disease. The abuses worsened once tests to detect HIV infection were developed in 1985. Governments authorized public health authorities—often working in tandem with the police—to carry out compulsory tests on groups presumed to be at high risk and to detain or isolate infected people. By the close of the epidemic's first decade, more than a hundred countries had passed special AIDS-related legislation, most of which violated the civil liberties of particular groups.

In addition, the broad sets of rights that are essential for human well-being had to be promoted, Mann said, pointing out that AIDS was disproportionately concentrated among populations whose human rights were least fulfilled. "In each society," he argued, "those people who, before HIV/AIDS arrived, were marginalized, stigmatized, and discriminated against become those at highest risk of HIV infection. . . . HIV is now becoming a problem mainly for *les exclus*, the 'excluded ones' living at the margins of society."

Mann insisted that the traditional, coercive public health approach was doomed to fail with AIDS. One crucial difference posed by HIV was that people remained asymptomatic and healthy for typically six to eight years from the time of initial infection, meaning that they could unwittingly pass on the virus to sexual partners during that period. Also, even resorting to mass testing to detect people with HIV offered no solution—short of the impossible one of quarantining millions till their eventual death. The use of extreme measures would worsen the already intense public hysteria about AIDS and drive individuals who were infected or at risk underground, away from health services.

All that made sense to me. From my earliest days in the United States in the 1980s, as the epidemic had swelled, I had witnessed the irrational hysteria and the abuses that had followed: the demonization and then the persecution of gay men, drug users, Haitians, and other groups associated with the disease in the popular imagination. Twenty states had considered laws to quarantine—presumably for the remainder of their lives—the tens of thousands who were HIV-positive or sick. HIV-positive children had been barred from schools; their homes had even been torched. Doctors who treated AIDS patients had been targeted. And the activism of gay American men had shown that AIDS was inherently a civil rights matter—as they battled against being thrown out of their homes or being fired from jobs, against the political indifference that stalled the search for cures, against the blatant hatred that led to them being denied medical care even when agonizingly sick.

I also knew from personal experience that criminalization and marginalization made gay and bisexual men, as a group, more vulnerable to the epidemic. The pathways were innumerable: by preventing us from having healthy, open relationships; by forcing us away from our families as well as from mainstream society; by giving us no option but to seek furtive, unsafe sex in parks and toilets; by keeping us from openly seeking information about safe-sex methods, buying condoms and lubricants, or getting tested to know our HIV status. It was only from Mann's teaching that I could begin to frame these handicaps in the formal human rights language of the "systematic unfulfillment of broader civil, political, economic, social and cultural rights."

But most of my classmates were midcareer health officials or practicing doctors. Almost unanimously, they had been taught that human rights could be legitimately set aside in light of public health imperatives, especially during epidemics of contagious diseases. "Leper colonies," in which countless men and women suffering from leprosy were forcibly confined for their lifetimes, exemplified the appeal of this approach. Even the Hippocratic Oath—which requires doctors to keep their patients' ailments secret—would have to be put aside in the face of the public good. It was no wonder that many of the students did not respond with ready comprehension during Mann's class sessions on human rights. It earned us his ire—any poor student who dared question him was frowned at as if she or he were a nitwit.

Despite the odds, Mann's powers of persuasion were such that, within a year of joining WHO, he had succeeded in getting the world's governments to disavow their reliance on the old coercive approaches and commit to a more humane strategy based on promoting knowledge about AIDS, responsible behavior, and human rights. Every year thereafter, he strategically pushed governments to make ever more explicit commitments at the WHO's World Health Assembly, the UN General Assembly, and other global bodies. The speed of change was astonishing.

The first global resolutions approved on AIDS, in 1987, did not explicitly mention human rights. But by the following year the world's health ministers had declared, at a London summit, "We emphasize the need in AIDS prevention programs to protect human rights and human dignity. Discrimination against, and stigmatization of, HIV-infected people and people with AIDS, and population groups undermine public health and must be avoided." And by 1991, a year after Mann's resignation, a UN General Assembly resolution explicitly committed governments and intergovernmental organizations to "protect the human rights and dignity of HIV-infected persons, persons with AIDS and members of particular population groups" as well as to "avoid discriminatory action against and stigmatization of them in the provision of services, and in employment and travel."

Those achievements by Mann and his team marked one of WHO's finest moments of global leadership in the organization's forty-year history. Mann had succeeded in ensuring that a disease spread by sex and drugs and associated with undesirable people be viewed rationally as a public policy priority. He had also convinced the world's governments to make written global commitments that, in their efforts to control the pandemic, they would respect the basic human rights of every individual—whether it concerned people stigmatized for being infected with AIDS or those of us who were so reviled for being gay, selling sex, or using drugs that governments would not even mention us in their declarations.

The fate of us outlaws hung tenuously on those coded, formalistic mentions of "particular population groups," of "discrimination" and "stigmatization," of "human rights" and "human dignity." Those elliptical words were the key to our very survival.

Would the world's governments take them seriously? Would the United Nations—that imperfect, embattled mediator between hostile nations—emerge as an honest advocate on our behalf?

If those commitments were honored, governments would move to provide sex workers, gay men, and drug users with effective HIV prevention services, as well as undertake legal and policy changes to address the terrible disadvantages we had long faced. If they were ignored, we were likely to be subjected to even more harm and persecution than ever before. Whatever the outcome, we would probably not even have had those opportunities if Mann hadn't pushed governments to agree that AIDS was a human rights issue just as much as it was a deadly disease.

⊹

The year rushed by at a speed that I could barely imagine. I missed Tandavan intensely—I phoned him every weekend and in turn would find rambling, loving letters from him in the mail, full of his endearments for me of *bébé* and *naikutti*, the writing interspersed with ink portraits of whichever friends he happened to be with—but there was scarcely any time to let it get me down. The weekdays were consumed by class; the weekends by readings and papers. There was no end of dinners and events to go to, not just with new friends among my fellow students but because Rosie, my beloved friend from college in Delhi, was now living in Boston with her husband, Badri.

I unwound once again as the tension that had accumulated from living in India fell away. I was again just myself—not evading the fact of being gay if professors or fellow students asked an innocuous personal question, not worried as in Delhi that my landlord and neighbors would ostracize me if they discovered I was gay, not apprehensive that some terrible persecution lay ahead.

I went half a dozen times to gay bars and to parties hosted by the Harvard gay group. I had two torrid affairs. One was an intensely sexual one, with a Mexican dancer whom I had first met when he was touring in India; he was now in New York City with the Martha Graham Dance Ensemble. He was beautiful like a male antelope, hard muscle stretched over fine bones, with buttocks of a breathtaking fullness.

The other affair was intensely emotional. That lovely man, Marc, was Louisiana Creole, a decade older than I, self-assured and caring, passionate about the arts as well as about social justice. Though there were moments when I felt I was headlong in love with him, soon enough some memory of Tandavan would make me realize that I was wedded to him. Perhaps Marc—whom I had told from the outset that I was in a committed relationship—also sensed that. When my second, final semester was drawing to a close, in his characteristic serious way he told me that he would be very happy if I stayed on in Boston with him, that we could get a dog and live together. He didn't reproach me when I said, some weeks later, that I could not stay on, merely said that Tandavan must be very special for me to love him so deeply. Fortunately, our relationship transitioned into an enduring friendship.

✥

In the spring of 1991, some weeks before the final semester was to end, I decided to get an HIV test. I dreaded that test even more than the previous one, back in Minneapolis in 1986. At that point, my anxiety had resulted from knowing very little about AIDS. Now I knew a lot about AIDS—and I knew I had many reasons to be worried.

Tandavan and I had stopped using condoms soon after we began living together. While living in India, I had once suggested to him that he get tested on one of his frequent visits back to France. But Tandavan had been terrified at the prospect, and I had let the matter drop, reasoning that it was too late to do anything even if he was infected; with the amount of unprotected intercourse we'd had, it was certain that I would have contracted HIV, too.

Adding to my apprehension, in the years since I had met Tandavan and become sexually active, I had had penetrative sex with at least two dozen men besides him. Though I had unfailingly used condoms with each one, I had not known that using petroleum jelly or oil as a lubricant multiplied the risk that a condom would tear, a fact that I had come to learn only during my Harvard course work.

A positive HIV result would stay on my medical records and affect my future medical insurance. So instead of going to Harvard's health services I sought out an LGBT-run HIV testing and counseling center in downtown Boston. It was housed in a nondescript building, a single large room flanked by enclosed small ones. I felt a rush of relief at seeing that instead of the clinical coldness of medical settings, it had the warmth of a community center, the sofas and chairs in the waiting area scuffed by use, newspapers and magazines piled untidily, casually dressed people busily going about their work.

But within minutes I realized that there was a palpable sense of tension despite the comforting ambience. The two other men sitting in the waiting area barely acknowledged me; their anxiety was obvious. And from one of the rooms, the unmistakable sound of uncontrolled weeping began to spill out through the glass walls and door. That weeping could mean only one thing. I was immediately swept with anxiety, imagining a similar fate for myself.

Soon enough, a young counselor guided me into one of the small rooms, shutting the door behind her. I was about to shake hands and tell her my name, but she quickly cut me off saying that the center did anonymous testing and as a matter of policy did not want to know my name. She explained that I would be given a slip with a sequence of random numbers and four days later the results would be given against that number, so I should carefully hold on to the slip.

On my way out of the center half an hour later, I felt a huge wave of gratitude for community-run HIV counseling centers. They made dealing with the terrors of AIDS less worrisome, because you knew you were with people who cared deeply and whom you could trust.

I returned to the center four days later, so frightened I feared I would faint. Somehow I found myself seated in one of the small consulting rooms, facing a counselor, who opened the sealed envelope that had my results, looked at it intently, and then said, the tone of her voice purposively unchanged, that my results were negative.

I called Tandavan in Paris, exulting on the phone that my HIV result had been negative—to his surprise, as I had deliberately not told him that I had decided to be tested—and that that was doubly wonderful as it definitely meant that he, too, was uninfected!

TEN

THE PERSECUTED

That summer, I flew to Paris to reunite with Tandavan. My joy was magnified because our immediate future plans had unexpectedly fallen into place. Starting in September, we were to move together to New York City, where I had a six-month assignment with the United Nations Development Programme. As a French national, Tandavan could stay in the United States for several months at a time without needing a visa.

He looked tired and older. The combination of dealing with diabetes and his demanding dance regimen was beginning to take a physical toll as he neared forty. I was relieved that our long months of separation were over and that I could now look after him. In our recent phone conversations, I had sensed that he was not his carefree Peter Pan self. We had both missed living with each other. But now, far from the risks of our Delhi life, we would be living together in a place where we need not live in fear. I described the apartment I'd already found for us, tiny but sunny, on the second floor of a Murray Hill town house, a ten-minute walk from the United Nations.

I had a week with Tandavan before heading to India, where I was to spend the next few months writing about the AIDS epidemic. The week was lovelier than even a honeymoon. Instead of feverish desire, there was the surety of knowing that I was deeply loved and needed.

✤

In those months of research in India, I thought often of Jonathan Mann because everything he had taught me about AIDS was visible there: the speed at which India's epidemic was growing, the challenges to action posed by the disease's long asymptomatic period, and, most graphically, the human rights abuses. Yet, despite all that I had learned in his class and despite being knowledgeable about Indian health matters, I was often overwhelmed by what I was seeing, this being my first attempt to investigate the ground realities of the epidemic.

Though it had been just five years since the first domestic cases of HIV had been detected in India—among Selvi and the five other sex workers in the Madras reformatory—more than half a million adults in the country were infected, WHO estimated. Yet fewer than a hundred cases of AIDS and fewer than six thousand known cases of HIV had been reported to the government through a screening program covering the major cities, mainly from hospitals as well as clinics treating sexually transmitted diseases.

I began my research in the handful of hospitals, almost all government-run, that were willing to care for people with AIDS. J.J. Hospital in Bombay, a grim, no-frills set of buildings teeming with patients and their families, was one of these rare places, under the supervision of Dr. Smita Gupta, head of the department of medicine. Brusque and no-nonsense, her one comment to me before leading me to her patients was that "even when the senior doctors look through the microscope at the HIV virus, they keep making funny remarks." Her frustration was visible. But the doctors' prejudice as well as their reasonable fears of contracting HIV, given the chronic shortages of gloves and other essential safety supplies, had far-reaching costs. They insisted that Dr. Gupta treat patients with HIV in a separate ward, even though that reinforced paranoia about the disease and made it likely that the patients' identities would become known publicly.

When Dr. Gupta took me to the ward, I noticed with relief that at least there was no sign identifying it as the "AIDS Ward"—like the one I had seen just days earlier at the All India Institute of Medical Sciences (AIIMS) in Delhi, the country's leading public hospital. The AIIMS ward had been completely empty in spite of the public expense that had gone into creating it, because doctors and nurses refused to care for patients with HIV. Here each one of the seven beds, crammed close together, was occupied. The ward at AIIMS was spanking new and pristine; this was a general ward with metal-frame beds, tattered sheets, and equipment worn down by overuse. In Delhi, with no patients to tend to, the staff stood around chatting. Here, they were so busy caring for the patients that they paid neither Dr. Gupta nor me any attention.

The patients! On every bed, there were sights of heartrending suffering, beyond anything I had seen except, perhaps, the leprosy-infected outcasts on the streets of Calcutta. My attention fixed on one patient in particular, because his physical suffering looked even more unbearable than that of the others. Across his long, emaciated body—only a thin sheet covered his groin—were suppurating dark boils, each the size of a clenched fist. What were they?

Whatever I had learned at Harvard about the myriad HIV-related opportunistic infections—candidiasis, Kaposi's sarcoma, *Pneumocystis carinii* pneumonia, tuberculosis, ulcerative herpes, and so on, the endless A to Z of torture spawned by HIV—deserted me when faced with that living proof. He was skeleton thin. This I recognized as the condition called "slim" disease in Africa because of the wasting caused by uncontrollable diarrheal infections. There were bandages tied onto so many parts of his body—one of his legs had been raised and tied to a pulleylike contraption—that it seemed as if the doctors were attempting to hold his limbs together as his flesh wasted away.

Those images from J.J. Hospital haunted the rest of my journey. I realized that each and every HIV-positive person I was meeting would inevitably suffer that kind of horror before the virus killed her or him off.

But no less harrowing than the physical suffering were the abuses spawned in reaction to AIDS. Mann memorably described those human rights abuses as the AIDS epidemic's "third wave," the first wave being the invisible epidemic of asymptomatic infection with HIV and the second the epidemic of illnesses that emerged some years later. I had learned that the third wave of abuses happened in almost every country, whether rich industrialized democracies such as the United States, Communist states such as Cuba or the constituent parts of the former Soviet Union, or impoverished developing countries. But from what I saw that summer in India, I began to feel that the abuses were spreading even faster than the virus itself, rather than as a subsequent wave, fueled by misinformed panic and the opprobrium attached to the disease.

Across India, men and women whose HIV status became publicly known—typically leaked by doctors and other medical staff—were being thrown out of their homes by their families. They were fired from jobs. Families were forced to flee their villages after being ostracized, barred from using roads or wells, their children forbidden from attending school, their homes torched. Newspapers reported uncritically on how patients found to have HIV had been ejected from hospitals, very often left to die uncared for on the streets. People from groups considered at high risk, such as drug users and prostitutes, were being forcibly tested for HIV by medical authorities and the police, often at the behest of the courts. A draconian AIDS control law, introduced in Parliament by the government two years earlier but still to be passed, would institute forced HIV testing, coercive tracing of past sexual partners, and even indefinite isolation of those found to be HIV-positive.

No group in India had been as badly hit by those human rights violations as women sex workers—that phrase had still not replaced the slur of "prostitute." From the outset, they had been associated with AIDS—because the first domestic cases had been discovered among Selvi and the other sex workers in the Madras reformatory—much as the United States' epidemic had been indelibly associated with gay men. The association had only intensified over the years.

Thus, in an article that very summer of 1991, *The Economist* asked, "Since sex is universal, why is AIDS primarily a disease of the poor countries?" The reasons, said the magazine, were that "prostitution and promiscuity are more common, and the traditional sexual diseases are less likely to be treated."

The most vital part of what needed to be done in developing countries, said *The Economist*, was to check the spread of HIV from prostitutes to their clients, a view widely espoused by public health experts. "Prostitutes in poor countries are often infected," the magazine wrote. "They and their clients played a significant role in the spread of AIDS in Africa . . . [and] prostitution seems to be at the heart of the disease's spread in Thailand, a country whose troubles are less well known but may prove cataclysmic." Those dynamics were expected to be no different in India and elsewhere in Asia.

And so the AIDS pandemic forced women sex workers everywhere squarely into the public eye and onto the agendas of health ministries. (Almost nowhere were transgender or male prostitutes mentioned; policy makers liked to pretend away any knowledge of such unspeakable persons in their nations.) The attention would have been a blessing had it led to actually protecting prostitutes against AIDS. They desperately needed help—and for too many it was too late already.

Extrapolations from studies suggested that 40 to 60 percent of prostitutes in several sub-Saharan African cities, and 10 to 30 percent of prostitutes in such major Asian cities as Bangkok and Bombay, were already infected. Prostitutes were being wiped out at a pace that dwarfed even the devastation among Western gay men.

To stem the epidemic among prostitutes and their clients, clients would have to use condoms unfailingly, protecting both the prostitutes and other clients from infection. That was an achievable goal in places where prostitutes were able to demand that their clients use condoms. In fact, at the onset of the AIDS epidemic, prostitutes in Western industrialized nations began to insist that clients use condoms or forgo having sex, and their clients usually agreed; as they were aware of the risks. Western prostitutes who contracted HIV did so overwhelmingly from injecting drugs, common among low-income prostitutes and their partners, not through sexual transmission, proving that prostitutes did not inevitably contract HIV as a consequence of their work.

To get clients of prostitutes in developing countries to use condoms was another matter altogether. In such nations, men were unused to condoms even as a means of birth control and disliked using them because they were perceived to reduce sexual pleasure. Condoms were in short supply anyway—few developing countries even manufactured condoms—and were a luxury for the average man, equal in price to that of a meal.

And many prostitutes, particularly in impoverished sub-Saharan Africa and South Asia, were illiterate or barely educated, criminalized by law in almost every country, vulnerable to all kinds of abuse, and so outcast that they rarely if ever had supportive advice or care from skilled medical personnel or social workers. So it was little wonder that it was difficult for them to grasp the threat posed by AIDS until years later, when they saw large numbers of other women falling sick and dying. Even the few women who were aware of the disease and convinced that condoms could prevent HIV transmission typically had little power to overcome their customers' opposition to using condoms. If a prostitute refused to have sex without a condom, the client would go elsewhere and the woman would lose her livelihood. Consequently, every factor conspired to push prostitutes in developing countries into dismissing the threat of AIDS.

Yet, in a parallel to the pattern in the West, HIV rates remained low among better-off prostitutes, such as those working in nightclubs or hotels or from their own homes, because they had more control over their working conditions, including condom use. Every study showed that the poorer the prostitutes, the higher the rate of HIV infection. Among the poorest groups of prostitutes in Kenya as well as

India and Thailand, some studies estimated that an astronomical 80 percent were infected by 1991 or so. Poorer women had to sell more sex to survive, and their poverty meant that they had little power in any aspect of their lives.

But if there was little that the women could realistically achieve themselves, governments certainly could not plead ignorance. WHO, under Mann's leadership of the Global Programme on AIDS, had provided detailed guidance on that issue.

WHO was initially ill-prepared for the task, as its past efforts to tackle the classic sexually transmitted diseases had focused on massive national identification and treatment programs. That blanket approach meant that the organization had not designed programs specifically for prostitutes and hence knew little about the health needs of women, men, and transgender prostitutes as well as the complex web of difficulties they faced. So Mann, in his iconoclastic but effective manner, had hired a feminist activist, Priscilla Alexander, a key figure in the nascent prostitutes' rights movement in the United States and Canada.

Alexander was a founding member of COYOTE, a pioneering prostitutes' rights organization established in San Francisco in 1973—the acronym stands, memorably, for "Call Off Your Old Tired Ethics"—as well as of the North American Task Force on Prostitution, a loose coalition of organizations working for the repeal of the punitive prostitution laws in the United States and Canada, launched in 1979. From the early years of the AIDS epidemic, Alexander had worked on HIV prevention projects for prostitutes. In addition to spearheading studies that improved understanding of the epidemiology of AIDS among prostitutes and other women, in 1987 she had helped found the California Prostitutes Education Project, the only AIDS prevention project in the United States organized by prostitutes on their own behalf. Her expertise and empathy could ensure that WHO's advice was made responsive to the realities of prostitution.

On Alexander's joining the Global Programme in early 1989,

she and Mann convened an unorthodox meeting on AIDS and prostitution. The participants included not just the usual public health
officials but also the tiny handful of prostitutes' rights advocates—
including current and former prostitutes—from both industrialized
and developing countries, ranging from the United States and Switzerland to India, Nigeria, and Thailand, where a handful of projects
(run mostly by local nongovernmental groups) had sprung up to help
protect prostitutes from HIV. From the perspective of the prostitutes
themselves, it was epochal progress: for the first time ever, they had a
seat at policy-making tables and a say in global discussions concerning themselves.

The guidelines that eventually emerged from that process emphasized that narrow HIV-specific efforts—such as merely educating women about the risks or providing condoms to their
clients—would fail because the factors that disempowered prostitutes remained unchanged. Instead, governments were urged to view
prostitution, when done by consenting adults—whether women,
men, or transgender—as legitimate work and in that context take
steps to improve their overall working conditions. That could be
done by establishing occupational safety standards, providing medical insurance and broad health-care services, and ensuring them
remunerative returns on their labor, all part of the panoply of rights
and benefits granted to other workers. United action by prostitutes
would be vital to tackling the myriad factors that left them helpless, and the guidelines emphasized the need for conscious efforts to
build solidarity.

To confront the stigma associated with the word "prostitute" and
emphasize their work as labor, deserving of rights and respect, WHO
introduced the new term "sex worker" in the guidelines. That marked
the first appearance of this term—coined a decade earlier by Carol
Leigh, a Bay Area activist, artist, and prostitute—in global policy documents. That positive term, emphasizing that they, like other workers,
worked for money and deserved the rights and respect given to all
workers, was soon widely embraced by those in the profession, with

translations appearing in countless languages around the world. My vocabulary changed, too.

The importance of those developments cannot be overstated: the health of sex workers was now an explicit part of WHO's responsibilities and policy agenda. And Mann had committed WHO, and through it arguably the entire UN system, to an approach focused on promoting their basic human rights as well as their participation.

❧

But Indian officials paid no heed to WHO's advice on sex work or, for that matter, the broader commitments about respecting human rights vis-à-vis AIDS that their government had made at the World Health Assembly as well as other international venues. That was so even though India arguably had the most to gain by putting into place effective HIV prevention programs for sex workers—the Ministry of Health and Family Welfare had recently estimated that the country had about 1 million women sex workers, far outstripping any other nation. Even Thailand, with its robust sex industry, was thought to have just a fraction of the Indian figure, at 150,000 sex workers.

Instead, like most other governments, India continued to take the opposite course of singling out women sex workers for mandatory HIV testing, imprisoning them if they were found to be infected, and making every effort to suppress sex work itself. Its disregard for WHO's advice on sex work was not surprising: the government's overall policy approach on HIV, embodied in the proposed AIDS Prevention Bill, was diametrically opposed to the numerous WHO recommendations it had formally agreed to.

Every year, the number of women in state custody rose. In the Madras reformatory where Selvi and the other five sex workers remained under imprisonment, as they had ever since April 1986, the number of inmates swelled in the summer of 1990. That, oddly enough, was the fallout of mass raids on Bombay's red-light areas.

Following a sensationalistic newspaper article in January 1990 claiming that two of every three of the city's sex workers were infected with HIV, the Bombay High Court directed the police to clear the city of HIV-infected sex workers. Subsequent raids over the next months led to the arrest of several thousand women. The court ordered that they be tested for HIV without their consent. Whether adults or minors, HIV-positive or -negative, all of them were held forcibly in Bombay's reformatories. When criticism from human rights activists about the abysmal, jail-like conditions at those institutions mounted, the state government decided to deport the women to their home states, as well as to Bangladesh and Nepal if they were from these countries.

And so it happened that nearly nine hundred women from Tamil Nadu and other southern states, along with eighty-five of their children, were transported to Madras by a chartered train. The organizers dubbed it the Mukthi Express—*mukthi* means "liberation"—implying that the women had found freedom from prostitution. It was Orwellian doublespeak. The women had had no freedom at all from the moment the raids began. Instead, they had been subjected to astounding human rights violations, made all the more inexcusable because the abusive actions had taken place at the express direction of a High Court judge.

They were imprisoned without charge for months. They were denied a court hearing. They were denied legal aid. The judge summarily rejected the plea made by several human rights groups that the vast majority of the women who had been arrested were adults and, not having been convicted of any crime, had a right to liberty. (The main Indian law on prostitution, drawing on the 1949 United Nations Convention for the Suppression of the Traffic in Persons and of the Exploitation of the Prostitution of Others, allows for "rescued" women to be held for three years, outrageously denying them the rights of due process and liberty on the specious assumption that they are defenseless and childlike.) The judge accused those groups of allying with the city's pimps and brothel keepers.

By the time the Mukthi Express reached Madras Central Station, the state government had passed an order to confine the women found to be HIV-positive until "a cure was found for AIDS." Tests forcibly carried out on the women showed that the vast majority were HIV-positive. Though the few uninfected women were released, the nearly six hundred HIV-positive women were imprisoned in appalling, overcrowded conditions in the state's reformatories—including the one in Madras where Selvi was imprisoned—as well as in jails and makeshift camps.

Those women would have remained imprisoned indefinitely but for a public interest case filed in November 1989, a few months before the Mukthi Express's journey. The case, filed by a maverick young journalist named Shyamala Nataraj, challenged the prolonged imprisonment of Selvi and the five other women in the Madras reformatory. Nataraj, formerly a correspondent for the *Indian Express*, had gone undercover in search of their story and gained entry to the reformatory by pretending to be a social worker.

She was devastated by her first visit. "Women who had tested positive since 1986 were kept in remand," Nataraj told me. "Each of them had been picked up along the way over those years, and then they were cordoned off. At that time, they were living in this large dilapidated building, which was so run-down that even the windows had caved in.

"All these women were summoned before me. This official from the remand home went out of the main building and shouted, 'Hey, AIDS, come here!' Just like that!

"For me to stand in the veranda and watch them approach from the building they were housed in was the most troubling moment of my life.

"They all filed in one by one. About two dozen women, all of them HIV-positive. They all stood against this wall, and the superintendent said, 'Listen, she has come to help you. She is a social worker. You talk to her.'

"And then this woman called Vijaya came up to me and screamed, 'Who do you think we are? Are we cattle that you come and look at us, you social workers? You just make money off us!'

"She looked hard at me and said, 'Look at you! You are carrying a child. I have a one-year-old child outside that I never get to meet.' And then she spat on my face and screamed, 'If another one of you comes along, I will commit suicide!' and ran out of the room.

"And then, one by one, they all followed Vijaya, sobbing. You can imagine how I felt!

"Selvi was the one who didn't say a word. She just cried silently. I noticed Selvi because there was so much anguish on her face."

Nataraj's subsequent visits to the reformatory and her questioning of the women made her realize that the women were being held against their will, despite the official line that they were staying there voluntarily. "Most women, when they talked to me, they simply said, 'There is something wrong with our blood.' And that seemed to be the extent to which they were aware of AIDS. The remand home officials had told them that they would be looked after till they were cured, and the women had been made to sign statements stating that they were willing to stay in the remand home."

Shyamala Nataraj

Nataraj, now convinced that she had to do whatever it took to ensure they were freed, filed the challenge to their imprisonment. Remarkably, in all those years, no one else had been moved enough to do so. I was struck that this epidemic was pushing people who did not have formal training in human rights law—from a public health expert such as Mann to a journalist such as Nataraj—to embrace its principles. The same thing was happening to me.

In response to the public interest case filed by Nataraj, the Madras High Court appointed an independent commissioner who asked the women if they had voluntarily agreed to remain at the reformatory. The women said they didn't know what they had signed. It became clear that the government officials had abused the women's illiteracy and powerlessness to keep them in confinement.

In July 1990, the court ordered that the women be freed, and all of them, including the hundreds deported from Bombay on the Mukthi Express and held elsewhere in the state, were released. It marked a welcome, if long overdue, improvement in the judiciary's attitude toward civil liberties and AIDS.

In spite of that, the government made no move to compensate the women for their unlawful incarceration—as if it bore no responsibility for their suffering. Nataraj despaired at thinking of the terrible odds facing those impoverished HIV-positive women and tried to track what had happened to them after their release. She found that some had been taken in by a Madras home funded by the American feminist charity Zonta International. Many had gone back to Bombay. Some might have tried going back to their families, but it was unlikely that they would have been accepted, given the implacable stigma against sex workers.

❖

I felt a strong commonality with sex workers. Sex workers and gays shared the fate of being demonized and persecuted because of prejudices about sex, the aspect of human life on which most societies displayed the worst irrationality and cruelty. People thought of us as vilely immoral, driven by greed or lust, with sex workers selling the use of their private parts for money and gays defiling theirs out of unnatural desire. They were literally being wiped out by AIDS yet were being blamed for the pandemic—and so it had been with gay men. I saw myself as a kindred soul, having known since childhood what it felt like to be reviled and cast out.

I sought out sex workers on that first research trip in the summer of 1991. I didn't go to Madras; the epidemic had spread so far that it didn't make sense to focus on the first women in whose blood the virus had been detected. As Mumbai's sex workers were known to be the hardest hit by the epidemic, I concentrated on them.

A day after my visit to the AIDS ward at J.J. Hospital, I visited a health clinic for sex workers in the city's major red-light district, Kamathipura. It was my first visit to a red-light area anywhere in the world. At least on that monsoon morning, there were no signs that the neighborhood housed countless brothels and sex workers, reputedly more than anywhere else in Asia. It was indistinguishable from other low-income parts of Mumbai, damp and nondescript. It had nothing of the heated sexuality I'd seen in Times Square in New York City, with its lurid sex stores and peep shows, and the in-your-face hookers and hustlers.

The clinic was a shallow, barely furnished room, reached directly from the street by a few shallow steps. It was dark because of the monsoon gloom. It seemed airless, too, though the main door had been left wide open. On rough wooden benches running along the wall, there were about a dozen young women sitting quietly, their heads bowed, dressed neatly in saris. Not one looked up as I entered and then walked past them.

The doctor at the clinic was no older than me. She ushered me into a small chamber—separated from the main room by floor-length curtains—where she did physical examinations, saying that she had time to answer only a few questions. She spoke in a low voice, almost a whisper, presumably concerned that the women sitting outside would realize that we were discussing them. Her consideration was touching, though I doubted if any of the women could understand English. "Almost all the women waiting in the outside room are HIV-positive," she said.

I asked her how old they were. "None of them is older than twenty," she said. "And the youngest is just fourteen." Some were already sick with HIV-related tuberculosis and other diseases. The doctor explained that they would not stop working until they were visibly ill; they had no savings and often had to pay off debts to their pimps and madams. There was nowhere else for them to go. Almost none of them had tried to return to their families in neighboring states or Nepal, because of the stigma of their work and now of being tainted with a disease associated with prostitution. And there were no charitable organizations in the city that would offer them succor.

The doctor asked if I wanted to speak to the women, but I said "No!" with such intensity that it must have struck her as odd. I didn't have the presence of mind to explain my reaction.

I had intended to interview sex workers as part of my research. I knew next to nothing about sex work by women beyond what I had read for class, all focused on the toll the disease was taking on them. I wanted to gain an understanding of their circumstances. But after coming here, all the sensible questions I had planned on asking seemed utterly pointless.

Those young women all knew they would die in a few years. They would suffer the tortures I had seen among the patients in the AIDS ward, but probably without any medical care. How could I possibly ask for their names, their ages, where they were from, their family backgrounds, or how they had ended up in Kamathipura? All those things had shrunk into irrelevance.

And I couldn't bear to ask any of the larger questions I had thought of because, while listening to the doctor recount how no one would help the women, it occurred to me that no matter what I wrote it would not dent the unyielding bigotry that kept officials and civic leaders from helping them—the same bigotry that kept many people in the West from aiding or even sympathizing with the countless gay men dying of AIDS. It was the first time I had ever felt such hopelessness in my years of working as a journalist.

Elsewhere on that research trip, the abuse and oppression were more obvious still. At a prison in Imphal, the capital of Manipur in India's northeast, several dozens of HIV-positive drug users had been segregated in one corner of the open central compound. Those young men and women sat with heads bowed, barely moving. I had never seen such palpable hopelessness. The jail warden seemed unconcerned by the fact that they were being kept imprisoned indefinitely without trial.

Yet the brief, distant interaction with the handful of HIV-positive sex workers at the Kamathipura clinic remained uppermost in my mind. Over the years, I often remembered the gloomy clinic and the strangely silent women. The disparity between how scornfully the outside world saw them and how absolutely vulnerable they appeared seemed cruelly unjust and was a deeply familiar feeling to me.

I was not the first gay man to feel such empathetic connections between all of us who were despised and outlawed for our desires. In a poem that I had loved ever since my undergraduate years, "Ode to Walt Whitman," Federico García Lorca—who, like me, had struggled with corrosive shame both about his homosexuality and femininity—expressed my feelings when he wrote, "That's why I don't raise my voice, old Walt Whitman, . . . against the boy . . . who dresses as a bride / in the darkness of the wardrobe, nor against the solitary men . . . who drink prostitution's water with revulsion, / nor against the men . . . who love other men and burn their lips in silence."

and other safer-sex practices, the official campaigns essentially went further than billboards and ads that, in frightening imagery, depicted ;uished men cursing their fate after contracting AIDS from "fallen" •men—the latter portrayed as nubile, malevolent figures who were king on the sidelines to waylay men.

I also knew that a significant (though unknown) percentage of the ⁄eral thousand men tabulated in official records as having contracted V heterosexually had instead been infected through unprotected ⅹual intercourse with other men or with trans women. But when •ctors or health officials asked how they had been infected, they sim- ⁻y said that they were heterosexual and had been with women sex ⅆorkers. By the end of 1990, just six cases of HIV in national health ⅼta were listed as homosexually acquired.

The only Indian gay men with any knowledge about the risks of ⅃IV infection through gay sex were the tiny English-speaking minority ⅃ncentrated in the main cities. Of even that minority, only a few of ⅼs had real knowledge about safer sex, either from traveling abroad ⅆⅽ from having had the confidence to subscribe to *Trikone*, a news- ⅈtter for South Asian gay men and women published in California, ⅽ *Bombay Dost*, India's pioneering gay magazine, published in small ⅆumbers since 1990.

An even smaller number of us knew, through our personal net- ⅴorks, of gay Indian men who were HIV-positive. Every year saw one ⅆr two more added to the roll call of the sick and dying. We began to ⅇe careful, by and large, when having sex. But we were an infinitesi- ⅿally tiny minority within the vast number of gay and bisexual men ⅈn India.

It was distressing to be faced with all the evidence that AIDS was spreading rapidly among us and in *hijra* communities. I feared that the devastation among us could eventually be as terrible as that being suffered by Western gay men. And it would spread even more widely, since almost all the men were married or were going to get married, as was the unbending social norm, with wives and babies who were likely to get infected, too. It was only if the government launched a frank

ELEVEN

THE INVISIBLE

On that research trip, I didn't seek out gay men for my analysis of India's unfolding epidemic in the same way as I did sex workers. In the half decade since HIV had emerged in India, the unrelenting focus on women sex workers had spared us blame and persecution for carrying the "gay plague." And so, to avoid drawing hostile attention, in the policy paper and articles I wrote I deliberately chose to keep silent about what I knew for a fact: that a significant proportion of Indian men had unprotected sex with other men, and that meant they stood an increasingly high risk of contracting HIV.

Virtually none of the men I knew or had witnessed having sex in public knew to use condoms and water-based lubricants. Though I did my part to educate my sexual partners—or others that I talked to— most of the men appeared bewildered. As they had heard that AIDS was a disease spread by women sex workers, they ended up concluding that it was spread only through vaginal sex. (Dismayingly, many of the men I spoke to would confidently assert that anal sex was, in fact, known to be safe; some even added that that conclusion had led them to pay *hijra*s for anal sex and stop going to female sex workers.) That was indeed what the government's amateurish AIDS education campaigns seemed to imply. Rather than providing useful, explicit education about condom use and other safer-sex practices, the official campaigns essentially went no further than billboards and ads that, in frightening imagery, depicted anguished men cursing their fate after contracting AIDS from "fallen" women—the latter portrayed as nubile, malevolent figures who were lurking on the sidelines to waylay men.

I also knew that a significant (though unknown) percentage of the several thousand men tabulated in official records as having contracted HIV heterosexually had instead been infected through unprotected sexual intercourse with other men or with trans women. But when doctors or health officials asked how they had been infected, they simply said that they were heterosexual and had been with women sex workers. By the end of 1990, just six cases of HIV in national health data were listed as homosexually acquired.

The only Indian gay men with any knowledge about the risks of HIV infection through gay sex were the tiny English-speaking minority concentrated in the main cities. Of even that minority, only a few of us had real knowledge about safer sex, either from traveling abroad or from having had the confidence to subscribe to *Trikone*, a newsletter for South Asian gay men and women published in California, or *Bombay Dost*, India's pioneering gay magazine, published in small numbers since 1990.

An even smaller number of us knew, through our personal networks, of gay Indian men who were HIV-positive. Every year saw one or two more added to the roll call of the sick and dying. We began to be careful, by and large, when having sex. But we were an infinitesimally tiny minority within the vast number of gay and bisexual men in India.

It was distressing to be faced with all the evidence that AIDS was spreading rapidly among us and in *hijra* communities. I feared that the devastation among us could eventually be as terrible as that being suffered by Western gay men. And it would spread even more widely, since almost all the men were married or were going to get married, as was the unbending social norm, with wives and babies who were likely to get infected, too. It was only if the government launched a frank nationwide effort to educate men about using condoms during anal sex that this mammoth tragedy could be prevented.

Yet, in the articles I published in 1991, I wrote strategically—saying not a word about the rising rates of HIV among India's gay and bisexual men—that in Africa, in contrast to the West, the overwhelming bulk of HIV infections had taken place through heterosexual intercourse, and that would be the primary mode of transmission in India, too. I was certain that the wiser course in these dangerous times was to maintain our invisibility.

⚜

I also decided against meeting Dominic D'Souza, the HIV-positive gay man who had been imprisoned in Goa in 1989. He had emerged as India's first HIV-positive activist, despite the dangers of an era when AIDS evoked hysterical fears of contagion even among well-educated people. Siddhartha urged me to go see him, but I didn't, not knowing that I was throwing away my last chance to meet him.

Far from going into hiding after his release in April 1989, Dominic became a resolute activist. His changed spirit shone in a letter written a few months after his release. Writing to a sympathetic Bombay doctor about three impoverished HIV-positive people—a young woman and two men—who had since been imprisoned at the very sanatorium where he had been held, Dominic said in frustration, "Believe me, not one word of counseling has been imparted to the isolated HIV carriers. I am proof to this unbelievable but true attitude of our health services and Goa medical authorities . . . How could the health services be so irresponsible? We have told them so many times to start educating people on how the AIDS virus is transmitted, but nothing has been done at all."

That newfound spirit of activism reflected the surprising alchemy about AIDS that turned many of its victims—as well as relatives and friends closest to them—into do-or-die activists. That was vividly evident in the United States, in the shape of the Gay Men's Health Crisis

(GMHC), ACT UP, and numerous other groups formed mainly by gay men, themselves HIV-positive or mourning lost lovers and friends. They had refused to accept defeat, instead pioneering HIV prevention programs, caring for the dying, challenging civil rights abuses, fighting to bring HIV into the scope of US disability laws, and forcing the Reagan administration as well as the drug industry to accelerate the search for effective treatments. Activism was a logical, almost inevitable reaction to the situation that HIV-infected individuals found themselves in everywhere in the world. They knew they would face harsh discrimination from almost every quarter until the disease killed them. And with death a looming certainty in the not-so-distant future, there was—ultimately—little at risk. All this transformed their personal calculus.

Shortly after Dominic's release, the Goa Legislative Assembly agreed—because of the advocacy of his mother and Professor Isabel Vaz—to substantially dilute the act that had instituted draconian anti-AIDS measures. Under the new amendments, the government still had the power to isolate HIV-positive persons, but it was an option to be used at the government's discretion, rather than being a mandated course of action. It effectively ended the practice in the state.

But, oddly, Dominic, Lucy D'Souza, and Vaz found that the courts were less responsive to human rights principles than the legislature. The Goa bench of the Bombay High Court refused to release the HIV-positive woman and men who were imprisoned in the TB sanatorium. Social class was the operative factor here; all three were from impoverished backgrounds, and so the court opined that, unlike Dominic, there was no guarantee that they would behave responsibly if freed. Eventually, the woman escaped, never to be found again, while one of the men died in captivity, cared for only by a local Catholic nun, as government doctors refused to tend to him.

Dominic himself continued to face devastating human rights abuses. On being incarcerated, he had been granted a year's leave without pay by the Goa office of the World Wildlife Fund (India). However, when Dominic reported back for work, the local head of the fund's committee, Dr. Sharad Vaidya, barred him from the office, saying that other staff members were refusing to work with an HIV-infected person.

"Dr. Vaidya didn't allow me to enter the office," Dominic wrote later. "I said I had every right to enter as the court has said I could go back to work. But he just refused to let me enter. If doctors behave in such a fashion, the common man is going to be even more terrified about AIDS." After months of fighting to regain his job, Dominic ulti-mately accepted voluntary retirement and a cash settlement, resigning himself to that outcome because he was "so fed up with all the dis-crimination."

Yet, at the same time, there were decent-minded people rallying to challenge that discrimination. A young human rights lawyer from Bombay named Anand Grover came forward to represent Dominic pro bono. Grover's involvement in fighting for Dominic became a last-ing commitment to HIV-related cases, eventually advancing not just the cause of people with HIV but also of sex workers and gays in ways that were simply unimaginable at the time.

Dominic, whom a later employer of his described as "the best am-bassador HIV-positive people could have," did not flag even when he began suffering from recurrent bouts of tuberculosis and oral thrush, an agonizing infection of the mouth and throat. Since his release, he had found that people in Goa who knew or feared that they were in-fected were turning to him for advice, given the perils of approaching a doctor or health official. In September 1991, he started a self-help group akin to New York City's GMHC. That group, known simply as Positive People, began operating out of Dominic's home, with funding from the Dutch development organization Hivos. It was India's first association of "positive people," providing confidential counseling and a support system for people "to share their grief, experiences and anxi-eties," as well as undertaking public awareness about AIDS.

But by then Dominic's illnesses had become life-threatening, in large part because Goa's hospitals refused to admit him for in-patient care. Finally, Isabel Vaz and his other friends admitted him to Bombay's Breach Candy Hospital, at that point one of the few private institutions in India willing to care for people with AIDS.

On May 27, 1992, Dominic died, two months short of his thirty-third birthday. He had lived for just three years from the horrifying morning of his imprisonment. With better medical care, he would certainly have lived much longer.

Remarkably, in that brief span of time, he had succeeded in improving public attitudes toward AIDS in Goa and beyond. In an obituary, the mainstream daily *Gomantak Times* wrote with evident pride in their native son, a sea change from the prejudice the press had displayed just a few years earlier. "This brave Goan did not quail under the burden of AIDS," the obituary said. "For every person who shrank from his very touch, Dominic taught ten people that there is nothing to fear . . . in interacting with HIV-positive people. He showed this country that except for a little virus in the bloodstream, they are exactly like any other normal human being."

While later piecing together Dominic's life, from all the vivid proof of his courage, I found that I was most moved by the bravery he maintained even on the verge of death.

In his will, written in the hospital just a few days before his death, he asked that a newspaper announcement be published to "boldly say that I died of AIDS and that I am not ashamed to say it." It took incredible personal courage and true dedication to combating the stigma against AIDS to insist on that, because, at that time, very few people anywhere in the world—even in the West—admitted to dying of AIDS. The *New York Times* obituaries, for instance, referred euphemistically to one young or middle-aged man or another as having died after a "long illness" or a "rare disorder"—or even that "the cause of his death was not immediately disclosed"—phrases widely known to be code for AIDS.

I also ached with sympathy at uncovering Dominic's struggles to come to terms with his orientation in matters of love and desire. Those struggles were made even more tortured by his feeling that it was his orientation that had led to his contracting the disease killing him. In a booklet published by Positive People shortly before his death, Dominic wrote, "I knew what AIDS was. But I never really educated myself. I knew how it was transmitted, but I never practiced safe sex. I had this feeling that it is not going to touch me." He then wrote, "I am a Roman Catholic. I kept thinking—is this His way of asking me to pay for what I have done? I felt that it was promiscuity that led me to getting this virus. I felt this was God's punishment."

It was painful to read those last anguished sentences suggesting that Dominic had not yet come to terms with those matters. That statement was the closest Dominic came to publicly disclosing his orientation. It is possible that he would have become increasingly candid had he lived longer. Already, in just the space of those few years, he had gone from maintaining that he had contracted HIV while donating blood to candidly saying that he had been infected sexually. In a few more years, he might have cast off fears about having to bear a terrible double stigma—of being known to be HIV-positive as well as gay.

It was possible that Dominic would have eventually done what I shirked from doing at that point, what I thought wise not to do: to make us gay people visible in India by speaking honestly about the epidemic that was beginning to devastate us. But as it happened, at the very time that Dominic was dying, another young gay man facing death took it upon himself to break the silence and end our invisibility.

TWELVE

A FIRST GLIMPSE OF FREEDOM

I should have guessed that my maverick friend Siddhartha would not let things stay quiet.

Siddhartha had given me an inkling of his intentions the last time we had met—on the first leg of my research trip to India in the summer of 1991. On arriving in Delhi from being with Tandavan in Paris, I rushed straight from the airport to his Defence Colony *barsati*. My longing to see Siddhartha was not merely because it had been a year since we had last seen each other; it was because his cancer had reemerged after years of remission. He was leaving in a few days for New York's Memorial Sloan Kettering Cancer Center, where he had been treated in the past.

Siddhartha was painfully thin, and his hair was only just growing back from his last stint of radiation at a Delhi hospital. Yet when I stood face-to-face with him, in the full wattage of his personality, I had no chance to voice the slightest of my worries. All I could pry out of Siddhartha was that he was delighted to have lost his hair because he now resembled the gorgeous Persis Khambatta in her recent appearance in a *Star Trek* movie. It had allowed him, he swore, to effortlessly seduce the male doctors at the hospital, and even the fitter of the patients! All discussions about his cancer were sidelined forever.

We talked through the day and into the evening, hugging each other tight as we lay in bed, full of love for each other. As always, our conversations careened from frivolity to seriousness.

He was full of questions about what I had learned from Jonathan Mann, whom he respected greatly, and about what I expected to cover in my AIDS research. I was even more impatient to know more about his own efforts on AIDS, which he had begun a few months before I had left for the United States, and his experiences working as a human rights lawyer at the Delhi High Court.

Siddhartha and several other activists had banded together to defend sex workers in Delhi's red-light area who were being forcibly tested for HIV by researchers from the Indian Council of Medical Research and the All India Institute of Medical Sciences (AIIMS). They had picketed those institutions day after day until they agreed to end forcible testing, at least in Delhi. (Those elite medical institutions had a disgraceful record through the epidemic's first decade. The council's top official, Avtar Singh Paintal, had pushed for prison terms for Indians who had sex with foreigners and then gone on to accuse Indian women of being "a lousy lot" for "cohabiting with foreigners." As for AIIMS, I hadn't forgotten its glossy AIDS ward standing empty even as legions of mortally sick people went untreated across the country, because of the hospital's unspoken refusal to handle AIDS patients.)

From that effort was born the activist collective AIDS Bhedbhav Virodhi Andolan (ABVA)—the AIDS Anti-Discrimination Movement, which fought AIDS-related abuses. It was an unusual organization, in which I knew several of its members through Siddhartha. The force behind the group was a Sikh doctor, Dr. P. S. Sahni, who lived a life of frugality in common cause with the destitute. Other key figures included an activist Catholic nun, a grassroots feminist, a "professional blood donor" (who sold his blood to blood banks for a living), a prominent orthopedic doctor, several lawyers, and Siddhartha.

On a shoestring budget raised through community donations—it refused funding from institutions on principle—ABVA not only operated a free health clinic for sex workers but also tackled some of the worst human rights abuses raised by the AIDS epidemic. Improbably, it had even succeeded in keeping the draconian AIDS Prevention Bill from being passed into law. The public rallies its members had held outside Parliament had drawn an astonishing range of people, including women sex workers, *hijra*s, gay men and lesbians, women from Delhi's slums, and leprosy patients (who knew well what it was to be the victims of unjust, cruel policies mandated in the name of public health). The AIDS Prevention Bill was now mired in controversy, and it seemed possible that it could be kept from being passed into law. It was thrilling to see that even a characteristically unresponsive government could sometimes be forced to heed the views of the downtrodden—and that that had happened only because of a group of unpaid grassroots activists.

To influence public opinion, ABVA had also published two pathbreaking reports over the previous year, one focusing on how women—including sex workers—were being blamed for the spread of AIDS, the other on how to make the blood supply system safe without banning "professional blood donors" from selling blood. Siddhartha added excitedly that they were planning to write one on the situation of gay men and women. That report was still nothing more than a resolve, said Siddhartha, and work on it had been stalled by reappearance of his cancer, but it would lay bare all the injustices faced by us.

When leaving Siddhartha late that evening, I felt a rush of inexplicable dread that I was going to lose him. I brushed it aside, putting it down to the usual sadness of having to say good-bye to a loved one.

Some six months later, I received a copy of the report on gay issues that Siddhartha had talked about. But it arrived under devastating circumstances.

Late on the night of January 12, 1992, Tandavan and I had returned to our Manhattan apartment after celebrating Tandavan's thirty-eighth birthday at a friend's home nearby. The flashing red numeral on the answering machine showed that we had received a message. It was from my close friend Nilita in Delhi. Her message was broken by sobbing—but it said that Siddhartha had died a few hours earlier. My premonition of loss when I had last met Siddhartha had been horribly true.

He had died after battling a high fever for two days, Nilita said when I called her: he had been at his Defence Colony flat, with his sister Anuja and friends caring for him.

None of us had expected that. Siddhartha's treatment at Sloan Kettering just a few months earlier had, by all indications, been successful. The doctors had expected him to do well for a long, if indeterminate, time. But it seemed that his immune system had been ruined by too much chemotherapy and radiation over the past decade. He was two weeks short of his twenty-eighth birthday.

It was several days before I could bear to leave our apartment and deal with the world. Tandavan stayed with me constantly, looking after me as though I were his fragile child. On the way out of our apartment building, I checked our mailbox. There was a letter from Siddhartha—the envelope bore his unmistakable looping handwriting, and there in the corner was his name and Delhi address.

It was a second walloping blow. I wished that I had never found the letter, that it had been lost en route. I went back upstairs, forcing Tandavan to take a break from caring for me because I needed to be alone, even though I dreaded opening the envelope.

Siddhartha had written the letter three days before his death. On every inch of the plain paper, front and back of both sheets, crowding every margin and corner, was the handwriting I had come to love from letters that I had received in one place or another, each one filling me with joy from his irrepressible spirit.

"My dearest, lovely, silly boy," Siddhartha wrote. "Your style of stringing adjectives is infectious. I note with envy your missives to Saleem and Nilita, but I'm sure you will write to me after this one."

I wept with remorse at not having written to him and knowing that it was too late to remedy my error. I wept even more knowing that I would never get to see Siddhartha's beloved face again, never hold him close as I used to, never be infected by his madcap giggling, never have him nearby to love and worry about and protect.

"I miss you immensely," he wrote at the end of the letter, "especially on these beautiful, misty winter days when all the Lodhi Garden trees miss you from their barks as I do too." It made me heartsick reading that, knowing that I would be the one missing him for the rest of my life.

But, characteristically of Siddhartha, the bulk of the letter was not about personal matters but about his causes. A full page focused on the efforts of the ABVA activist collective. Its energies were now focused on the World Bank, which was in discussions with the government over providing a $100 million soft loan to India for expanding its AIDS control efforts. Siddhartha and his colleagues had been pressing the Bank to approve the loan only if the government explicitly agreed to human rights safeguards that would put an end to its current punitive policies. If the Bank could be forced to insist on human rights protections, Siddhartha wrote, the government would, in turn, have to fall into line at this time, when India was in the throes of one of its worst foreign exchange crises and was beholden to the Bank for its support. For once, the Bank's use of "conditionalities" as preconditions could be a positive thing.

"Please see if you can get some further information on the specifics of what the World Bank is planning," Siddhartha wrote. "Also, see if you can write about it—possibly interview people in charge in Washington, DC. If you do, please try and include questions from the point of view expressed in our memo. The World Bank team will be visiting India again in February to wrap up the contract. If you speak to them, ask them what their response is to our memo, and what concretely they plan to do to ensure their money doesn't finance AIDS-related human rights violations here."

Despite my grief, I couldn't help but chuckle at Siddhartha's unrelenting determination. He was doing his utmost to leave the Bank no wiggle room.

Sure enough, just a few months later, the Bank approved India's AIDS control loan after the government gave it private guarantees that it would end the harsh policies it had pursued ever since AIDS had first surfaced in the country. Prime Minister Narasimha Rao withdrew the draconian AIDS Prevention Bill from Parliament, and with that, the government—at least in principle—resolved to adhere to internationally agreed strategies on AIDS.

And then, with such evident passion, Siddhartha wrote, "I wanted you to have a copy of our latest report on homosexuality. It's a real labor of love. I've never worked so hard in my life—while pulling it together, I worked eighteen hours a day on the computer continuously for two weeks. Nor have I felt such utter isolation, of the kind that engulfed me almost wave after wave while working on it."

He continued, "It's strange, I have for many years wanted to write something like this. Now when the chance came, my deepest impulse was to run away, postpone the whole thing. To actually sit and articulate what I wanted to say in the Indian context, to bring together years of insights, readings, mullings, wanderings, along with journalistic material, and to do it through a group of die-hard activists which includes Naxalites, Gandhians and a nun, seemed an impossible feat. But you have the product with you now, and I await your critical comments."

The report was a pink-jacketed booklet titled—in the smudgy type print of that time—"Less than Gay: Citizens' Report on the Status of Homosexuality in India."

Those ninety-five pages were a revelation. It was in the pages of "Less than Gay" that I saw, for the first time in systematic fashion, the historical evidence showing that homophobia was a British colonial legacy—epitomized in the laws that mandated criminal prosecution for male same-sex acts as well as for gender-ambiguous males—and that Indian traditions had been immeasurably more accepting of same-sex desires, of diverse expressions of gender identity, and of sexuality in general. It was a relief to know that not all major cultures had treated those matters with the destructive loathing that Christianity and the West had displayed since the Dark Ages.

"Indigenous texts, concepts and traditions revered and even celebrated sexual ambiguity," Siddhartha and his coauthors wrote. The *Kamasutra*, the famed ancient guide to erotic love and sexual pleasure, they noted, contained an entire chapter on the pleasures and techniques of oral sex between people of the same sex. (Fellatio was regarded as the defining male homosexual act in ancient India; sodomy was discussed only in the context of heterosexual sex.) Vatsyayana, the sage who compiled the *Kamasutra*, emphasized that these practices were allowed by the *Dharma Shastras*, the texts that detail *dharmic* or ethical behaviors.

Hinduism's epics were rife with mutable, androgynous gods and heroes who displayed a stunning variety of sexual desires, Siddhartha and his colleagues wrote. The erotic sculptures that decorated numerous early-medieval temples—such as the renowned ones in Khajuraho and Konark—celebrated the Hindu metaphysical understanding that sex and desire are not impure impulses but lie at the root of all creation and routinely included same-sex acts among the other uninhibited, ecstatic forms of lovemaking. Hinduism even had a god embodying sensual love and desire: Kamadeva, a son of the creator god, Brahma.

And, strikingly, Hindu metaphysics did not make rigid male/female and masculine/feminine distinctions, in contrast to Christianity and other Abrahamic traditions. The worship of Shiva as *Ardha-narishwara*—half woman, half man, portrayed with the secondary sexual characteristics of both sexes—embodying the gender dualism present in each being, was an idea as old as India itself, they wrote. Indian mystics and spiritual seekers saw themselves in androgynous terms, as beings that combined male and female energies or in a state where the lines separating masculinity and femininity had collapsed.

In the past, generations of ordinary Hindus had accepted all those ideas without surprise or discomfort. That acceptance sprang from the ethical relativism that is fundamental to Hinduism, where nothing is unnatural, as the universal spirit pervades all things and humans can never know the absolute truth of things.

Siddhartha and his coauthors maintained that those tolerant attitudes to erotic desire and gender expression had not been destroyed by the Muslim dynasties that had come to power in the subcontinent from the tenth century onward, as many people assumed. In Sufism, the liberal, mystic tradition that has been more important on the subcontinent than orthodox Islam, "homosexual eroticism was a major metaphorical expression of the spiritual relationship between god and man" and Sufis saw themselves as genderless.

The rupture came only with British colonial rule, said Siddhartha and his coauthors, particularly from 1858, when India was brought under the direct heavy-handed rule of the British Crown. The chasm between British and contemporaneous Indian views on same-sex relations and gender expression, and more generally on both men's and women's sexuality, could not have been more enormous, setting in motion a true clash of civilizations, one with lasting retrograde impacts on Indian society.

Raised with harshly prudish notions, the colonial elite was appalled by Indian sights and customs—the bare-breasted women, loincloth-clad men, naked toddlers, and flagrantly cross-dressing "eunuchs"; regional traditions that encouraged maternal uncles to marry their young nieces, younger brothers to sire children with their older brothers' wives, and women in matrilineal communities to freely take male lovers; and the *tawaif*s and *devadasi*s who ascended to power and wealth. Even Hindu gods are "absolute monsters of lust," William Wilberforce, the slavery abolitionist and Christian proselytizer, thundered in Parliament in 1813, no doubt thinking of the legions that worshipped glistening *lingam*s and *yoni*s. (Wilberforce was as unabashed in condemning Hinduism as he was in glorifying Christianity, maintaining, "Our religion is sublime, pure, beneficent . . . theirs is mean, licentious, and cruel.") Lord Elgin, the viceroy of India, warned that British military camps could become "replicas of Sodom and Gomorrah" as soldiers acquired "special Oriental vices." Ridding the world of sexual sin became a key aspect of Britain's imperial civilizing mission, the "White Man's Burden" of bringing Christian morality to their "new-caught, sullen peoples, half devil and half child."

Britain's effort to prevent "sodomy" in its prized Indian colony, whether among its own people in this outpost or the degenerate "natives," was eventually wrought through the Indian Penal Code of 1860, Section 377 of which criminalized "carnal intercourse against the order of nature." Out of Victorian prudishness, Section 377 did not explicitly mention buggery or sodomy, unlike earlier English and North American laws that had been written with raw bluntness. Lord Macaulay, the main drafter of the Penal Code as well as of that particular section, spoke elliptically of "an odious class of offences respecting which it is desirable that as little as possible should be said." But the intent of Section 377 was clear to the colonial administration, courts, and police: to harshly punish any form of sex between males, even if it was between consenting adults. Arrests under Section 377 did not require a warrant and were also nonbailable. Convictions could lead to life imprisonment or ten years of rigorous imprisonment. Those punishments were so harsh, "Less than Gay" noted, that only murder, rape, and kidnapping were treated more severely.

There was more persecution to follow. In 1897, the colonial Criminal Tribes Act was amended to expressly include "eunuchs"—which is how the British recast India's *hijras*—who could now be arrested without warrant and imprisoned for up to two years merely for appearing "dressed or ornamented like a woman in a public street" or of being "reasonably suspected" of "committing offences under Section 377 of the Indian Penal Code," without need of proof of an actual act.

With those punitive laws, for the first time in the Indian subcontinent's recorded history same-sex relations as well as nonconformist gender identities were criminalized and became the target of active prosecution and brutal punishment. India was one of the first of the colonized lands to which Great Britain exported its pathological condemnation of male same-sex desire; by the end of the nineteenth century, laws identical or similar to Section 377 were firmly in place across Africa, the Americas, the Caribbean, Asia, and Australasia, often replacing accepting traditions with cruel persecution.

The arguments in "Less than Gay" helped me make sense of what I had gradually come to feel over my years of adulthood in India as I grew more knowledgeable about the country. "Macaulay's Children," such as my father and most people of my background, were almost invariably hostile to same-sex desire as well as to any perceived feminine qualities or behaviors in men. Even those of them—my father being a perfect example—who knew intimately the ancient Hindu myths of gender ambiguity and same-sex desire as well as their foundational place in Hindu metaphysics didn't allow these concepts to impact their thinking or behavior, so overpowering was the hold of the Victorian notions that had been drilled into them.

In contrast, as Siddhartha and his colleagues wrote, "notions of same-sex friendship, romance and love still suffuse the lives of ordinary men and women," whose thinking was not as heavily shaped by Raj-era cultural influences. Both Siddhartha and I had often sensed that in our encounters with nonelite Indian men, a surprisingly large number of them treated their desires with astonishing naturalness. And we had both seen convincing evidence that our more traditional relatives, such as my aunts from small-town Madhya Pradesh, treated same-sex desire as well as femininity in men with simple acceptance or, at the very least, with a relative tolerance.

But from the tortured personal testimonies in "Less than Gay," it was clear that India's older traditions had shrunk dangerously over the 130 years since Section 377 had come into force. "Because of its existence, gay men are subjected to systematic harassment, blackmail and extortion at the hands of enforcement agencies and the public . . . the law exists solely to criminalize and terrorize a section of society," Siddhartha and his coauthors wrote. The outcome by now was that though the homophobia was not as pervasive and virulent as I had seen in the United States—even the grounds given for condemning homosexuality lacked the bred-in-the-bone vehemence of Christian cultures, a sign that this animus was a relatively recent transplant—it was potent enough to make gay men and women live in great fear.

It was the report's opening and closing pages that had the most profound impact on me, fundamentally changing my thoughts on a crucial aspect of this matter.

On the third page of "Less than Gay" was this paragraph: "ABVA views homosexuality (and heterosexuality) as a political issue. We will strive to get consensual, adult homosexual acts decriminalized and fight for the right of gay men, lesbians and other 'sexual minorities,' like *hijra*s, to enjoy equal benefits of the laws on marriage, inheritance, adoption, and privacy, among others. We feel that a clear and unambiguous stand should be taken by political parties and civil rights organizations on the human rights of gay men and lesbians. How much longer will the British-framed law on sodomy be tolerated by us? When will the Indian State recognize the equal rights of 'sexual minorities'?"

There it was, unambiguous and powerfully worded, what I had never yet seen stated in print: the demand that same-sex relations be decriminalized in India.

And at the report's very end was an astonishing charter of emancipatory demands, breathtaking in its boldness—if realized, gay Indians would no longer be criminals but equal and proud citizens.

The first demand, of course, was for the repeal of Section 377. But then there was the demand for the Constitution to be amended to include equality before the law on the basis of "sex" and "sexual orientation." There was the demand that police policies be reformed to end the abuse of gay people and gender minorities and that a human rights commission be available to monitor rights violations. There were demands for "judgment-free health education related to sexuality, homosexuality, sexually transmitted diseases . . . and AIDS." For tackling homophobia, they demanded "positive images and role models of gay men and lesbians, and of homosexuality as a viable, healthy alternative lifestyle" from school onward. Ending the charter were demands for full equality in those vital matters of love, relationships, and families: "Amend the Special Marriages Act to allow for marriages between people of the same sex . . . All consequential legal benefits of marriage should extend to gay marriages as well, including the right to adopt children, to execute a partner's will, to inherit, etc."

I read that charter with astonishment, followed by mounting excitement. I had never even dared to imagine such freedom in India—of not being criminalized, of not being perpetually fearful, of having a constitutional guarantee that I would be treated equally in every aspect of life, of having the right to marry and have a family—let alone imagine that I should begin to expect and fight for this in my lifetime.

Those were audacious, almost outlandish demands to make in the first years of the 1990s. Homosexual conduct was a criminal offense not only in India but also in an overwhelming majority of the world's nations, besides half the states in the United States. The United Nations' human rights bodies were still several years away from making the pioneering rulings establishing that "sodomy" laws violated international human rights norms. No country, so far, provided constitutional guarantees of equality or antidiscrimination for gays or gender minorities. Just one country—Denmark—recognized same-sex civil unions, and only Sweden had laws protecting gays and lesbians in matters pertaining to social services, taxes, and inheritance.

Yet Siddhartha, with his colleagues in the ABVA group, asked for complete equality, even though there was no proof as yet that any modern society, let alone India—still mired in colonial ways of thinking and doing—was capable of providing such justice. Perhaps individuals on the verge of death were blessed with such prescience.

Let alone the practicality of such ambitious changes, Siddhartha and I had often heatedly argued about the possibility of throwing out Section 377. His view was that we needed to build a mass movement in India seeking this goal, akin to the 1960s African American civil rights effort or the ongoing antiapartheid struggle in South Africa. My reaction had always been that something like that was simply not possible in the India of our time. It was too dangerous. There were too few of us who were openly gay and even fewer with a determined sense of activism. And we had almost no allies—just a handful of supportive friends and families and an even smaller number of forward-thinking lawyers, journalists, and activists.

I argued that we would face a terrible backlash. No Indian civil rights groups considered matters of sexuality to be of any relevance to their work—even abroad, Amnesty International had only just begun to fight for people imprisoned because of their sexual orientation. I pointed out that in Margaret Thatcher's right-wing Great Britain, homophobia had intensified—the police were harassing and entrapping gay men in unprecedented numbers, and the antigay "Section 28" had been passed into law—while in Reaganite America, the Supreme Court had upheld sodomy laws as recently as 1986. I was sometimes even dismissive while arguing with Siddhartha, my irritation at his impractical idealism rising to a head.

In a practical sense, I was correct. For a start, very few of even the relatively open gay men and women in India were activists to any great degree. Given the real risks of discrimination and persecution, it made sense to remain largely guarded, which would have been impossible as an activist. Tellingly, Siddhartha wrote in his letter to me, "None of my gay friends bothered to come for the press conference or to collect a copy until a month later! Somehow I felt shocked by what seemed to be a betrayal . . . [I]t seemed that all our parties and bonhomie and friendships had come to naught . . . [W]hat explains the apathy and indifference?"

And it was clear that the matter of decriminalization of same-sex relations, let alone equal human rights for us, was taboo in almost every realm of India. Thus, on releasing "Less than Gay," Siddhartha and his ABVA colleagues presented a formal list of demands to the petitions committee of the Lok Sabha, the lower house of Parliament—but not a single member of Parliament even acknowledged the petition, let alone championed it. Of the dozens of prominent people and organizations they had written to (including legislators, bureaucrats, police officials, health experts, feminists, and human rights leaders) while researching the report, only nineteen had written back.

But on reading those brave, fighting words that morning in 1992—"We will strive to get consensual, adult homosexual acts decriminalized and fight for the right of gay men, lesbians and other 'sexual minorities,' like *hijra*s, to enjoy equal benefits of the law"—for the first time I didn't care that the odds were so heavily arrayed against us. Though I realized that I had come to feel this because of the circumstances, because the ache for that freedom had literally been my beloved friend's last sentiment, it proved to be a personal turning point. I began to feel that it was only right to fight against Section 377, even if the effort lasted decades and even beyond my lifetime, instead of simply fearing it as I had and choosing to live abroad.

And so Siddhartha, in dying, forever changed my views. In a magazine review of "Less than Gay," I wrote that the report "is potentially a powerful weapon with which gay Indians and activists can fight the government . . . [It] contains every detail necessary to challenge the Indian sodomy law as unconstitutional."

The power of what Siddhartha had set into motion through "Less than Gay" soon became potently evident. In early 1994, two years after Siddhartha's death, ABVA filed a public interest case in the Delhi High Court asking that Section 377 be declared unconstitutional and void on the grounds that it violated the constitutional fundamental rights to life, liberty, and nondiscrimination and obstructed AIDS prevention efforts. The immediate cause of ABVA's action was the refusal by officials at Delhi's Tihar Jail to supply condoms to prisoners—despite evidence of male homosexual conduct as well as several HIV-positive cases—on the grounds that homosexuality was a criminal offense.

The fight against Section 377 had now moved from words to reality. India's establishment was being forced to address, as a matter of constitutional principle, something it had long refused to acknowledge even as existing in India.

And Siddhartha, aesthete and satyr, madcap and visionary, revolutionary and intellectual, had been the driving force for all this in the span of his short, wondrous life.

THIRTEEN

MORE RIGHTS—TO CORRECT THE WRONGS

In early 1993, I joined the World Bank in Washington, DC. It was a difficult and unlikely decision for me, given my socialist-democratic views and the Bank's record of promoting policies that favored the interests of rich countries and rich people over the well-being of the poor.

I reasoned that I was joining the part of the Bank—the health policy division—that was encouraging genuine progress by promoting public health and even defending human rights, as demonstrated by its role in convincing the Indian government to disavow its punitive AIDS control policies. And at my young age of thirty-one and having recently embarked on a fresh career focused on public health and development policy, I needed work experience that was as broad as possible, I told myself.

But the truth was that my decision was almost entirely driven by personal reasons, not professional ones. I had desperately needed to escape from New York City, and lacking US work papers, the Bank was one of very few employment options open to me.

My desperation to leave New York City was because my relationship with Tandavan had disintegrated, five years from the time we had met and fallen in love. We still loved each other deeply—that had made the process of separating drag on painfully. But we both also knew that we were no longer the happy couple we had been. There seemed no chance of resolving our problems, though we had long tried.

They were garden-variety problems. They ranged from our not being able to strike a balance between my neurotic tidiness and Tandavan's messiness to Tandavan being even more dangerously impractical about finances than I was. Those tensions had existed when we lived in Delhi, too, but had taken on a destructive power in New York City. After a first year of exceptional happiness—overjoyed to be together again and to be living for the first time in an environment where we didn't fear persecution—the particular stresses of New York City hit home: the cramped living space, the high rents, and, not least, the dismal, dangerous state of the city, no less grim than when I had lived there last in 1986. When I returned to New York City after traveling to Africa and Asia for the United Nations, I invariably found it even more depressing than the impoverished, strife-torn places I had visited. (The violence was so extreme that on a per capita basis the yearly death toll from guns and other violent causes exceeded that of Punjab, the northern Indian state then in the midst of civil war, I calculated.) Our relationship spiraled downward into ugly tension and fights, doing both of us damage.

Tandavan and I never concretely decided that we were breaking up, evading the fact though we both recognized it. I told him I was going to move to DC to work at the Bank; perhaps in time he could move there too. He would stay on in New York for now, he replied, because his US work papers had come through and a large number of people had signed on to learn Bharatanatyam from him.

On the morning that I left to drive down to DC in a rented car, I kissed him on the cheeks and said that we would see each other soon. I started sobbing only when I couldn't see him any longer in the car's rearview mirror. I called briefly once I reached DC to say I'd arrived safely. Then neither of us called the other for over a month. The hiatus established everything we were unable to say to each other.

I struggled for months with my sense of loss, despite being in a new city with demanding new work. It took me a year even to go out on a date. A momentous, happy epoch of my life—in which I had gone from being a virginal, lonely young man to experiencing great love and becoming a fulfilled adult—had come to an unhappy end. A love I had thought would last a lifetime had lasted just those few years.

❖

In small ways and big, the Bank's entitlements and power crippled its ability to promote genuine, broad-based well-being in the countries it worked in. That became clear to me on a firsthand basis from public health projects that I worked on in India, Kenya, and Uganda.

While on "mission" to design or monitor those projects, a majority of my colleagues flew first-class from DC to the capital cities of those countries. A few of us stuck to business class. ("Mission" is the bizarre term used in the international development industry to describe, typically, a quick visit by foreign experts to dispense advice. It remains a mystery whether the term came into use because we were supposedly doing charitable work like missionaries or because we imagined we belonged to the heady world of military espionage.) We stayed at the grandest hotels. We spent without limit on meals and taxis, rather than being constrained by the generous but capped daily allowances of UN staff. On our return leg, we had "rest stops" in attractive European cities. Taxpayers' money gathered from the world over paid for us to enjoy the lifestyles of the global superrich.

In Africa in particular, our work mainly consisted of meeting top bureaucrats and politicians. Though they were of the rank of health secretaries and health ministers, they would be visibly deferential to the Bank's team leader—even though he or she was no more than a mid-ranking staffer. All we glimpsed of reality was when we were whisked off in air-conditioned SUVs to visit some carefully selected hospital or nongovernmental organization. There we were treated with a reverence appropriate for visiting heads of state. We shook hands, asked a few questions, murmured comments that demonstrated our exceptional expertise, and were then chauffeured back to our luxury hotels.

Our reports were written from the best hotels in country capitals or in even more salubrious settings. On one memorable occasion, our whole team of two dozen was jetted off to a famed boutique hotel in Maasai Mara. Each of our house-sized "huts" had outdoor Jacuzzis where we could take bubble baths, sip cocktails, and hear the predators on the savanna far below. All that purportedly was because we required restfulness to meet our deadlines.

Despite several visits to such countries, I knew next to nothing about them, feeling much like a rich First World tourist gazing uncomprehendingly at Third World sights from a cocoon of luxury. I was soon convinced that many of my colleagues—armed with Ivy League and Oxbridge degrees—would not be able to recognize an impoverished person if they saw one. Yet they remained convinced that they knew best what the masses needed—an arrogance that led them to chronically misdiagnose and worsen the problems faced by poor countries and impoverished people.

I was often reminded of a poem satirizing the "development set" I'd read at Tufts:

> The Development Set is bright and noble
> Our thoughts are deep and our vision global;
> Although we move with the better classes
> Our thoughts are always with the masses.
>
> . . .
>
> We discuss malnutrition over steaks
> And plan hunger talks during coffee breaks.
> Whether Asian floods or African drought,
> We face each issue with open mouth.
>
> . . .
>
> Enough of these verses—on with the mission!
> Our task is as broad as the human condition!

Just pray god the biblical promise is true:
The poor ye shall always have with you.

In India, where I was part of a team in mid-1994 to monitor the Bank's loan for the national AIDS program, I could be an insightful judge of the Bank's work because of my own prior knowledge.

Disbursement of funds had begun two years earlier, and there was evidence that the Bank's money and related technical support were being used well to implement the national AIDS program. That was conducted through the National AIDS Control Organization, or NACO, which was led by an experienced senior bureaucrat. His staff was energetic and committed, and quite a few had technical expertise. They worked with almost every state government to raise official concern, build HIV prevention programs, and improve medical care. Actual performance varied from state to state, depending on the overall quality of the state administration. NACO was backing the Bank's demand that poorly performing states be pulled up. It was a relief to see that in India, by virtue of the professionalism of its senior bureaucrats, there was a largely productive working relationship between Bank staff and the government, rather than the harmfully lopsided relationships I had witnessed in Kenya and Uganda.

But even there, and that, too, with a project that had no complex issues of equity or harm involved, the weakness of the Bank's work was glaringly evident. Bank staff remained utterly cut off from reality. On one leg of our monitoring visit we were put up in the lap of luxury at the Taj Fort Aguada in charming Goa and on the next leg an equally plush beachfront resort in Kovalam, Kerala. "Why?" I wondered to myself.

On our second day in Goa, with a senior state government official fussing over us, we were ferried two hours south to Baina, which was, at that point, home to one of the major sex-work sites in western India. We alighted from our luxury minibus. From a great distance, we watched sari-clad women standing along the seafront or sitting on the low wall and scores of men propositioning them. We noted the unending expanse of the shanties where the women lived and sold sex.

We took in the windswept beauty of the site, with the monsoon waves rising dramatically in the background. We asked the solicitous government official a few questions. Then we drove away.

The whole episode was surreal. I was left with scarcely any understanding of what I had just seen, beyond the rudimentary facts that our government colleague seemed to know himself. (The gist was that the women were mainly from the impoverished regions of neighboring states and came to Baina to sell sex during the lean agricultural months. Their clients were both locals and tourists; the day of our visit, several busloads of schoolteachers had been their main customers.) Even a foreign tourist visiting the Taj Mahal would have learned more than what we did on that Baina visit. I would have plumbed far deeper by working as a journalist in a single day, pen and notepad in hand and feet on the ground, than on those ten days of jet-setting and official visits.

Nonetheless, for all the *Lords of Poverty* buffoonery on display, the Bank was attempting at that point to refashion itself into a poverty-focused institution. It was faced with mounting criticism that the harshly inequitable policies that it and the International Monetary Fund had enforced through the 1980s debt crisis had led to the impoverishment and destabilization of entire nations in Africa and Latin America, a pattern now being repeated in Russia and the former Soviet Union. The campaigners' slogan, "Fifty Years Is Enough"—the Bank and the IMF had been established in 1944 as the linchpins of a US-designed postwar global economic order—had sent a chill down the spines of the top officials of those institutions.

Advocates for the Third World noted that the men governing those twin institutions were the very ones—rich white men—who had been exploitative colonial lords until forcibly ousted just a few decades back and were now plundering poorer countries using discreet neo-colonialist methods rather than bloody conquest. The Bank president is always a US political appointee, more often than not a former bank CEO or a secretary of defense, and the IMF managing director a Western European.

Whether the changes under way would lead to a fundamental break with the past in policies and impact or would amount to window dressing was too early to tell. (I had strong doubts. These twin institutions seemed incapable of moving even to recommend the democratic socialism of the Nordic nations over the winner-takes-all-and-losers-be-damned capitalism of the United States.)

The upshot of that repositioning was that the Bank's leaders realized they now needed to know the impoverished, the disenfranchised, and the excluded—to understand them, speak their language, and woo them. That process had begun by the time I joined the Bank, and the Bank's responsiveness to ABVA's demands that it should not lend to India for AIDS prevention until the government agreed to end its draconian policies was an early sign of its new responsiveness that was now gathering momentum.

The Bank began to hire staff from nongovernmental and activist organizations so as to improve communication at the grassroots level. It began to invest in operational research that solicited the views of the poor. Infrastructural projects began to address how to resettle those who were displaced. The Bank also began to require all its staffers to spend a week or so every second year in impoverished urban or rural settings, de facto admitting that its technocrats knew scarcely anything about the realities they were supposed to be improving. (Tellingly, the Bank's intranet was soon full of unintentionally hilarious commentary by staff members who—seemingly for the first time—realized that people in shantytowns and impoverished villages lived in hovels, did not have toilets or running water, and often went hungry.) It moved large numbers of staff from Washington, DC, to country offices, to stay closer to their areas of responsibility and keep their ears to the ground.

The Bank also began to take an unexpected interest in the health of gay men and sex workers. It was an outgrowth of the Bank's work on AIDS: the economic devastation caused by the pandemic had led the Bank to rapidly become the largest funder of national AIDS prevention programs in developing countries.

Management already had some firsthand understanding of the

subject of gay men, from the considerable number of staffers who were open about their orientation. Within days of joining the Bank, I had found, to my astonishment, advertisements on hallway notice boards and the intranet announcing meetings of a gay group for Bank and IMF staff—the World Bank/IMF Gay Lesbian and Other Bisexual Employees Association. The first meeting I could attend was, I found, held openly on the premises, its atmosphere cheery and unafraid. The group had several dozen members, largely American and European men, but there was a sprinkling of people like me from developing countries. It was reassuring to see several senior staff members at the meeting.

In my two years at the Bank, I found that the management was fairly responsive to our demands that we, and our partners, be acknowledged and treated on a par with heterosexual staff and their families. Haltingly, the Bank began to provide basic benefits and legal protection, such as medical insurance for same-sex partners and prohibition of discrimination on the basis of sexual orientation. Some managers did all they could to secure visas for partners of staff wherever they were posted.

Just those small steps put the Bank far ahead of the UN system, where gay and lesbian staff continued to work in fear and secrecy. Indeed, at that point, the Bank was also ahead of the US government. This was the era of the homophobic Defense of Marriage Act, which denied recognition to same-sex partners for all federal benefits and rights. Many factors contributed to that—including the value placed by top management on job performance, the Bank's operational autonomy from member countries, and the singular outspokenness of the prominent Bank economist Hans Binswanger about being both gay and HIV-positive.

However, none of that convivial familiarity applied to the other set of sexual outlaws: sex workers. To all intents and purposes, they were still unidimensional, faceless ciphers that were of interest only in terms of slowing the pandemic.

But then, in August 1994, at the 10th International Conference on

AIDS in Yokohama—where I was part of a small team of Bank staffers—I felt something change tentatively.

At one of the plenary sessions, I heard a former sex worker and activist for sex workers' rights, Ms. K, speak about the epidemic's impact on sex workers. She spoke with outrage about how AIDS had been decimating sex workers since the pandemic's earliest days, even as those with the power to help them did not act because of overpowering bigotry. Everyone in that massive hall kept exceptionally quiet through the speech, as if ashamed by the truth of her words.

In that speech, I heard Ms. K call for reforming the laws that criminalized sex work in country after country. Decriminalize sex work! It immediately made sense to me—just as decriminalizing homosexuality was the first step that gay men and women needed to emancipate ourselves, so, too, women, trans women, and men who sold sex needed to be freed from the fear of criminal prosecution in order to begin tackling the myriad hardships they faced, of which HIV was the latest. Coming from Ms. K—someone with as personal an experience of sex work as I had of being gay—the call had an unquestionable authenticity.

I sought out Ms. K, a self-assured woman with the charismatic style of a nightclub singer, to ask if she would contribute an article to the health policy newsletter that I edited at the Bank. Would she write about what sex workers thought the World Bank should do to turn around the pandemic's onslaught on sex workers and their clients? She agreed on the condition that she ask a colleague to author the article, given the short deadline.

A week later, the article arrived by email. It turned out to be written by Priscilla Alexander, the activist and researcher on sex work whom Jonathan Mann had recruited to WHO's Global Programme on AIDS in 1989. Alexander had left WHO in 1993 to coordinate the efforts of the National Task Force on Prostitution, a coalition of US and Canadian organizations for sex workers' rights.

Alexander's article began by discussing the terrible stigma and persecution that have been visited on women sex workers for eons in most societies. "Prostitution has often been called the oldest profession," Alexander wrote. "However, it has rarely, if ever, been respected as a profession." Following centuries of overwhelming discrimination, the emergence of AIDS and "epidemiologic characterizations of female prostitutes as vectors who will speed up transmission of HIV to men, to men's wives, and to babies" had worsened the vilification of sex workers. It had also legitimized a spate of brutal, unjust health regulations.

"Papers in prestigious medical journals have described female prostitutes as 'reservoirs of infection,' 'pools of contagion,' 'vectors,' and—my favorite—'core groups of high-frequency transmitters,'" Alexander wrote acerbically. (For all her frankness, Alexander was being diplomatic—she could have noted that the Bank was also a leading offender in using exactly these alarmist, blame-the-victim terms in its documents on HIV and sex workers.)

Sex work was illegal in all but twenty-odd countries, with countries varying only on the extent of criminalization and the specific aspects of sex work that were prohibited. Though many countries specifically criminalized the selling of sex, others, such as the United States, also criminalized buying it. Great Britain and many of its former colonies, including India, had adopted the contradictory approach of the 1949 United Nations Convention for the Suppression of the Traffic in Persons and of the Exploitation of the Prostitution of Others, which targeted sex workers despite its ostensible goal of protecting the women as victims of criminal exploitation; these countries made it impossible for sex workers to engage in their profession without breaking the law, as they criminalized every aspect of selling sex—such as soliciting, advertising, using their homes to sell sex, being found in a brothel, or selling sex near any "public place"—rather than the sale of sex itself.

Revealing the depth of animus against sex workers, most countries used every possible law to prosecute them, typically combining specific antiprostitution laws with the discriminatory use of broad laws targeting vagrancy, public nuisance, adultery, or sodomy (in the case of male or transgender sex workers). The punishments were stunningly harsh, including monetary fines, jail terms, indefinite incarceration in reformatories, eviction from their homes, forced removal of their children, and being listed in public records as a "common prostitute" or "sexual offender"; in a handful of countries, women convicted of prostitution were put to death. The pattern that sex workers bore the brunt of the punishment was true both in India—where virtually every arrest was of sex workers, even though the law did not directly criminalize them—as well as in the United States, where three-fourths of the annual 125,000 arrests were of women and transgender sex workers (disproportionately black) and just 10 percent of arrests were of clients or pimps.

"At the present time, as we near the end of the 20th century, there are essentially three dominant paradigms for how society should approach the subject of prostitution," Alexander wrote. "The oldest one is 'control the prostitute,' which has, as its corollaries, 'protect the client,' 'protect the neighborhood' or 'protect society' from the prostitute. The second is 'rescue the prostitute,' from herself, from the clients, from the pimps." Those two traditional paradigms were the ones that had "left sex workers so vulnerable to violence and disease."

In contrast, she said, "A new voice has begun to make itself heard, the voice of sex workers powerfully enunciating a new paradigm. This paradigm is 'control working conditions,' in the context of sex work as a legitimate occupation." She ended with a half-dozen bullet points, stripped of any flourishes, laying out what sex workers' organizations wanted the World Bank and governments to act on. They included decriminalization of adult, consensual sex work, alongside a crackdown on forced prostitution and child prostitution, avoiding prostitution-specific legislation in favor of improved and well-enforced general laws against rape, sexual assault, kidnapping, and child abuse. (Decriminalization differs from legalized regimes, such as that in Nevada, since it focuses on empowering sex workers themselves, rather than the state, to have greater control over their work.) She laid out ways to ensure better work conditions for sex workers through paid sick leave, medical and disability insurance, retirement pensions, and broad health care. She emphasized that sex workers needed the right to engage in collective bargaining and other kinds of advocacy, just like workers in other industries.

From everything I had seen, read, and understood of sex work so far, those demands seemed legitimate and reasonable. I thought that my Bank colleagues' notions about sex work and HIV would be usefully challenged by Alexander's article. But Alexander now wrote, her frustration evident, "With any other occupation, such basic demands would not be controversial, but with sex work, few policy makers are even willing to participate in an open discussion." Those closing words of hers were prophetic.

My immediate boss read the draft and curtly told me that he would not allow it to be published in the Bank's health policy newsletter. I was appalled: he had been wholeheartedly enthusiastic about the idea when I had checked with him before asking Ms. K to contribute to the newsletter. But he now maintained that it was inappropriate for sex workers to tell the Bank and its partner governments what they wanted, and that, too, in such forceful terms.

I argued that we had made a commitment to both Ms. K and Alexander, that, too, on a sensitive matter, and we could not renege on it. He retorted that if I didn't like his decision, I was free to resign. From his expression, it was clear that he hoped I would.

It took several weeks and several meetings with the director of the division and other senior staff to present my case, but eventually the director told me that he had decided that Alexander's article should be published in its entirety. I was overjoyed; I knew that almost no other international organization would have run such an article. Whatever my criticisms of the Bank's wasteful functioning and damaging impact on the world, there was no doubt that there was greater freedom for debate there than at other comparable institutions.

Eventually, Alexander's article appeared as the lead front-page item in the fall 1994 issue of the Bank's health policy newsletter, distributed among Bank staff as well as to the public. I noted candidly in the introduction that the Bank had solicited the article "because of the continuing disregard by decision-makers of the views of sex workers' rights organizations." As I expected, the article attracted more attention than any other in the newsletter's history. One reason was that it marked the first time a community so severely affected by AIDS had the chance to convey to Bank staff, indelibly in print, their view of what the Bank and its partner governments needed to do to make real headway against the epidemic. Several years later, when the Bank first fully enunciated its thinking on HIV prevention among sex workers and their clients, I was gratified to see that it was informed by Alexander's perspective—particularly her vital insight that criminalization harmed the well-being of sex workers as well as the goal of tackling the spread of HIV.

But though I felt glad that I had played a role in opening a dialogue, I was never confident that it would deepen into genuine understanding. We gay people were no longer outcasts at the Bank; we were welcomed on staff and even in senior positions, and the Bank now understood that our fundamental human rights needed to be assured. But sex workers remained outcasts, even more of an alien species than the merely impoverished, whose needs the Bank struggled to respond to anyhow. I wondered whether that great distance could ever be bridged.

FOURTEEN

"THIS NAKED, HUNGRY MASS"

In the fall of 1994, at the time that my dispute over Alexander's article was unfolding, I was awarded a grant by a US foundation that would enable me to research and write a book that I had long dreamed of: a nonfiction book that would use the first-person story of a destitute Indian family to depict the larger account of how India's impoverished masses had fared in the country's first half century of independence, coming up soon on August 15, 1997.

Faced with the prospect of actually moving back to India, which I had fled with Tandavan just four years back after the terrifying incident with the police, I hesitated. But I had dreamed of writing this book for many years—indeed, the seeds had been sowed more than a decade back, in my undergraduate years. I felt that nothing I might achieve personally could be more important than this book because the history of the poor in India was *the* history of India. And soon the generations who had lived through the epochal first decades of independence would die and their history would be forever lost. I had to write this book.

So at the end of 1994, age thirty-three, I left the World Bank to return to India. As with my first return—back in 1986—my work passions propelled me homeward, despite my knowing that to live in

India as a gay man was fraught with the potential for disaster. As in the past, Delhi was my base. I was hosted as a visiting fellow by the Centre for the Study of Developing Societies, a progressive think tank I had long admired.

For my field research, however, I had chosen an area far from the capital, in the outback of Uttar Pradesh, the vast state that was then home to nearly one in five of India's 950 million people. Baba ka Gaon, the small village of a hundred families that I had settled on, was marked only on detailed maps of the state, roughly a hundred miles from Lucknow, the state capital. I had selected the area because it was there in 1920, during a fierce revolt that had pitted impoverished peasants and landless laborers against rapacious *zamindar* landlords and the British colonial government, that Jawaharlal Nehru—already a leader of the Indian National Congress and eventually to become independent India's first prime minister—had first confronted the country's poverty.

In his autobiography, Nehru confessed that encountering "this naked, hungry mass" had filled him with "shame and sorrow." The peasants had looked at him and the other Congress leaders with "loving and hopeful eyes, as if we were . . . the guides who were to lead them to the promised land." What more fascinating perspective could there be than to record what a representative family from this area's "naked, hungry mass" truly felt about how far Nehru and his successors had led them toward "the promised land"?

Every month, I drove the exhausting seventeen-hour stretch from Delhi to Baba ka Gaon, stopping only to sleep over in Lucknow. The tarmac road ended over two miles from the village, following which the jeep clawed its way across a dirt track cratered with potholes and swampy irrigation channels. At the village, the track broke into two, the one to the right broad and sweeping, the other a broken mud rut that eventually ground to a halt. The broad, motorable track led to large homes and numerous temples in the areas occupied by Brahmins and Thakurs.

The broken track took me to the area that I soon came to know like a second home—where those formerly called "untouchables" and other impoverished communities lived in mud-and-thatch huts cramped close to one another, so tiny that fifty would fit into one of the dominant-caste mansions. The men and women there were visibly poorer, thinner, and smaller than on the wealthy side—they were the tiny, sinewy people seen everywhere in India doing every kind of back-breaking, dangerous, and inhuman work for a pittance, pulling rick-shaws and carts, ferrying head loads in quarries and kilns, handling industrial waste, swabbing floors and bathrooms in home after home, cleaning stinking garbage dumps barefoot and barehanded, clamber-ing neck-deep into manholes to clean shit-choked sewers.

Here, on the impoverished side of Baba ka Gaon, I began docu-menting the life of several generations of the extended family headed by Ram Dass Pasi and Prayaga Devi. They were both born in the 1930s in nearby villages to Dalit landless laborers, bonded by gen-erations of debt to the local landlords. Ram Dass was one of the few individuals who knew for certain, from family lore, that his father and other relatives had fought in the revolt that had drawn Nehru to this area seventy-five years back. Gradually, through recording tape after tape of oral histories, I began to piece together the lives of Ram Dass, Prayaga Devi, their two adult children, and their older grandchildren, as well as more distant relatives living in Baba ka Gaon and other nearby villages.

✦

The days in Baba ka Gaon usually sped by. In the mornings, there were inevitably practical things to help with: ferry kids who had been bitten by a rabid dog to the hospital an hour's drive away, try to arrange a wheelchair for a young man severely crippled by polio, take someone to the district government offices to sort out land ownership titles or secure their pension (invariably eaten up by a network of corrupt of-ficials). In the afternoons, I waited patiently to get an hour or two of interviews with Ram Dass and the others when they finished working in the fields.

Apart from a few nights spent in the village itself, I would set out before dusk back to my room at the "circuit house"—the Indian term for a government guesthouse for officials on tour—a half-hour drive away. I made it a point to return before dark, as the interior roads were deserted and it was risky for me to be driving alone.

From then on until I returned to Baba ka Gaon the next morning, the hours would stretch endlessly and bleakly. If the electricity did not fail—especially in summer it was cut for hours at a stretch through the day and night—I would read from the stacks of Agatha Christie, Ruth Rendell, and P. G. Wodehouse books that I had brought along from Delhi. Dinner would be *daal* or vegetables from the roadside *dhaba*.

On one or two evenings a week I queued up at the sole telephone booth—it being some years before mobile phones or internet access came into use in India—to call my friends in Delhi or New York, my brothers or my father. Even that inevitably had mixed results, as on hearing about their full lives, replete with the everyday pleasures of movies, good meals, and convivial time, I ended up feeling acutely that I had set out on a foolish, quixotic search. My forays into rural India had until now all been time-bound and consequently had had a feeling of adventure to them—but this one stretched on and on, without a foreseeable end, as though I were undertaking a solitary, risky swim across an unmapped ocean. At many moments, I wished fervently that I had not begun at all and had settled for life and relationships in surroundings to which I belonged.

❖

Every three weeks or so, I drove back to Delhi. That time back in my quiet apartment was a desperately needed respite. I was invariably physically exhausted and would sleep endlessly. For days, I would barely leave the apartment, grateful to be in a clean space, to have a veranda from which to admire the *seesham* and *semul* trees, to be among my familiar things, to have home-cooked food again, to have friends over. All those prosaic things had become wondrous treats.

Even though I was never there for long, that apartment felt like home. My beloved friend Nilita had lived here when Tandavan and I were still living in Delhi. She had left everything as it had been then—and the familiar books, the homey furniture, the earthy rugs, the cheery blue-and-white Jaipur crockery, and the posters of her documentary movies felt as though they were mine, too.

It was a haunting place as well, full of memories of Siddhartha. He, Nilita, and I had often whiled away happy hours here, drinking cups of *chai*, cuddling on the bed. In my first months there, I was certain that I felt Siddhartha embracing me, wrapping his cool, thin arms around my neck or resting his head on my shoulder. I would choke with tears and fight away those memories. Things that I had thought were sureties, that would last my lifetime, had ended forever. Siddhartha was dead. My relationship with Tandavan was extinguished. Those were the kinds of seismic losses I had naively imagined happened when one was old, not in one's thirties.

This time, I was unable to connect more broadly with life in Delhi. I couldn't overcome a sense of alienation to do with the unbridgeable differences to the life of the people I knew in Baba ka Gaon and the thoughtless relishing of comfort and privilege here as India's embryonic economic boom and the beginnings of globalized culture eroded the self-denying values that had defined the post-Independence decades.

So, too, beyond being with old friends, I found myself unable to participate in gay life in Delhi. From the handful of gay parties that my friends dragged me to, I saw there were striking new developments. In the late 1980s there had invariably been just a dozen or so of the same faces of gay men and women at those gatherings. But, to my astonishment, there were now hundreds of men at the parties. And although the essentially tame affairs of the past had always been hosted at someone's home, they were now thrown at the palatial country houses on Delhi's outskirts that the rich were building as weekend retreats, and behind the high walls and secured gates men freely kissed and made out in the swimming pool, bedrooms, and grounds.

The changes were not confined to the rich. At a huge dance party held at the community center of a middle-class housing association, I was struck that so many middle- and lower-income young men unequivocally told me that they were gay, a notable break with the earlier norm when men had invariably said they were merely having fun with men because women and men were prohibited from dating or having premarital sexual relations.

Though it seemed that the lives of wealthy and middle-class gay men and women in Delhi and Bombay were changing in unexpected ways, it seemed doubtful that those changes augured any kind of broad, nationwide progress. The legal challenge to the sodomy law filed in the Delhi High Court in early 1994 by Siddhartha's ABVA had made no headway. India seemed not to care one whit about the progress on gay rights that was visible on every continent—that countries from Albania to Venezuela had recently decriminalized same-sex relations; that numerous others were moving toward equality by passing antidiscrimination laws and equalizing the age of consent; that South Africa had become the world's first nation to explicitly prohibit discrimination based on sexual orientation in its constitution; that the UN Human Rights Committee had ruled that sexual orientation was included as a protected status under the UN International Covenant on Civil and Political Rights, making sodomy laws illegal.

❖

The snatches of time I had in Delhi over those years were so transitory as to leave me feeling that I had not even lived there. But there was one lasting, wonderful development: my relationship with my father deepened in transformative ways.

On moving back to India, I found that my father's life was in a state of upheaval. Some weeks before my departure from Washington, DC, he had told me on the phone that he had moved out of our family home in Calcutta and was going to live apart from my mother.

He would continue to look after her, he explained, but her worsening mental illness made it impossible for them to inhabit the same space.

My brothers and I empathized. Over the past decade, our mother's mental illness had become incapacitating. Her moods swung between depression and rage, and it was only in rare moments that I could still see the gentle, loving person to whom I had been so deeply attached as a child. She had angrily refused to allow a psychiatrist friend of ours to visit her at home to see if he could help. After our father moved out, she isolated herself completely, living alone in a worsening spiral of disrepair. My father's staff would deliver cooked food, groceries, and asthma medicines but would inevitably have to leave them at the front door as she refused to answer it. Our worries were intensified because her chronic asthma every so often spiked into a life-threatening emergency. She soon refused to even speak to any of us, her sons, on the phone, let alone to let us visit. Months began to go by without her seeing another person, speaking on the phone, or leaving the house. We got updates only when her doctor made a house call or she was admitted to his clinic in an emergency. The only shred of comfort came from knowing that our father could always be counted on to do his best to look after her.

Meanwhile, his businesses were hemorrhaging funds. A decade earlier, after a damaging rupture with the vast tea company that he had long headed, he had begun an ambitious project to grow tea in areas where it had never been grown before, including the central reaches of Orissa state, three hundred miles to the southwest of Calcutta. This area was home to indigenous *adivasi* communities who had been pauperized as the bountiful tropical forests where they had lived for generations had been razed by illegal timber operations and large-scale mineral mining. My father dreamed of reforesting those hills with tea bushes and shade trees, and of working with the *adivasi*s to provide them with an ecologically sustainable livelihood that respected their bonds with nature.

Against all the odds, he had succeeded. On my visits over the years, I had seen barren hills transformed back into verdant green, once again alive with wild animals, including sloth bears and leopards. More than a thousand *adivasi* women and men were now employed there, earning far more than their peers anywhere else in the region. My father was now praised not just by other tea experts but also by leading advocates for indigenous peoples' rights. He dreamed of turning over ownership of the land to the *adivasi*s so they could run it as a self-sustaining cooperative of smallholders and reap direct benefits forever.

But the mammoth investments needed to establish the plantation—coupled with the state government's failure to provide the infrastructural support it had promised—were now draining his finances. For years, he had pumped the profits from his other businesses into the plantation, but those ventures were coming to an end. He refused to think of closing down the plantation, given the countless defenseless people who would lose their jobs, let alone his own investments of money and effort. There seemed no solution in sight.

My father began to visit me in Delhi virtually the moment I returned there from my research trips. I always welcomed him, and we began to talk in a way that we hadn't before. He had always spoken candidly to me since we had begun to grow close in my last year at Doon, but now, perhaps because he was grappling with the course of his own life, on which blow after unrelenting blow had fallen, he left out nothing. It was just how I was getting to know Ram Dass in Baba ka Gaon, of exactly my father's generation but from a background that couldn't be more different.

He told me how strange it was to have spent his entire childhood in a state of embattled fear, knowing that it was only his grand-uncle's protectiveness that had kept him and his mother from being dispossessed or even killed by his relatives after the murder of his father. Even Doon School and its savagery had been preferable to life at home. He had gone on to St. Stephen's College, graduated, and walked away from his inheritance, saying he wouldn't touch something that was tainted by his father's murder.

One evening, sitting on the veranda at dusk, he told me about how he had fallen in love with my mother. I knew the story of their first accidental encounter well already, from being told as a child, but I could see that he was longing to tell me again now, almost as if it would help him make sense of what had gone wrong since. Age twenty and already working as an expert tea taster in Calcutta, he was visiting relatives in a small Madhya Pradesh town, when, on a drive into the countryside, he found the road blocked by a car from which a beautiful young woman was leaning out of the driver's window, waving at the crows pecking at something on the road in front of her. She was beseeching them in Hindi, "Crows, please move, please, come on, how can I drive if you keep sitting there!" He was smitten by that vision— and on coming to know her during his stay there he had fallen in love, drawn by her gentleness and love of nature, a world apart from the sophisticated women he had dated so far.

He fell silent. We were both quiet for a long while. I wondered whether, like me, he was thinking about how much each of us in our family, my mother foremost, had lost to her mental illness.

I had always admired my father's ability to remain balanced and cheerful at the most stressful moments. (Even when he had run a business empire, he had somehow set aside those preoccupations the minute he reached home, and we children had had his undivided attention.) Even at this nadir, when life would have seemed unbearable to most others, there was never any complaint, no bitterness even toward those who had wronged him needlessly or cruelly. His joie de vivre was undimmed. He relished every routine pleasure—his morning yoga and prayers; sports; whisky and cigarettes—while his determination to save his beloved tea plantation for the *adivasi*s never flagged.

I can only describe what I saw revealed in him not as stoicism but as an upbeat resilience, an astonishing ability to remain joyous in the face of tragedy. It reminded me of Albert Camus's counterintuitive reading of the myth of Sisyphus, where Camus writes that despite Sisyphus's full awareness of his doomed predicament, condemned by cruel gods to eternally pushing a boulder up a hill, he succeeds in triumphing over that punishment and indeed the gods themselves by somehow remaining joyous. Camus wrote, in words that moved me profoundly, "The struggle itself toward the heights is enough to fill a man's heart. One must imagine Sisyphus happy." It struck me that my father was becoming more and more heroic to me at the precise time that he was losing the wealth and power that had made him an admired, larger-than-life figure to many others.

✤

We took huge steps forward in addressing the one cause of awkward-ness and discomfort between us: my orientation. Perhaps simply be-cause of our growing closeness he came to reach a level of relaxed comfort about this matter that transformed our equation for the re-mainder of his life.

His views on same-sex matters were rife with contradictions that I could never resolve. "Son, did I ever tell you that Uncle X was gay?" he asked once, smiling, as he was telling me a story about his college days. X had been one of his closest friends from St. Stephen's and was now married with children. I took the chance to ask as many questions as I could. How did you know he was gay? "Oh, son, he was having sex with lots of other Stephanians who lived on campus. He was gorgeous then, probably the best-looking man I've known."

And his being homosexual didn't bother you? "Not at all! He was one of my closest friends. Constantly flirted with me. I guess he was in love with me, though we never talked about it. One of his favorite pranks was to arrive in my room at night, wet from the shower and wearing just his towel, holding his toothbrush, grinning away, saying 'Basant, I want you to use my toothbrush to clean my bum, it's still not clean.' Oh, he was hilarious."

And nobody persecuted him? "Nobody would have dared. I would have beaten up anyone who hassled him. Anyhow, he was a great sportsman and everyone liked him."

I was puzzled. How could my father combine his unqualified com-fort with that friend and his lasting affection for him with the patently homophobic views he had expressed when I was younger? I didn't ask, mainly because we had both moved far beyond those harrowing years, and that was all that mattered to me.

But that opening up led us to a new level of comfort. One of my father's favorite bantering habits whenever women friends of mine were around was to say to them and me both, in a tone that was at once jesting and yet hopeful, "Come on, son, why don't you and she fall in love. Isn't it time you tried a woman?"

In the past, I'd ignore his comments or snap at him in irritation. But now, in one instance, I retorted, "Dad, if you try a man, I'll try a woman. Which of your friends will it be?"

My father guffawed at that retort, as did my friends. "You never know, son, stranger things have happened!" he quipped. My friends erupted in cheers and catcalls. The banter melted away the last of our tensions.

⚜

The years hurtled past, such strange years, so utterly different from anything else I had lived. By mid-1997, two and a half years from the time I had begun the research, I had a close-to-final draft of my manuscript. The end of what had once seemed an impossible task was in sight.

In the meanwhile, I had lived some of the most meaningful years of my life, despite the hardships and despite all that I had forgone in terms of having a normal, settled life.

Years of exhaustive research had added immeasurably to my knowledge about poverty and the challenges of social justice. It had, ironically, left me more ambivalent than ever about India's track record.

There was so much evidence to show that on matters of social justice India had advanced at breathtaking speed in the fifty years since the end of colonial rule and its ruinous depredations. Famines and epidemics no longer killed millions. Feudalism had been ended so effectively that old elites no longer dominated politics. The most extreme forms of oppression and exploitation had been vastly reduced. Poor people voted increasingly freely in record numbers—their choices could make or break electoral prospects. The impact of affirmative action programs, the world's largest, was stunning. India's president in its fiftieth year was a Dalit man, the widely admired K. R. Narayanan, and a forty-one-year-old Dalit woman, Kumari Mayawati, had twice become the chief minister of Uttar Pradesh. In numerous other states, women like her had achieved commanding political power through their own prowess rather than dynastic inheritance. I sometimes felt that independent India was more strongly committed to correcting old wrongs and achieving social justice than almost any other country.

But more often I felt frustration and anger. The striking gains made in addressing the gargantuan accumulated wrongs of colonialism were the result of socialistic commitments made at Independence. Both the strength of those commitments and their impact seemed to be fading precipitously by the late 1990s. Nearly one in two Indians still lived in dire poverty, a number that outstripped the country's entire population at Independence. None of the basic building blocks needed for the poor to advance— whether schools and health care, safe drinking water and sanitation, housing, or guaranteed-employment programs—existed or functioned in most parts of the country. As a result, India's performance on social indicators was worse than that of most other developing countries, including several of its neighbors. (Only the handful of Communist-ruled states and southern states performed significantly better.) Nobody was ever held to account for this chronic misgovernance. When the poor sought help or simply fair treatment, they were treated with a dehumanizing disdain—by even the lowest-ranking functionaries—that I had never seen elsewhere in the world. Seeing all that left me to draw the bleak conclusion that as a nation India was callously indifferent to its citizens' well-being and would forever remain the land of poverty that the British had reduced it to.

All that knowledge was important to me, but more precious still was the relationship I had developed with Ram Dass, Prayaga Devi, and others in Baba ka Gaon. It had evolved gradually, like all deep-rooted relationships, marked with moments of epiphany that bridged the vast divides between our lives.

There was the afternoon, just a month into my research, when Ram Dass had cut off my apology for burdening him with questions after his arduous day at work. "You never need to apologize for asking me questions," he said firmly, the first time he had spoken to me without deference. "Until you came to the village, no rich person had ever asked me how my life was or what I felt. And if I don't tell you my history, how will people learn from what I've suffered?"

There was the day, months later, that I realized that Ram Dass and the other Dalits in Baba ka Gaon had come to trust me wholly, thought of me as one of them because I had stood by them unflinchingly through a violent attack by the Thakur landowners.

There was the time that I asked Prayaga Devi what she thought of trapeze artists wearing skirts instead of saris—I had taken her and her grandchildren to their first circus—and she replied in her characteristic measured manner, "Everyone must dress according to their needs. They cannot wear saris while swinging upside down! Just like we Dalit women cannot pull our *pallu*s over our faces like upper-caste women, because we'd cut off our hands while harvesting."

There was the day in Bombay that I asked Ram Dass what had been his favorite haunt in the city when he had lived there many decades back. His voice ringing with excitement, he said that he loved the Kala Ghoda museum, the colloquial name for the Prince of Wales Museum of Western India, more than anything else to gaze at the ancient sculptures of the Buddha. "The first time I came to the museum, I was so astounded by it that I spent half the day here," Ram Dass said. He had taken every member of his family to the museum, visiting it more than a dozen times.

And then there were the days, most moving of all, whenever I left Baba ka Gaon, that I saw Prayaga Devi weeping at my leaving, saw Ram Dass and so many others in the crowd fighting back tears, too, and saw me struggling not to sob openly like Prayaga Devi. I had become part of another family that I loved deeply.

FIFTEEN

DEATHS—AND WOMEN'S REVOLUTIONS

In the summer of 1997, with the manuscript of the book delivered to the publishers, I left Delhi to join UNICEF's health policy division in New York City. Just eighteen months later, in late 1999, I turned around and went back again, this time to write a book about India's escalating AIDS epidemic, my research underwritten by a Ford Foundation grant. For the next many years, my writing and advocacy focused overwhelmingly on AIDS and its devastating impact on sexual outlaws.

By that point, the AIDS pandemic had become one of the world's defining threats. More than 50 million adults and children had contracted HIV, of whom nearly 20 million had died. An estimated 13 million children had lost one or both parents to the disease. Almost all that toll was concentrated in low- and middle-income countries—all from a disease practically unknown just seventeen years before.

Even worse devastation lay ahead, the United Nations' newly formed AIDS program, the Joint United Nations Programme on HIV/AIDS, known as UNAIDS, warned. In 1999 alone, 5.8 million adults and children contracted HIV, a daily average of nearly 16,000 people. In that year, 2.5 million people died of AIDS—equivalent to more than a hundred Boeing 747s crashing every day with no survivors. Only a handful of developing countries had managed to lower their infection rates, notably including Thailand, Uganda, and several West African and Latin American nations. And even though the newly launched antiretroviral drug combinations were, Lazarus-like, literally bringing dying people in rich countries back to healthy life, there was no hope that developing countries could ever afford them, as a year's treatment for an individual cost $20,000, many times the average income in even the best-off of those nations.

To many experts, India was the greatest source of worry outside sub-Saharan Africa. Though just a dozen years had passed since the first indigenous cases of HIV had been detected among Selvi and other sex workers, more people were infected with HIV there than in any other country, according to estimates by the UN and other international groups. UNAIDS estimated that it had affected somewhere between 4 million and 5 million adults, approximately 1 percent of the adult population. As many as half a million more were contracting HIV every year, and more than 150,000 were dying annually of AIDS, its estimates suggested. The US government's National Intelligence Council, an expert research arm of the CIA, warned that an astronomical 25 million Indians could be infected within years—with India's billion-strong population, even a small increase in rates made a difference of millions of people in absolute numbers.

The consensus among close observers was that the Indian government's prevention efforts were too patchy to check the epidemic, given how widely it had spread. Every aspect of the response was imperiled by the abysmal condition of public health programs, chronically underfunded by the government, which left all but the well-off practically without access to even basic health-care services. Only a handful of well-run state governments had rolled out comprehensive HIV prevention efforts.

Within days into my research, I could sense the shocking change in scale. From previous AIDS research trips, I could remember virtually every encounter with people hit by the epidemic—an artifact of the long lead time from infection with HIV to actual sickness. Now there were countless HIV-positive individuals. In every city, they waited in unending lines in the outpatient departments that specialized in sexually transmitted diseases or tuberculosis (the most common AIDS-related opportunistic infection in poorer countries). They gathered at "positive people" associations and HIV-focused nongovernmental groups, their worries and sickness overriding fears of persecution, desperately seeking confidential HIV tests as well as advice on where to find doctors who didn't discriminate and how to hide their illness so that they would not be evicted by landlords or fired by employers.

I met impoverished manual laborers, low-income truck drivers, and upper-income professionals. There were sex workers and housewives. There were injecting drug users as well as policemen. They had had nothing in common to draw them together earlier—but now they had been forced together by AIDS.

Their suffering was exacerbated by the real threat of persecution facing anyone whose HIV status became known to others. Though the federal government had formally ended coercive AIDS policies in 1992, a myriad of abuses continued, so widespread as to defy cataloguing.

Both public and private hospitals continued to eject patients found to have HIV and leaked positive HIV test results to the press, employers and health-care insurers. In 1998, the Supreme Court ruled that any man with HIV would be prohibited from marrying, "as the marriage would have the effect of spreading the infection of his own disease, which is obviously dangerous to life, to the woman he marries." Newspapers all over the country carried reports about individuals or even entire families who had killed themselves because of the AIDS-related persecution they feared or had suffered.

Sex workers continued to bear the brunt of the persecution. On the orders of the courts or government, sex workers were routinely rounded up in raids and forcibly tested for HIV, with those testing positive incarcerated indefinitely. In 1994, the Maharashtra government attempted to pass legislation that would have allowed it to brand HIV-positive sex workers with indelible ink. In 1996, the Mumbai

High Court ordered the arrest and mandatory HIV testing of more than four hundred sex workers; many of the women were incarcerated for over a year, and seven died in that time. The Supreme Court made several rulings that further legitimized the persecution and abuse of sex workers.

My notebooks were soon overflowing. Every one of the interviews with those who were HIV-positive was heartbreaking because of the desperation they exuded, so different from the philosophical resignation with which I had seen Indians accept more conventional catastrophes, however awful or unremitting. Their terror leached through as relentless anxiety. Every conversation returned to the looming prospect of death. For those with children, there was the added feverish dread about which relative or friend could be trusted to house them, how to set aside some money to provide for them, how to ensure their well-being.

The one constant I found in my research was that AIDS had devastated the lives of India's sex workers like no force ever before. In the dozen years since Selvi and the five other sex workers in the Madras reformatory had been found to have HIV, countless more sex workers had contracted HIV, had fallen mortally sick, or had died. No one knew exactly how many—or even exactly where.

Given the rudimentary state of India's vital registration systems, many deaths among the poor were never recorded, particularly those of unknown women dying on the roadside. The governmental National AIDS Control Organization had established serosurveillance sites in major urban red-light areas, which blind-tested for HIV blood samples drawn from the women, but even by 1997 there was just a tiny handful of sites and even fewer that provided consistent trend data. Those sites reported infection rates ranging from under 5 percent to nearly 50 percent, with the highest rates in the cities of western and southern India. The estimates from Bombay were harrowing, suggesting that every second woman sex worker in the central red-light areas had contracted HIV—as high as the peak rates recorded among gay men in New York City. And though those results were unlikely to be representative of the many areas where sex work did not take place from brothels, the nongovernmental organizations that had sprung up to undertake HIV prevention with those women reported, anecdotally, that considerable numbers of sex workers were falling sick and dying. Adding to the imprecision, there was still very little empirical knowledge about sex work in India; much of what was known was still more guesswork than fact.

But it soon became evident, to my great surprise, that alongside the havoc AIDS was wreaking in the lives of sex workers, the epidemic had also catalyzed positive changes for them, perhaps even transformative changes for those who might survive the epidemic. That dynamic reminded me of the impact that AIDS had rapidly had on gay activism in the United States and elsewhere in the West, evident in the revitalized push for equal rights as well as the landmark success in forcing the pharmaceutical industry and US government to develop lifesaving drugs at record speed.

In India, those changes were driven by a handful of unusual HIV prevention efforts focused on sex workers. They rapidly evolved from being standard, top-down public health projects into collectives run by the sex workers themselves that began to catalyze once unimaginable changes—from forcing the government and the women's movement in India to pay heed to sex workers and their right to self-determination to profoundly influencing global thinking about sex work.

Over the years, I got to know well three of the most remarkable of those sex workers' collectives. They were coincidentally founded in the very same year, 1992, but in far-flung reaches of the country—Calcutta, Madras, and the small agricultural town of Sangli in Maharashtra, hundreds of miles apart. And though they developed independently, the common thread linking the groups was that their founders acted on the evidence that when sex workers saw that their overall welfare was genuinely at the heart of their efforts—that their most hated burdens were being tackled—they themselves rose up to fight determinedly for their well-being, of which protection from HIV was an urgent part.

Their commitment to the women's well-being and their right to self-determination set the collectives far apart from mainstream HIV prevention projects focused on sex workers. Those had begun to multiply because of the millions in funds available from the National AIDS Control Organization. The mainstream projects—largely established by Indian and foreign not-for-profits that had so far worked on other health issues—struggled to make headway on even their narrow goal of trying to control the spread of HIV, once faced with the difficult realities of sex work. Indeed, the worst of them did the sex workers outright harm by aiding authorities with forcible testing, raids, and imprisonment or by duplicitously helping pharmaceutical companies use them as guinea pigs for testing drugs and purported cures.

The Madras organization, the South India AIDS Action Programme, or SIAAP, owed part of its astonishing success to the very woman who, years before, had been among the first to be subjected to the state's brutality: Selvi, the sex worker who had been imprisoned in the reformatory for four years. It had been set up by Shyamala Nataraj, the journalist who, in 1989, had filed the legal challenge that had won hundreds of HIV-positive sex workers imprisoned in Tamil Nadu, including Selvi, their freedom.

By the time I first visited SIAAP, two thousand sex workers had joined local collectives launched by the group in villages, towns, and cities across Tamil Nadu. This was a world away from its start just six years earlier, when the fledgling organization had begun with no budget at all, operating out of a tiny rented room, with its staff comprising just Nataraj and a part-time assistant. I quizzed Nataraj—a woman of my age with a boyish figure, cropped hair, and an unsettlingly direct gaze—about its evolution.

Nataraj admitted candidly that she had begun with no clear plan, let alone a blueprint for action. She had had no prior training in grassroots work, and there had been no bank of knowledge anywhere on the most effective ways to support sex workers. But the fledgling organization had rapidly taken on an effective shape—because Selvi and several of the other women from the Madras reformatory had found their way to it and would change it in ways that Nataraj said she could never have foreseen.

As Natraj understood it, Selvi had first gone back to Ulundurpettai to live with her husband, to try to make things work with him. "But she found once again that she could not get along with her husband and her in-laws. She came back to Madras with her son but decided she was not going to sell sex anymore. She heard through the grapevine that I had set up a place to work on AIDS. So one day she walked into my office and just said, 'I want to work with you.'

"Realizing that I clearly did not recognize her, she said, 'Don't you remember me? You met me in jail, in the remand home. I am one of the women you freed.'

"I asked her, 'What work will you do?' There was no money available at that time to hire anyone to work on AIDS. She gave that question some thought and then answered, 'I will tell other people what I went through. Whether you pay me or not, I will come and work.'

"And then for the next many years, until her death just some months earlier this year, Selvi was really a tireless crusader. She would go to other sex workers and say, 'Hey, I had sex without a condom. Look at me now. Don't let this happen to you. This doesn't need to happen.'"

That is how "peer education"—as the strategy of relying on credible community members to influence community behavior and norms is known in development parlance—became a core element of SIAAP's strategy. Though sex workers were loath to trust outsiders or authority figures, they trusted Selvi. Soon, overcoming their fear of informers, they began to attend educational meetings at the organization and from there began working as part-time peer educators themselves. It exponentially expanded the group's reach and impact.

From all that Selvi had suffered in her life—her abusive marriage, her years of selling sex to support herself and her young son, her HIV diagnosis, and her long years of imprisonment—she knew better than any outsider about the realities faced by those women and what exactly would help them the most. That had enabled the group to tailor itself to the characteristics of sex work in Madras, Nataraj explained.

In Madras, and generally across Tamil Nadu, brothels were a rarity and sex work happened in almost exactly the kind of places that men who had sex with men sought out. Once sex workers picked up clients from crowded areas such as bus stops and railway stations, cinema halls and highway rest sites, they showed the same ingenuity as homosexual men in finding places to have sex in this crowded country where privacy and space are luxuries available only to a minuscule elite. Any nook and cranny was used to have sex, literally any building or dark space in which two people copulating for a few minutes, fully dressed, might not be discovered: a patch of bushes near a bus stop, the ditches off highways or railway lines, corners of construction sites, city parks, and, if the men could afford them, huts and tenements that called themselves "lodges" and "hotels" but provided tiny rooms by the hour. And just like us homosexual men, they made do with whatever they could find—even if that meant that they lay on shit and garbage while having sex or risked being caught by the police.

So Selvi and the other sex workers who had joined SIAAP began to identify convenient spots in which to leave supplies of condoms that the women could access. They were placed in public toilets or inside broken lampposts or left with helpful vegetable vendors or tea stall owners. They even negotiated with "lodge" owners about placing condoms in rooms.

The more I learned from Nataraj and other women at the group about Selvi's transformation—from the silent, traumatized young woman held captive in the Madras reformatory to a trailblazing activist—the more intensely I regretted that I had not gotten to meet her. (Selvi had died in 1998 just a few months before I reached Chennai.) It was a revelation to see how deeply Selvi had inspired others even in such a truncated life. One of her closest friends at the collective, Mary Thomas, a sex worker from the neighboring state of Kerala, was so inspired by Selvi's dedication to others that she established a grassroots charity honoring her friend—the Selvi Memorial Illam Society. *Illam* means "shelter" in Tamil, and the charity runs a shelter for people sick with AIDS, along with providing home-based care, child care, and support groups.

Selvi

Nataraj quickly realized that the women desperately needed practical support. She began building alliances with health-care institutions, lawyers, and the government's women's rights and human rights agencies. Gynecologists came to brief the women on sexual infections and HIV. Feminist activists and lawyers introduced the women to issues related to their rights as citizens and to debates about gender and patriarchy. They, in turn, were sensitized to the particularly harsh difficulties faced by sex workers, marking the beginning of a long-term engagement.

From the discussions at the group meetings, Nataraj realized that she had to do something to help the women "build their self-respect and stop viewing themselves as 'doing wrong.'" She was struck that they castigated themselves so bitterly for selling sex, despite the compulsions that had propelled them into the work. "Many of these women entered sex work because they had been abused or deserted by husbands, lovers, or family members," said Nataraj. "Others wanted to supplement their husbands' earnings because the money they made was too little for their families to survive on. In any case, entry into sex work also displayed the autonomy of these women, rather than solely their victimhood.

"So we encouraged them to share their life experiences—not only about the desertion, abuse, and violence but also about survival as well as hopes and aspirations for their children and their own relationships with husbands, lovers, and other family members. They gradually began to see themselves as strong women, women who would not be easily cowed."

That awareness was very evident in the women I talked to. Thus, Mary Thomas said, "Every time something goes wrong, men put the blame on the women! Men say they go astray because of women. Men say they take to drink and drugs because of women. Men say they get HIV because of the prostitutes. The men never bear responsibility!"

One of the fronts that the group focused on almost immediately was tackling the violence the women suffered at the hands of the police. From the regular group meetings with the sex workers Nataraj realized that their "one common desire was to get the police off their backs."

SIAAP first used persuasion. "Selvi, some sex workers from the locality, and I would go together to the local police station and discuss the issue," said Nataraj. "The key was to touch the humanity of the cop in a completely nonjudgmental way. We pointed out that sex work had existed through the ages and often was a product of sexual desire of the client, on the one hand, and the poverty of the woman, on the other. We would tell them that there was no right or wrong involved, and the risk of HIV made it urgent for them to help both parties protect themselves—rather than take a moralistic stand.

"I think the cops bought the logic because many of them were also clients of sex workers. They appreciated our approach as well as the condoms and education material we left behind.

"For their part, the women became more circumspect in their behavior at the pickup sites, making sure that they did not show up tipsy or disheveled. They also made a pact among themselves to stop pimps from exploiting underage girls, threatening to report them to the police with SIAAP's help. In any case, over time, the police in Madras began to treat the women better. The abuse and arrests reduced considerably, even more so when we began to regularly send letters of appreciation to police stations."

Even so, confrontation was unavoidable, because a core of policemen continued to exploit and abuse sex workers. The group decided to challenge the police whenever any of the sex workers belonging to or known to the organization was arrested. On closely analyzing the federal law under which many sex workers were arrested, Nataraj and the human rights lawyers supporting SIAAP realized that it did not criminalize the act of selling sex itself but penalized every activity related to it—such as soliciting, renting premises for prostitution, pimping, or operating a brothel.

"Everybody—the women themselves as well as the police and lawyers—thought that sex work was clearly illegal in India, rather than a gray area," Nataraj recalled. It was because of that assumption that sex workers helplessly and unquestioningly pled guilty to whatever charges the police filed against them when produced in court, even if they were false.

The confusion reflected an unresolved contradiction in the law, which had remained largely unchanged since its first version had been enacted in 1923 by the British colonial government and had inherited the tensions dating back to that time between the government's goal of squashing prostitution and a reluctance to be seen as punishing the "victimized" women too harshly. The damaging result was a law that criminalized sex workers not in principle but in practice. Tellingly, even though the law is purportedly aimed at preventing the sexual exploitation of women—it is titled the Immoral Traffic (Prevention) Act—its real goal is to punish women in sex work. (This contradictory approach had spread worldwide through being institutionalized in the UN Convention for the Suppression of the Traffic in Persons and of the Exploitation of the Prostitution of Others of 1949. In contrast, in

the harshly prohibitionist approach of the United States, both prostitutes and their clients are explicitly criminalized in almost every state.)
Nataraj and the lawyers saw an opportunity in that confusion.

Nataraj and the lawyers knew that it would be difficult for the
police to provide hard proof that sex workers were soliciting—unless they had been entrapped by the police—and decided to focus on
that weakness in challenging future arrests. "We knew that the women
would win if only they found the confidence to plead not guilty," said
Nataraj.

"But, given the risks," said Nataraj, "it took a few years before one
brave woman—Saroja—agreed. But she won! And then more women
began to challenge their arrests. And they won, too. We had soon overturned dozens of arrests in the state." The sex workers were soon confident enough to challenge arrests on their own, without turning to
Nataraj or Madras-based lawyers.

Drawn by SIAAP's proven utility, increasing numbers of sex workers joined the local collectives that the group launched in cities and
towns across Tamil Nadu. Those collectives were run by the sex workers themselves, with officers chosen through regular elections. In the
formative years, SIAAP provided seed funding and matching grants,
but, in time, the local collectives' expenses were met entirely by mem-
bership fees.

From my visits to the local collectives over the years, I could see
the immeasurable benefits of participation. In the one I came to know
best, in the tiny town of Theni, three hundred miles south of Chennai,
the two dozen women would meet once or twice a week, always in
the morning, as they sold sex in the late afternoon and early evenings
before returning home. By 9:00 a.m., they would be grouped in a circle
on the mud floor of the rented hut that functioned as their office. It was
foremost a gathering of close friends, and there was much hugging,
chattering, giggling, and sharing of snacks, alongside the work-related
discussions.

Most of the women were in their twenties, a few in their thirties,
the two eldest in their early forties. Every one of them had two or

more children. Every one of them was married or had been married before being widowed or abandoned or before leaving an abusive husband. Like other married Tamil women they wore *mangalsutra* pendants, traditional jewelry and saris, a *bindi* on their foreheads, and a bunch of fragrant jasmine flowers pinned in their hair. Almost every one of them had regular employment, working for daily wages on construction sites or in agriculture like their husbands, virtually the only jobs available in that essentially rural area. The men invariably earned three to four times what women were paid for labor. But selling sex, discreetly and without their families' knowledge, was an even more lucrative earner for the women, providing the largest earnings for their families. I was surprised to learn that most of them were not from particularly impoverished backgrounds or castes. That was one striking indication of the dire financial pressures on average families in the area, the other being the fact that a surprisingly large proportion of local women—perhaps as many as one in twenty-five—sold sex on the side to earn money for their families.

What struck me most at every one of those meetings was their confidence. The women knew that they had one another as well as a formal organization to help them. From experience, I knew that having a community to turn to means the difference between hopelessness and hopefulness, especially for those of us who do not have a natal or visible community to begin with.

Their change in outlook and behavior had helped them negotiate as a group with local politicians, government officials, and the police, gradually winning the rights and welfare benefits they were entitled to, particularly vital for the significant number of single mothers among them. The state and local administration provided the women with voter identity cards as well as ration cards to buy subsidized staple foods and changed the rule for school admissions so that children would be admitted on the basis of the mother's guardianship alone (rather than requiring a father's presence).

The police began to treat those newly assertive women with

caution. Their old practice of arresting the women on trumped-up charges—to extract bribes or free sex or simply as moralistic punishment—diminished. They also began to act against men who harassed or exploited the women. Giggling, her tone almost incredulous, one of the women said, "Now the policemen request us to have a seat if we ever go to the police station to lodge a complaint!"

The on-the-ground gains won by SIAAP across Tamil Nadu in that short time were remarkable. The group's impact had also, however, stretched far beyond the grass roots: it had succeeded in pushing the issue of sex workers' rights and well-being onto the agenda of the Indian government. I was astonished to see that, as my experience of grassroots groups in India had been that even those who dealt successfully with local administrations struggled to make a measurable impact on national policy makers.

In 1995, the new chairperson of the National Commission for Women, the prominent social activist V. Mohini Giri, committed the commission to issuing an in-depth report on sex work. She supported Nataraj's plea that the commission's members pay heed to sex workers' views and demands, rather than deciding matters without their participation. Eventually Giri herself met more than two thousand sex workers across the country, and the penultimate draft of the report was opened up for comments from forty sex workers, notably including Selvi and Mary Thomas. That set a hugely important precedent in India, establishing that sex workers—no less than other women and other citizens—had a right to be heard in matters concerning them, even at the rarefied level of national policy making. They were now legitimate participants in public policy making.

Sex work was an unlikely choice of issues for the National Commission for Women, a governmental body. Until AIDS brought sex workers to the government's attention, every branch of the state had shunned those women, their only contact with the state being the predations of the police force, harsh sentences from the lower courts, and punitive incarceration in reformatories. And across the decades since Independence, the women's movement had paid no heed to women in sex work, focusing its energies on more broad-based concerns such as domestic violence, "dowry killings," and inheritance rights. The wider nongovernmental sector had ignored sex workers as well, at the most offering high-handed rehabilitation efforts predicated on the women's forswearing sex work and forever after living as impoverished penitents.

As Nataraj remarked to me, only overt prejudice against women who sold sex could explain such sweeping neglect. Even in a country where innumerable women, often cutting across class, face severe disadvantages, sex workers were arguably the most disempowered, worst treated, and most critically in need of support from feminists and other activists. It said everything that it was journalists and public health professionals, not mainstream activists or feminists, who had most strongly taken up the cause of those women and were instituting progressive and feminist models of empowerment.

The commission's report—*Societal Violence on Women and Children in Prostitution*—was published in early 1996. It was a bombshell of a document. The opening page said, "Women in prostitution are first and foremost equal citizens of India. . . . The fundamental rights toward basic amenities, comfort, freedom and dignity should be available to these women as much as they are to all the citizens of India." I had never imagined that a report bearing the imprimatur of the Indian government would ever take such a respectful position, given how disgracefully it had treated them so far.

Indeed, the report—in essence—was a catalogue of the grievous wrongs done to sex workers by varied branches of the state. "The state's key institutions, such as the police, schools and hospitals, are dismal in their attitudes and responses to these women," said the report. "In fact, most of them have served as the opposite of their designated functions; they double their exploitation and extortion, along with exerting violence of varying degrees upon these women and their children." Even basic social services such as government clinics and hospitals "are virtually beyond their access due to discriminatory attitudes and behavior of both the medical and the para-medical and the administrative personnel."

The commission reserved its most scathing criticism for the police. "The one constant refrain from women at all meetings held by the National Commission for Women was to 'do something about the police,' " the report noted bluntly. "The women are arrested under charges of 'possession of condoms,' or even on false charges of 'possession of narcotics.' . . . The women are rounded up at the end of the month when the target for petty/minor offences are not met by the particular police station . . . Some police officers are known by name to be self-avowed crusaders against 'prostitutes.'" Adding insult to injury, the police raked in a fortune from the hard work of those impoverished women through the massive bribes they extorted, the commission noted.

The commission lambasted India's laws and judiciary. The laws and their prejudiced application—whether it was the federal anti-prostitution law or the myriad state and local laws employed against sex workers—"victimizes the women," the report emphasized. For instance, antivagrancy laws that regulate the uses of public spaces, including footpaths and parks, were routinely used to arrest sex work-ers. "No other citizen is usually charged for the offence of vagrancy, which is the law most often operating against the women in sex work," the commission wrote sharply.

One egregious section of the federal antiprostitution law gave mag-istrates unchecked power to have a sex worker evicted from her home or premises in the "interests of the general public" or "if there is a com-plaint against her." The commission asked, with palpable outrage, "How will such a procedure stand the test of 'reasonable restriction'?" (While reading the report, it struck me just how completely all those anti–sex work laws were no less an alien legacy than Section 377 of the Indian Penal Code that criminalized gay men, all of them malignant hand-me-downs from British colonial rule. Recent research by both British and Indian historians showed that in precolonial India the diverse categories of women who were entertainers or sold sex had not been considered immoral, much less been criminalized—with temple dancers and cour-tesans commanding social respect, and less elevated categories being treated with at least relative tolerance. But during the nineteenth century their social and legal status was destructively and lastingly redefined as the East India Company and then the colonial government promoted regulated brothel prostitution to service British soldiers at the same time as criminalizing these women and portraying them as congenitally immoral individuals from degraded "prostitute castes.")

That sweeping survey was followed by reams of recommendations. The commission asked for legal reform, an end to police abuse, guaranteed affordable housing, ration cards to enable sex workers to buy subsidized food staples, and electoral identity cards so that they could exercise their basic citizenship right to vote—heartbreaking to read, because they confirmed just how much had been denied to them. The commission even had to urge that condoms be considered "life saving equipment," not used as a pretext for police to arrest sex workers. The recommendations were not legally enforceable, but the institution had been established to advise the government, and its views carried weight.

I was filled with admiration to note that Mohini Giri had left intact the views of sex workers, prominently highlighted in boxed sections, even when they sharply disagreed with the commission.

Their disagreement was blistering on the crucial issue of legal reforms. The sex workers clearly felt that the commission had not gone far enough. They called for real emancipation—and for that, they stressed, the law and the police would have to be entirely removed from their lives through a complete repeal of all prostitution-related laws. They had no patience for reforms that implicitly disapproved of sex work and sought its ending, when it was the most lucrative of the work options available to them as impoverished, largely illiterate women. They wanted adequate protections for sex workers so that they could continue to earn well from this livelihood option.

"There should not be any laws against prostitution," they stated categorically. "There should be no fines; there should not be 'demand reduction' in our services or else we will starve." (I was struck that India's sex workers had arrived at many of the conclusions of Priscilla Alexander and other Western advocates for sex workers' rights, despite hailing from a completely different setting.)

The most moving revelation of all came in the report's very last pages. It was the text of a recent petition by Selvi and six other sex workers, addressed to the government's National Human Rights Commission. Their petition focused on the arrest of several hundred sex workers in Mumbai in February 1996—on the orders of the High Court—who had then been forcibly tested for HIV and either deported to their home states or held captive indefinitely.

Selvi and her cosignatories had submitted the petition as members of the Representative Inter-State Committee of Sex Workers in India, urging the National Human Rights Commission to demand the release of those sex workers. "The members of this committee," they wrote, "have discussed this situation and the violations, and wish to record their anger and deep sorrow at the gross injustice that is being done. We submit that the below mentioned parties be held responsible, and urged to remedy the inhuman and illegal situation thus created." They named Mumbai's commissioner of police, the National AIDS Control Organization, and state health officials as the responsible parties.

The petition had come almost exactly a decade from the time Selvi had been imprisoned in the Madras reformatory. There she was, in those words, fighting to free hapless women who were in exactly the same cruel situation she had been in, of being incarcerated not for a substantiated crime but simply because they were HIV-infected and sold sex.

The dramatic change in Selvi's situation seemed to embody a tantalizing turning point. Though the abuses of sex workers hadn't diminished, many people were now challenging those abuses. The sex workers' cause was so visibly just that it had moved and drawn in people from a diversity of backgrounds, from activist journalists to public health specialists, and now even to influential establishment feminists and human rights defenders. Most promising, thousands of sex workers were themselves on the front lines of those battles, not only having succeeded in overcoming the crippling shame and self-loathing that had been foisted on them but having united to fight for their own emancipation. Things had changed in breathtaking ways that would have seemed unimaginable just a few years back.

✤

Everywhere in those years there were signs of what seemed to be the stirring of a revolution for India's sex workers. India was celebrating its fiftieth anniversary of independence, and more than anything else I knew of, that development, that the most cruelly stigmatized women seemed to be on the path to winning their rights to dignity, self-determination, and inclusion, filled me with hope that the country was set on a progressive, inspiring path.

In November 1997, just a few months after India had celebrated its fiftieth anniversary, Shyamala Nataraj and a dozen others from SIAAP were among five thousand sex workers and activists who reached Calcutta from far-flung parts of the country for the first national conference of sex workers. I longed to go, especially as the conference was in my hometown, but I had just moved to New York City to join UNICEF. The conference was the work of another pathbreaking sex workers' collective with the assertive name of Durbar Mahila Samanwaya Committee—Bengali for Indomitable Women's Collaborative Committee.

Durbar, as the group is popularly known, like Nataraj's group in Madras, had originated from an HIV prevention effort begun as recently as 1992 in Calcutta's largest red-light area, Sonagachi. It had proved to be so useful that about thirty thousand sex workers had joined the collective; its staff included 261 sex workers as educators and team leaders, besides a hundred other professionals, many of them the adult children of sex workers; it operated a network of vital services from health clinics to crèches to vocational training programs; its cooperative savings bank had freed the women from the stranglehold of local moneylenders; and the establishment of self-regulatory boards with strong government and community representation was bringing to an end the trafficking of girls and women.

Sex workers and activists from all across the country excitedly crowded into Salt Lake Stadium, an iconic venue. Those who understood contemporary Bengal's politics realized what volumes that fact itself—that their conference was being held at that historic place—spoke of how much headway their cause had already made in the state. The stadium had been the gathering point for fiery political rallies since the 1960s, by impoverished Bengalis who backed the local Marxist Party—with its commitment to direly needed pro-poor reforms—against the ossified and increasingly repressive Congress Party. Now here were women, *hijras*, and men who sold sex for a living insisting that their demand for respect and rights was a legitimate political cause.

None other than India's home minister, the legendary freedom fighter and Communist leader Indrajit Gupta, came to the function as its chief guest. It was an astonishing political statement, as Gupta's post was the most influential national position after that of the prime minister. "The women from SIAAP I was with almost couldn't believe it," Nataraj recalled. "And when he appeared on the dais we were blown away, because he was this distinguished, grandfatherly figure who exuded a huge moral authority."

In an opening speech delivered in Bengali, Gupta told the wildly cheering audience that he empathized with sex workers. No one should be allowed to abuse or persecute them, he said, and explicitly not the police, pointing to his armed bodyguards. To a crescendo of cheers and clapping, Gupta said he supported their demands for decriminalizing sex work and providing them the full panoply of human rights. He assured them that he would take the fight to Parliament.

It was testimony to how far India's political democracy had progressed. In the 1920s, when a group of Bengali sex workers had repeatedly volunteered to join Mahatma Gandhi in the anticolonial struggle, he had angrily refused unless they repented and left the trade, describing them as "unrepentant professional murderers" and "more dangerous than thieves, because they steal virtue." Gandhi's harshness—all the more inexcusable given his pleas for compassion for other stigmatized people, such as "untouchables," whom he called "Children of God"—sprang from his obsessive hostility to sexual desire. It had to do partly with guilt-ridden incidents in his youth, when he had come close to having sex with sex workers and experienced conflicted desires that, like the usual run of men, he blamed on the women rather than on himself. But now, so in contrast, here was India's incumbent home minister speaking of them with respect and fighting for their rights!

Indrajit Gupta didn't get the chance to deliver on the promise he made at Salt Lake Stadium, as the fragile coalition government fell just a few months later. The right-wing government that came to power in 1998—led by the Bharatiya Janata Party, or BJP—was fundamentally opposed to social progress for the marginalized. I knew it would abort the commitments made by Gupta as well as the recent recommendations of the National Commission for Women; but even that disappointing setback at the time seemed a blip in an inexorable and astonishingly fast march forward for sex workers.

The Durbar sex workers demonstrate against punitive laws

In March 2001, remembering my regret at missing the 1997 national conference, I made sure to go to the Millennium Milan Mela, or "celebratory fair," organized by the Durbar. My book on AIDS had just been published, and I was in Calcutta for the first leg of a nationwide speaking tour. The fair was intended to mark the dawn of a new millennium of progress for sex workers, and its opening day—March 3—would henceforth be celebrated as International Sex Workers' Rights Day, the Durbar, Indian, and worldwide sex worker groups announced. (By that time, with increased internet and mobile phone access in India and other developing countries, sex workers' rights groups worldwide had begun to come together and some years later would form the Global Network of Sex Work Projects.) What I witnessed at the Mela left me awestruck at what those women had managed to achieve in less than a decade.

Outside Salt Lake Stadium, huge crowds were milling and queuing up for tickets, the atmosphere carnival-like with loud music and announcements blaring from speakers. Inside, the crowd of thousands consisted overwhelmingly of everyday couples and families with children of all ages. They seemed interested in every aspect of the fair—relishing the food stalls and folk dances from all over India or listening intently to the panel discussions about the realities of sex work and the need for decriminalization and other changes. Nobody seemed to notice or remark, let alone react negatively to knowing, that the people manning the stalls, doing the dance performances, and speaking with great passion during the discussions were women sex workers and their children, with a sprinkling of *hijra* and *kothi* sex workers. There was no leering. There was no rudeness. All present acted exactly as they would at a more routine fair.

It was thrilling to witness, and I felt enormous pride in being a child of this state, with its century-long history of progressive politics, where people had come to so deeply value egalitarianism and justice. Wandering through the fair that afternoon, watching the confident, cheerful sex workers and the engrossed crowds, I felt optimistic about India in a way that I never had before. Perhaps the marked gentleness characteristic of many Indians and the lack of polarized views on most social matters—in such sharp contrast to the United States, where many people seem to be permanently inflamed with self-righteous moralizing—meant that we Indians now had the unique potential for building a just and humane society? Otherwise, what would be the point of the egalitarian possibilities offered by the democracy that had taken such strong roots in the past half century as well as the highs of philosophical understanding that had emerged here over the millennia? As I stood there at the fair amid the crowds and the noise and the music and the sex workers, every kind of progress seemed thrillingly possible.

SIXTEEN

AN ERA OF UNCERTAINTY

The AIDS epidemic was also ravaging gay men and *hijras* across India, but for them there were there were no feisty path-breaking collectives, let alone carnivals and national conferences attended by national leaders. For all that, the changes for gay men and *hijras*—our sisters in arms—were real.

I began to learn about many of those changes in the company of V. Sekar, a gay man in Chennai who in 1999 generously volunteered to help me with research for the book on AIDS that I was working on. Sekar was resolutely open not just about being gay but also about being HIV-positive. I felt afraid for him on both counts.

Barely anyone outside elite circles was open about being gay. And even now, a dozen years into India's epidemic, people discovered to be HIV-positive were facing horrific persecution, driven to suicide in many cases. But here was Sekar, a slight figure in a colorless safari suit that hinted at his precarious finances, looking immeasurably older than his mid-thirties because of his thinning hair and skin turned gray from ill health, insisting on speaking out on both matters.

Sekar had been diagnosed with HIV in the early 1990s. Desperate for help, he had soon reached out to Shyamala Nataraj at SIAAP, and there he had been befriended by activist sex workers, including Selvi and Mary Thomas. He had ended up becoming an AIDS activist, as resolute and outspoken as the women he emulated. Much like what Selvi had done with other sex workers in SIAAP's formative days—literally going up to them and saying she had AIDS and wanted others to be spared it—Sekar started doing in gay cruising areas, encouraging men to start using condoms and counseling those who turned to him with their fears about AIDS.

In 1996, with counseling experience of his own and with seed funding and technical advice from SIAAP, Sekar set up Anbu Illam, or House of Love, to provide counseling on HIV to the city's gay and bisexual men. But at that point, the Tamil Nadu state government dismissed Sekar's urging that large numbers of men were contracting HIV from sex with other men or *hijra*s. "The government kept insisting that the 'MSM' population is very small," Sekar explained. ("MSM" is the acronym for "men who have sex with men," an umbrella term that became widespread in the field of HIV prevention to describe the reality in India and elsewhere that men who enjoy sex with other men or with trans women often do so without considering themselves to be gay or even bisexual. Its poor fit vis-à-vis trans women is self-evident, as usually they themselves and the men who have sex with them consider them to be women or of an alternative gender, but certainly not men.)

"I told them that the population is, in fact, large and that many were getting infected," said Sekar. "It is only that these men are not visible—that it is a hidden, invisible population. But the government did not listen. They didn't understand that whenever a man who is gay goes to the hospital and doctors ask him questions about how he got infected with HIV or an STD, he always says that it happened from sex with women. No man will admit that he had sex with another man or *aravani*!" (*Aravani* is the preferred Tamil term for *hijra*.)

Without consistent financial support, Anbu Illam folded in a matter of years. But Sekar continued to be doggedly open about having contracted HIV from gay sex, turning him into living, incontrovertible proof that the AIDS epidemic was taking its toll among our ranks and that HIV prevention services were desperately needed. He didn't seem perturbed to take on that fraught role, which even Dominic D'Souza, for all his public courage, had avoided less than a decade earlier.

I wondered at Sekar's courage, but I found that every community direly affected by AIDS was producing its own leaders who transformed how that community dealt with that disease in terms of overcoming denial and of spearheading prevention and support. Among Chennai's sex workers there had been Selvi. Among gay men, there was Sekar. And among the city's *aravani*s or *hijra*s, it was Noori.

Noori was working with a "positive people" network when we first met but soon thereafter started her own grassroots group, focused on aiding *aravani*s. She was a striking figure—forceful and tall, her sari wound awkwardly around her like wrapping paper, wearing traditional makeup on her strong, square-jawed features. She didn't know her age and brushed off my queries, but from what I could tell she was in her late forties. "I found out many years ago that I was infected with AIDS," Noori told me. "I was in Bombay then, living in a rented house with other *aravani*s. I earned most of my money through sex with men. But after finding out that I was infected, I never sold sex again.

"I moved back to Chennai once I fell very sick, as I longed to be with other Tamil people. And it's cheaper here, so my savings will last longer. They also treat you better in Chennai hospitals. In Mumbai, hospitals won't treat *aravani*s even if they don't have AIDS. The prejudice in that city is so bad, the police won't even allow *aravani*s to beg.

"Anyway, most of my *aravani* friends in Mumbai are dead or dying. But now so are many of the *aravani*s here and in other parts of Tamil Nadu." Her voice grew taut with anger. "We finally got some money from the government to educate ourselves about AIDS. But it's too late for most of us!"

At some point, in the course of the days I spent with her, I realized that Noori's forcefulness went far beyond the obvious. She was the only person living with HIV who seemed dismissive about the disease and its death sentence. There was none of the desperation and anxiety that I witnessed with virtually every other HIV-positive person in India. Even in the preternaturally calm Sekar, those anxieties broke through occasionally. But Noori talked about AIDS as if it were just another one of the many unpleasant things life had dealt her.

I came to appreciate just how essential it was for *aravani*s to develop that toughness while interviewing several younger ones in the city. The dangers and hardships that beset them were of a horrific extreme. The minute they left the neighborhoods they lived in—where, by their accounts, they typically found tolerance and even support and affection, as people knew them personally—they faced hostility.

"There are always problems when an *aravani* ventures outside her area," a young trans woman, who looked more adolescent than adult, told me. "I go twice a week to Mount Road to beg. But we can't travel in the public bus in peace! Even educated men, especially the youngsters, behave indecently. They speak such filthy words! The young men will say a thousand insulting things, call us dirty names, and sing obscene songs. No one will help us. They will just watch. But if we say one thing in response, that will become a big fight."

This harassment was a mere irritant compared to the terrible sexual violence they suffered. The most gentle of the *aravani*s I met, a slight, dark woman in her twenties, told me in a trembling voice that, just a few weeks before, she had been staying overnight at her mother's hut when a gang of men had broken open the door, lifted her up, and tried to carry her away. She had been saved only by the intervention of her mother's immediate neighbors.

Almost every one of those younger trans women had been raped, sometimes by gangs of thuggish men or policemen. The sexual violence against them was of the same unhinged intensity as that against women sex workers—as if the association with sex had debased them so much that their abusers felt they had forfeited their claim to be treated as humans. From their accounts, it seemed that many men thought of them only as sexual objects for having voluntarily chosen to become female, almost as if they imagined that they had changed their gender out of an unquenchable desire to be fucked.

From every one of the *aravani*s I spoke to, including Noori, it was apparent that once again the police, far from providing help, were their worst oppressors. Though the colonial-era Criminal Tribes Act that had criminalized "eunuchs" had been scrapped in 1949, almost everywhere in India the police retained the notion that *hijra*s were inveterate criminals. They were accused of all manner of crime—of being prostitutes, of kidnapping young boys to castrate and force into prostitution, and of petty theft and extortion. The policemen well knew that the *aravani*s had no choice but to beg, dance in public, or sell sex to survive, as almost no one would hire them for conventional jobs because of the depth of popular intolerance, but that did not lead them to act with sympathy. (This being paradoxical India, there were simultaneously also isolated cases of *hijra*s being treated with the acceptance and respect they had enjoyed in precolonial India. Bafflingly, that seemed to occur most in the conservative northern states, such as in the case of Shabnam Mausi—"Mausi" means "aunt"—a forty-five-year-old *hijra* elected to the state legislature of Madhya Pradesh in 1999, and others elected to the post of mayor in two northern towns.)

The upshot of those prejudices was that trans women were routinely persecuted by the police under Section 377 as well as India's multitude of vagrancy, public nuisance, and antibegging laws, all dating back to the colonial era. (A 1989 amendment to the federal anti-prostitution law introduced gender-neutral language, in effect criminalizing soliciting and other aspects of sex work by men and trans women, but this law continued to be applied almost exclusively to women.) The police singled them out, emboldened to act against them en masse—for instance, fining or imprisoning dozens in antibegging drives or for unsolved thefts, irrespective of whether any of them was likely to have been involved or not—treating them as a homogeneous mass of criminality and perversion.

Those interviews left me shaken and enraged in no small part because I could see myself in the younger *aravani*s, with their stories of how they had felt feminine from childhood and had wished to dance and wear women's finery. If I had been born to an impoverished or average Indian family rather than a wealthy, Anglicized one, I might have had no choice but to live like them, the only other alternative being to lead an isolated, fearful double life as a closeted married man. They had, at least, a ready-made community, which no doubt explained why I found such large numbers of *aravani*s in Tamil Nadu—in Theni district, where SIAAP worked, I heard from numerous sources that as many as one in a hundred men, or persons considered male at birth, were *aravani*s.

By the close of the 1990s, the open advocacy by Sekar and Noori in Chennai as well as a handful of pioneering activists in other major cities—not all of whom were HIV-positive and some of whom were just concerned, decent-minded heterosexual women and men—had begun to convince key government officials that a significant proportion of Indian men had sex with other men as well as trans women and that increasingly large numbers were contracting HIV. By now there were also data to back those claims. Studies in Chennai, Goa, and Mumbai—typically conducted by the fledgling groups that had recently launched HIV prevention efforts among gay and bisexual men and trans women—reported HIV prevalence rates ranging from 2 percent to over 50 percent. (The huge variations reflected not only genuine differences but also small sample sizes and the use of differing methodologies.) Broader research about Indian sexual behaviors, commissioned by the government's National AIDS Control Organization, showed that a substantial share of men, whether in cities or smaller places, were bisexual or pansexual, variously having sex with women, other men, or trans women. A 2001 nationwide survey found that nearly one in three men who visited female sex workers had also had sex with one or more male or transgender partners in the past year alone.

An inflow of international funding now made it possible for grassroots activists and groups to begin expanding HIV prevention services for gay and bisexual men as well as trans women. Even till the late

1990s, there had probably been no more than half a dozen such grass-roots groups, all concentrated in major cities. But by 2005, there were dozens, spread across even provincial capitals and small towns.

So gay and bisexual men as well as *hijra*s in cities and towns nationwide now began to encounter outreach workers—typically, local gay men or trans women—in their cruising areas after nightfall. They advised them about safer sex, provided free condoms and illustrated booklets on safe sex, urged them to join their support groups or meet their counselors, and offered to help intervene in family conflicts or with police raids. Telephone help lines run by those groups gave advice and support to those unwilling to risk being seen at the offices of HIV-focused organizations.

It was very far from being enough to end the epidemic's onslaught among them, but it was still a quantum leap from the utter neglect of the past. And given the relatively small numbers of men who could be open to any degree about their orientation, those groups couldn't bring about the larger structural changes that had been generated by the sex work collectives. Even so, the spread of the groups began to fuel activism for gay and transgender rights across India.

❖

By the end of the 1990s, as the economy boomed, the India of Gandhian austerity and socialist rationing that I had always known was in retreat, to be replaced by a fractured, unequal nation where billionaires, yuppies, and the middle class jostled with a hinterland of mass poverty, squalor, and want.

That epochal shift in India's fortunes held all kinds of opportunities for gay men and women among the multiplying numbers of the upwardly mobile. Successful gay people were suddenly visible at the forefront of the swelling ranks of fashion designers, interior decorators, beauticians, hoteliers, and artists. They had the financial freedom and self-confidence to be increasingly open about their orientation within well-off urban enclaves. Support groups for English-speaking gay men and women began to emerge in the major cities. Upmarket bars began to discreetly host weekly gay evenings. English-language TV channels aired Hollywood films as well as documentaries and newscasts about gay issues. Local programming began to cover metrosexuals, gay men, drag queens, and transgender people, often as fabulous, frivolous creatures but sometimes more empathetically. Indian publishers released a slew of gay- and lesbian-themed books, ranging from novels to scholarly works. At least in affluent urban circles, those changes began to breed a public familiarity with gay people that had never existed before.

❖

The backlash came with breathtaking speed, the work of Hindu-supremacist political parties and their vigilantes, who had surged in assertiveness with the dawn of this gilded age, India's first moment in the sun after centuries.

The initial flash point was a 1998 movie *Fire* depicting a lesbian relationship between two of its main characters, the first time an Indian film had explicitly shown homosexual relations. Directed by the Canadian Indian Deepa Mehta, the award-winning movie was running to full houses when Hindu supremacist mobs linked to the ruling Shiv Sena and BJP vandalized theaters in several cities in Maharashtra, as well as in Delhi and Uttar Pradesh. Maharashtra's chief minister (a position similar to a state's governor) supported the vandals, remarking "I congratulate them for what they have done. The film's theme is alien to our culture."

The thuggish Shiv Sena leader, Balasaheb Thackeray, a fervent admirer of Adolf Hitler who had just been named in a judicial inquiry as a provocateur of mobs that in 1992 had slaughtered 1,200 Muslims in Bombay, rhetorically asked in a magazine interview, "Is it fair to show such things which are not part of Indian culture?" And then, without waiting for a reply, he answered, "It can corrupt tender minds. It is a sort of a social AIDS."

The BJP ideologue and right-wing columnist Swapan Dasgupta wrote, "So widespread is the new gay evangelism that . . . there were loud claims of homosexuality and lesbianism being part of the Indian 'heritage,' a claim that angered many Hindu activists."

The victimization of gay people was part of a larger assault by the BJP and its Hindu-supremacist backers on what they alleged was a new wave of colonization by Western culture, especially in the realms of sexuality and morality. Anything even tangentially relating to romance or sexuality became an excuse for government censorship combined with mob violence. The minister of information and broadcasting banned educational programs on sexual health from the national TV broadcaster Doordarshan, despite the vital role they played in AIDS prevention efforts. Vigilantes were given a free hand to operate as moral police, assaulting women who wore jeans rather than saris or *salwar*s, thrashing couples spotted holding hands, and torching bookshops that sold Valentine's Day cards. India seemed to be at war with itself, some of its people ambitious to shape the twenty-first-century world, while others were bent on enforcing oppression in the name of contrived tradition.

Low-income gay men and *hijra*s were hit worse than anyone else, as they could not sequester themselves away in enclaves of privilege. Persecution and sexual violence by policemen and thugs multiplied. The police used Section 377 with far greater frequency, in addition to the old abuses of extorting money and sex.

The gay men and trans women working on the front line to promote HIV prevention among their peers became a special target. Conservatives accused them of being conduits for Western powers to promote homosexuality and pedophilia. The brutal murder of two gay men in Delhi, one of whom worked for USAID, rather than eliciting any sympathy from the right-wing commentator Swapan Dasgupta, led him to allege "a nexus between employees of international aid agencies and the gay underworld," with "the lavishly funded anti-AIDS campaign being misused . . . to buy cheap sex with poor slum kids."

An investigation by Human Rights Watch documented serious

police abuse of the staff of such organizations in half a dozen cities and towns. In the most concerted case of persecution, four staff members of Naz Foundation International and Bharosa Trust—two accredited nongovernmental groups working on HIV prevention in Uttar Pradesh's capital, Lucknow—were jailed after the police raided their offices in July 2001, accusing them of "promoting homosexuality," running a gay "sex racket," and selling pornography. Even though there was no evidence of sexual acts, they were charged under Section 377, along with charges of criminal conspiracy, abetment, and obscenity. Although both these groups were recognized by the state government's AIDS Control Society and were working within the guidelines laid down by the National AIDS Control Organization, the city's chief judicial magistrate accused them of "polluting the entire society by encouraging the young persons and abating [sic] them to committing the offence of sodomy."

One of the men arrested, Naz Foundation International's Lucknow director, Arif Jafar, later told Human Rights Watch researchers, "For the first ten days, they provided nothing for us, not even clean water. We were not provided utensils for eating, and we couldn't take baths. We were cleaning drains and toilets with the same utensils that were all we had for eating. . . . We were harassed. The first news reports that came out about our arrest said that we ran a 'gay den' and had made seventy lakh [roughly $150,000], so the police had the impression that we had money, and that, combined with their idea that we were doing 'unnatural' things, made them harass us. We were abused and beaten and threatened. . . . I have kidney stones, and in prison they would not allow me to have medication. I was in terrible pain. It was so painful—at that time, I wished to die."

The four men were imprisoned for nearly two months before a higher court ruled against the police, reprimanding them for attempting to frame the men. Jafar, a Muslim, said that the police had told him that he was "trying to destroy our country by promoting homosexuality" and that "Hindus don't have these practices—these are all perversions of the Muslims."

I feared the worst in those dark years of BJP rule. The intense hope I had felt for India at the sex workers' *mela* in Calcutta now seemed a chimera. The courage of Sekar and Noori appeared to be a flimsy defense against the bigotry and violence of Hindu supremacists. Perhaps the old India of fearful invisibility had been a safer, better place for most gay men, after all, than this new India, where homophobia had been politicized and turned into a rallying call for thugs.

SEVENTEEN

A NEW MILLENNIUM

In the spring of 2000, exhausted by the unsettled life of the past few years, I decided to settle in New York City. Since leaving the World Bank at the end of 1994, I had moved homes repeatedly and traveled constantly, often for months on end. They had been rewarding years for learning and for my work, but I ached to be in one place, to have the simple pleasures of a home and a settled life again.

I was also suddenly aware that my thirties had vanished. My fortieth birthday lay just ahead, in September 2001. And since breaking up with Tandavan in 1993 I had not had the time for relationships. In all those years, there had been just two brief relationships, more affairs than anything else. One had stretched through my second year at the World Bank, with a Spanish man, Jesús, whom I had met while visiting Madrid. Jesús, a gardener and landscape architect, was the one man I had dated who loved trees with even more passion than I did. But the stress of the long-distance relationship had become overwhelming when I had moved to India and could no longer afford to travel to Spain frequently. Without discussing it, both Jesús and I knew that our relationship was ultimately hopeless because none of the countries to which we belonged—whether Spain, the United States, or India—recognized same-sex relationships for immigration purposes, so we could never hope to live together. The other, short relationship had been in Delhi while I was writing the poverty book and had spluttered out of its own accord.

I resolved from now on to put my personal life ahead of my work passions. I stuck firmly to that decision, turning down a fascinating job at the World Health Organization in Geneva to lead its advocacy on the interrelationships between health and poverty, a tailor-made responsibility given my years of work on precisely those matters. Fortunately, I had no dearth of consulting assignments that I could undertake from New York City with the World Health Organization and UNAIDS, the Geneva-headquartered secretariat of the United Nations' collective efforts on AIDS.

New York City had come to feel like home in the year and a half that I had lived there while working with UNICEF, beginning in the summer of 1997. A half dozen of my closest friends now lived there, including Nilita and Sankar. I had four godchildren in the city, all toddlers. I had a loving family in that group of dear friends to whom I could entrust my life without worry. I had been very lucky in my adult friendships: a psychoanalyst friend remarked that I gave more importance to my dearest friendships and to my relationship with my father than to my romantic relationships—a healthy thing but possibly also an explanation for why I hadn't sustained a relationship since Tandavan.

The city itself now seemed to be in a golden era, an exhilarating balance between being safe yet wildly edgy. There was no better place for a nonconformist, liberal immigrant like me to feel at home. I once again rented the small apartment in the West Village where I had lived while on my previous stint with UNICEF. It was in a prewar building at the crossing of Grove and Bedford streets, architecturally unremarkable but vividly bohemian in spirit. (I was not the only person struck by the building's originality—it had been featured as Jackson Pollock's Village home in the 2000 movie *Pollock*.) The main door was a brilliant green, opening onto a narrow corridor with bright yellow stucco walls. The tiny elevator, big enough for no more than three people squeezed tightly together, was of the same exciting green color as the main door.

My neighbors were just as exciting as the building. Most unforgettable to me were a zestful gay man whose bushy hair seemed to stand up on end of its own accord and an intense young Spanish woman who resembled a Pedro Almodóvar femme fatale. Someone or other from the building was invariably sitting out on the stoop smoking or chatting; it meant setting aside time for conversation every time one entered or exited.

And I loved my apartment, up on the fifth floor. It was all of five hundred square feet, but the high ceilings, the numerous windows, and the elongated layout—the bedroom was separated from the living areas by a long, narrow corridor—somehow made it seem spacious. A graceful ginkgo tree stood outside one window and an exuberant honey locust outside the other. The area was a haven for birds, including nesting red-tailed hawks. I felt I had a private balcony because two people could squeeze onto the fire escape.

I shipped in my few possessions from India. At Pottery Barn, I splurged on a solid frame bed, a capacious sofa bed, linen curtains, an expanding dinner table and chairs, a bookcase, and an armoire; it was all I needed and all that would fit into the little apartment. Then I began to unwind in ways that I couldn't back in the country of my birth.

In India, I felt conflicted about eating out at restaurants, using a swimming pool, or even living near a green park to walk in—those were luxuries available only to a privileged handful. In New York, I relished the simple joys of going Rollerblading along the Hudson, working out at New York Sports Club, and eating at the city's plethora of good, cheap restaurants. Of course, I realized that it was absurd that my psychological conflict eased merely because I was several thousand miles away from the sights of suffering, but those were the fabricated stratagems I used to quiet my conscience.

I could also finally unwind about being gay. I exulted at living right near Christopher Street. In 1986, less than a decade and a half before, when I had first lived in New York, I had skulked through the area, an outsider peeping nervously at sights that I lacked the courage to participate in. But now I lived here! Lived right in the heart of what I had come to think of as the world's sacred place for gay and trans people—our Benares, our Bodh Gaya, our Jerusalem, our Mecca, our Vatican!

That patch of small city blocks embodied the resilience of our spirit, enduring despite the terrible things we had suffered. Though the full-scale slaughter of the AIDS epidemic had waned, it still felt like a country recovering from war—the missing generations, the numbed silence about the past, the hopelessness on the faces of those who had lost unbearably too much, the skeletal survivors on the brink resting outside Bailey-Holt House, which provided a home for people living with AIDS.

And all of us who lived there, or flocked there in the evenings, knew that the neighborhood was a ghetto in a city and nation rife with hate and threats. A friend and I once mapped out, based on our own experiences, that the only safe area for gay and transgenders in Manhattan extended precisely from Leroy Street on the south to Seventh Avenue on the east and the Hudson River on the west, stretching up merely to Twenty-Third Street in Chelsea.

But it spoke volumes about our spirit that straight people had never created such a liberated holy spot or such a welcoming and fun ghetto. I was soon affected by Christopher Street's buoyant spirit. I looked at myself in dismay—I was surely the most boring gay man ever to live in those precincts. My clothes were all preppy, baggy cottons from Gap. I wore sensible Naot sandals or waterproof shoes. I'd never yet had a full shot of anything stronger than beer or done more than puff at a cigarette. I was more boring than even the most boring straight man.

So I set about reinventing myself.

At the gym, I rapidly became as fit as I had been in my days as an undergraduate competitive swimmer. Under the tutelage of Sankar—who was now a muscular hunk, not the geeky genius I had known at school—and my sexy friend Kamala, I splurged on French Connection jeans and T-shirts, all woven with spandex that clung to my musculature. I soon had a veritable collection of Valentino hot pants that barely covered my crotch and bum. I had party shirts, too—form-fitting black Armani, shiny metallic things with zips, even a leopard print in some velvety fabric.

I learned the joys of drinking. One night, dressed in my *beau monde* finery, I headed to Wonder Bar, the tiny East Village dive that had been Tandavan's and my favorite when we had lived together all those years back. I gulped down two vodka martinis in the space of a few minutes. The results were magical. Brimming with derring-do, I deep-kissed several men at the bar, letting my hands and theirs do whatever they wanted. I bummed a cigarette and inhaled deeply, suppressing my coughs but feeling mature and sexy, an irresistible mix of Marlboro Man and femme fatale.

So began the years of mindless fun that I'd never had in my teenage years or as a young adult. I tried out and relished everything that I hadn't done yet in my life. My days, whether the weekdays or the weekend, became a happy routine of concentrated work, followed by the gym or Rollerblading, and then invariably dinner with friends. And then I went for a drink to Bar d'O or the Monster in my neighborhood or dancing on weekends to Splash or La Nueva Escuelita. I reveled in knowing that after downing four drinks I was slurring and even weaving drunkenly. I tried out pot, poppers, Ecstasy, and cocaine. On the weekends, I would invariably return home after dawn, both exhausted and energized, usually after hours of sex with a hunky stranger. It was all a welcome break after being relentlessly serious.

❖

At the LGBT Community Center on West Twelfth Street, a short walk from my home, I saw a Keith Haring mural that was worlds removed from the popular matchstick figures emblazoned on mugs and shirts, so different that it was difficult to believe they were the work of the same artist. The gigantic work of black-on-white line drawings, which covered the walls of a small room, was of countless men and their mouths, cocks, and assholes joined in an orgiastic daisy chain of sexual pleasure, of fucking, sucking, rimming, jacking off, and coming. It had been the second-floor men's bathroom when Haring completed the mural in May 1989 as part of an artists' commemoration of the twentieth anniversary of the Stonewall Riots. That was why the mural began at the chest-high height where the urinals would have been fixed at that time. Haring's distinctive signature was on one corner. Below it he had written, "Once Upon a Time."

It was Haring's ode to sexual freedom for us gay men—our victory over the endless centuries during which acting on our desires triggered the risk of our being shunned, jailed, thrashed, or killed. It was also Haring's final act of up-yours defiance against AIDS—he died eight months later of the disease, age thirty-one.

The mural hit me with the force that Picasso's *Guernica* had— the force of unvarnished honesty and truth telling. "Once Upon a Time"—a fleeting, glorious time when we could savor every pleasure that had long been demonized and outlawed.

And though that halcyon time had long passed, I had sex like that more times than I can count in those years in New York. With unknown groups of men, dozens strong, in sex clubs. Those endless nights of pleasure were the zenith of my sexual life, both physically and intellectually, which had begun to flower just over a decade earlier with Tandavan.

I would be shivering with excitement by the time I reached the door of El Mirage, my favorite club, on the Lower East Side, the prospect of what lay ahead overcoming even the two drinks I'd had to unwind. It would be close to midnight and this eastern stretch of Houston Street deserted. Anyone who didn't know the number of the building would miss the unmarked door. You pressed a bell. Someone unseen checked you out from behind a one-way glass panel embedded in the door. You entered to find many other men standing in line to pay at the windowed booth, you were then frisked by the muscular bouncer, you unzipped and showed your penis to him—evidently police regulations prohibited policemen from exposing their penises, so that kept out undercover cops—and only then did you make it to the rooms of pleasure beyond.

By the time I left, after three or four hours of almost nonstop sex (with no worries, this time, about AIDS: I unfailingly used lubricants and condoms), I felt as though I'd had the most consuming gym workout but one of utter pleasure. I had no regrets or psychological conflicts about those nights, at least nothing more than ruefulness if I was exhausted the next morning. If anything, I felt those were precious hours of utter honesty, such a rarity in human social life.

Walking back home, as I invariably did despite the late hour and the distance back to the West Village, I would often remember lines from a favorite Cavafy poem, one that celebrated outlawed desires and secret rooms like the ones I had been in:

> *When I went to that house of pleasure*
> *. . .*
> *I went into the secret rooms*
> *considered shameful even to name.*
> *But not shameful to me—because if they were,*
> *what kind of poet, what kind of artist would I be?*

✤

In those first years back in New York City, I tentatively began to feel an optimism about global progress that I had not known before. I wasn't certain, though, whether my optimism stemmed from the general euphoria about the new millennium and my distance from events in BJP-ruled India or was built on firmer foundations. Were Thomas Friedman and Francis Fukuyama right in positing that with the Cold War ended, the world less bloodied by wars, and the United States providing a benevolent Pax Americana, globalization would spread Western liberal democracy, modernity, the rule of law, and material comforts universally, ushering in a golden epoch for all of humankind?

Surely there were good grounds for hope that humankind would have learned sufficiently from the horrors of the previous millennium—from its record of slavery, imperial conquest, mass poverty, famines, genocides, world wars, and nuclear weapons—so as to not repeat them.

Even with the AIDS pandemic, for the first time, it seemed as though real change was happening globally, two decades since the disease had come to scientific attention and with more than 60 million people infected or dead.

In January 2000, a special session of the UN Security Council declared the pandemic to be a threat to the security of nations because of its catastrophic toll on economies and societies, the first time that the council had identified a disease thus. A year later, at a special session of the UN General Assembly dedicated to the pandemic, the world's governments agreed to a global plan of action for slowing the spread of HIV. UN secretary-general Kofi Annan called for a superfund to fight AIDS, with a target of raising and spending $7 billion to $10 billion a year. His idea quickly began to turn into reality, with large new commitments from donor governments—including the promise of foreign-debt relief for poor countries to free their money for AIDS-related efforts—and major foundations, raising the money available for combating AIDS in developing countries into the billions of dollars from the inadequate hundreds of millions spent yearly through the 1990s. It was now possible to substantially scale up national responses in the next years.

And, crucially, there was now global agreement that it was unconscionable to let tens of millions of impoverished people in developing countries die from AIDS when lifesaving medicines existed. What had seemed impossible just a few years before even to those of us who wished for it fervently was now becoming a reality. Activist coalitions demanding treatment for themselves and others, patent-busting generic drug manufacturers, and a handful of committed developing-country governments had fought the multinational pharmaceutical manufacturers of the antiretroviral drugs and the Bill Clinton administration (which threatened to impose punishing trade sanctions), forcing down the price of the drugs to less than a dollar a day from the original

$20,000 annual cost. Though the details were still to be worked out, it was now definite that a global effort to ensure antiretroviral treatment to even the poorest of people in the poorest of nations was in the offing. It rapidly proved to be one of the greatest victories in the history of modern public health—saving millions in developing countries and turning AIDS from an implacable force into a solvable challenge.

❖

Unexpectedly, in the summer of 2001, I plummeted into a frightening bout of depression. It was about a year into my settling into New York City, just a few months before my fortieth birthday. It began one ordinary weekday evening, not provoked by any incident or trauma. But in the space of hours my normal, carefully maintained equilibrium had been smashed.

My joy in my home and city drained away. So did the satisfaction I had gained from the books I had written. My sense of being special for having the deep love of my father, my siblings, and many close friends emptied of meaning. The sense of self-worth I normally felt about being a principled person no longer moved me. The cartwheeling, childlike joy that would, unbidden, invariably transport me for many minutes every day now felt like a cruel figment of my imagination.

All those things were swept away. And in their place was a bleakness so heavy that I felt powerless against it. My life had amounted to nothing. I had no one. I would never have love or children. Life would never improve. I was a failure.

At some point I pulled all the curtains close so that there was no light and turned off the phone ringer. Unwashed, unshaven, teeth unbrushed, I lay endlessly in bed in the darkness with that despair choking me, sometimes squeezing exhausting bouts of sobbing out of me.

It took me days to recover enough emotional strength to answer the worried calls that had filled up my answering machine—from my friends, my father, my brother Bharat. I was so embarrassed and loath to tell them the truth that I made up some lie about the answering machine having malfunctioned.

It was only with two close women friends who insisted on visiting me immediately that I admitted what had happened. Though I cried while telling them, it was from relief at being able to trust and savor human connections again. I promised those two friends that I would unfailingly call them if I ever began to feel like that again. It was only while saying it that I realized how strange it was that although I was unfailingly candid about every personal matter with my close friends and family, until now I had not been able to admit to anyone that I was lonely and unhappy.

Though I soon found my way back to my old equilibrium of appreciating life, I noticed that the episode had changed me. Whether those were positive changes, I wasn't sure, but I didn't fight them. I felt I knew myself far better now, and I accepted as legitimate these feelings rather than insisting to myself that I had to emulate the heroic people I admired for overcoming adversity uncomplainingly, those I knew intimately, such as my father and my eldest brother, or the legion of impoverished or oppressed people I had interviewed over the years. But it also felt that my awareness of my sadness had begun to color my life, as though a dye had been mixed into it, taking away some of the passion for living—and for social justice causes—that had emerged since my undergraduate years.

There was no confusion in my mind about the precise causes of the disquiet. I was turning forty but even at that late stage my life didn't seem to have any moorings, anything that I could point to and say "This is mine," in the sense of a child or a long-term boyfriend. I had two books, lots of learning, and some success to show for my thirties—things that had filled my life with meaning when I was doing them but seemed pointless seen against the larger, empty canvas of my life.

And though I had been in New York City for just a year, I had quickly become pessimistic about finding a long-term relationship there. For all that I had made a determined effort to fit into the city's gay life, I realized that at heart I didn't belong.

I had zero interest in fashion once the initial fun of getting a wardrobe together had ended. I couldn't discuss *Queer as Folk*; I didn't even own a television. I disliked the shallowness of mainstream Chelsea bars and Fire Island's Pines. The blatant pecking order based on looks, wealth, and race, and the scornful exclusion of those who didn't make the grade, left me appalled, wondering how those of us who had suffered endlessly ourselves could act so heartlessly. I wished I could find a way of meeting gay men interested in the things I cared about, but online dating was in its infancy. It spoke volumes about the dysfunction of gay life in New York City that there were countless others in exactly my situation, endlessly single and endlessly searching for romantic love.

I knew I was not blameless for the lonely predicament I found myself in. I was drawn far too much to good looks and missed out on relationships with a number of men whom I liked deeply. Through my own brand of immaturity I also destroyed the one relationship that had true promise. It was with a Cuban American a few years older than I. I was drawn to Sebastian's gravitas—it made me realize that the only men I now had a lasting connection with were those who had suffered deeply and had emerged wise and upbeat.

Sebastian's suffering had come from AIDS—he had been on his deathbed in 1996 when the antiretroviral combinations had come into use and saved him. I had no worries about his being HIV-positive in the sense of contracting HIV—I had had sex with many men whom I knew for a fact were positive. But I couldn't bear to face the prospect that he might die. Antiretroviral treatment had been introduced so recently that there was no certainty about how long people on it would live. I wanted an assurance of happiness, not the prospect of tragedy just down the line. Our mutual attraction and liking were so strong that our relationship continued in some form for years before turning into friendship, fortunately a close and enduring one.

The one wholly positive outcome of my emotional crisis, some months later, was that I got myself a puppy, something I had ached to do for years but hadn't because of my peripatetic life. My puppy was a

Portuguese Water Dog, and his black-and-white curls made him look more like a stuffed toy than a dog. Even at three months of age, he was so sweet-tempered that I felt blessed. I named him Lorca after my great idol Federico García Lorca—and I was soon convinced that the illustrious Lorca would have approved, as my Lorca had all the loving-ness and decency that I imagined García Lorca had had in abundance. I finally had the child I knew I would never otherwise have.

EIGHTEEN

THINGS FALL APART

I was doing my morning yoga when I heard a plane roar past, sounding so close that I rushed up to the window, catching a glimpse of the massive jetliner as it seemed to almost touch the town houses on the far side of Grove Street and head, seemingly, for the Hudson River.

Shaken, I woke my father, who was visiting me at the time, saying that it seemed that a plane was crash-landing in the river. Rushing out minutes later to get to work at UNICEF, I met one of my neighbors, looking stunned, who told me that the television news was saying that a plane had crashed into the World Trade Center's twin towers in a terrorist attack.

At the crossing of Seventh Avenue, joining a crowd of strangely silent people staring downtown, I could see not one but two planes sticking out of the twin towers, the upper floors of the buildings wrapped in flames and smoke. For moments, I refused to believe what I was seeing, my mind telling me that surely a movie crew was simulating the events for a *Towering Inferno* sequel.

I called my father at home to tell him to stay put. I then caught a taxi to work, my instinctive response to horror being to work even harder at trying to do something useful. But the UN buildings were soon evacuated. I walked back home, staring at the figures shrouded in gray ash and dust who were streaming uptown.

For days, the sounds of ambulance and police sirens made the city sound like an elephant in mortal agony, trumpeting out its pain.

I grieved for a city I loved dearly—but also because the optimism I had momentarily felt for the new millennium had been wishful thinking. This millennium, like the one before, would be blood-soaked.

⚜

Things fell apart, everywhere.

George W. Bush's Orwellian "war on terror" burgeoned. Afghanistan was invaded in Operation Enduring Freedom, Iraq was devastated in the search for "weapons of mass destruction," Iran and North Korea were targeted as the "axis of evil." The whole world was going to burn from Bush's warmongering.

One evening, at the end of February 2002, my father called from his home in Kolkata, his voice so anguished that my heart thudded in anxiety.

"Son, I am ashamed to be a Hindu today," he said—words that I had never imagined I would ever hear him say. "If I could change my surname, I would do so immediately. Have you seen what those scum are doing to Muslims in Gujarat, raping women, killing little children, butchering and torching people? This is not what my religion is!"

In that pogrom, an estimated two thousand Muslims were killed by Hindu supremacists, in several documented instances at the direction of BJP politicians and sympathizers in the police and bureaucracy. Thousands more were raped or brutally injured. An estimated 150,000 lost their homes and often every possession. The intervention of the state government, led by the BJP's Narendra Modi (who was later to become India's prime minister), could have ended the violence in hours, but both Modi and India's prime minister, Atal Bihari Vajpayee—often lauded as the BJP's "moderate" face—stood by silently, inescapably suggesting their acquiescence and perhaps complicity.

Those atrocities marked my father's loss of faith that his Hinduism was too complex to be enduringly politicized, with its embrace of philosophical ambiguities and absence of an all-defining holy book or centralized church. For me they marked the end of hopefulness. It was strange but telling that father and son—him a devout Hindu, me an agnostic who admired Hindu philosophy—were losing faith in their society's future because of a party that claimed to represent the best interests of us Hindus, particularly of us elite, dominant castes who had always profited from venal appeals to "Hindu" orthodoxy or identity.

⚜

The world's sexual outlaws were made scapegoats in those hate-filled times, along with drug users, Muslims, and other easy targets.

In many parts of the world, much of the tenuous recent progress in challenging our criminalization and stigma was a reaction to the devastation caused by the AIDS pandemic. Now reactionary changes in global AIDS policies, driven by the Bush administration, would do us grievous harm, especially in the low- and middle-income nations where the pandemic was at its worst.

In his January 2003 State of the Union address, President Bush described his newfound commitment to battling AIDS as a "work of mercy." The pandemic was a baffling choice for Bush to adopt as his personal charitable cause. He had shown not a glimmer of compassion so far in his career for the million Americans living with HIV or the forty thousand newly infected every year, or the half million killed by this disease. In his years as governor of Texas, Bush had done nothing to address the state's abidingly severe HIV problem. AIDS had not figured in his 2000 presidential election campaign: none of the populations among whom the United States' epidemic was concentrated—gay men, injecting drug users, and African Americans—mattered to his electoral chances. In his first years as president, Bush considered closing the White House Office of National AIDS Policy.

He cared so little about the pandemic's calamitous global toll that he failed to join world leaders at the 2001 UN General Assembly summit on AIDS, even though he had the shortest distance to travel. Instead, in the preparatory negotiations on the Declaration of Commitment, the global road map on AIDS that would be endorsed by leaders at the summit, his administration led some of the world's most reactionary governments—including Egypt, Libya, and the Vatican delegation—in undermining the document's emphasis on human rights.

They deleted every mention of sex workers and gays from the declaration, perpetuating the denial of the past and sabotaging vital prevention efforts for those populations. The Bush administration even scuppered UNAIDS's efforts to have the assembled leaders endorse the *International Guidelines on HIV/AIDS and Human Rights,* killing the one opportunity to have that meticulously developed guidance adopted widely around the world. And just days after the UN Summit, USAID chief Andrew Natsios, opposing the summit's pledge to fund lifesaving antiretroviral treatment for the tens of millions in poorer countries infected with HIV, proclaimed that Africans would not take the drugs in accordance with the prescribed schedule because they "don't know what Western time is . . . They know morning, they know noon, they know evening, they know the darkness at night."

Unsurprisingly, realpolitik led Bush to break with this callous record. The 2003 State of the Union address justified Bush's impending invasion of Iraq as well as the launch of his worldwide "war on terror." "As our nation moves troops and builds alliances to make our world safer, we must also remember our calling as a blessed country to make this world better," Bush pronounced. The $15 billion in foreign assistance provided by the President's Emergency Plan for AIDS Relief (PEPFAR) was to be the public relations cover for his militarism.

Though the United States was now providing nearly twice as much to the global effort against AIDS as the rest of the world's richest governments combined, those billions of dollars brought with them a legion of problems. The Bush administration concertedly began to use the funds to impose destructive policies on the governments of poorer countries, the United Nations, and grassroots and civil society groups. At precisely the point when Bush was insisting that the world accept his trumped-up claims about "weapons of mass destruction" in Iraq, those diktats were yet more proof of his schoolyard-bully approach to foreign relations.

One set of these demands focused on HIV prevention strategies. Bush's AIDS team pushed to replace evidence-based programs with interventions inspired by puritanical Christian notions. (Another set of demands, eventually defeated, related to AIDS treatment, with the Bush administration putting American profits before saving lives by insisting that pricey branded drugs made by American pharmaceutical giants be used in all the countries aided by the United States—rather than the cheap, easier-to-use, and equally effective generic copies that were being used in the larger UN-led global effort.) The epidemic could be defeated by encouraging Africans to embrace "biblical values and sexual purity," proclaimed Senator Jesse Helms.

"Abstinence-only" programs were what Helms and President Bush, both animated by Christian fervor, had in mind. (I was perennially astounded by the sanction given to Christian dogma, however obscurantist, in shaping US public policy matters, far dwarfing the role Hinduism is permitted in India and making a mockery of the United States' claims to separate church and state.) Those programs maintained that heterosexual intercourse within marriage was the only acceptable form of sexual behavior and contraception and the only fail-safe means of preventing the spread of HIV. The truth, of course was that "abstinence-only" interventions were demonstrably ineffectual. Every domestic US abstinence-only effort ever evaluated had failed to reduce rates of teen pregnancy or sexually transmitted diseases. Abstinence and fidelity were valuable options only when promoted within a comprehensive approach to safe-sex behaviors, alongside condoms, so individuals would know all the effective ways of protecting themselves from HIV and choose those best suited to them. Yet PEPFAR earmarked—and certainly wasted—a billion dollars for abstinence-only education abroad.

The damage was magnified because, astonishingly, the Bush team simultaneously attacked the efficacy of condoms in preventing HIV. The government's most respected health bodies—such as the US Centers for Disease Control and Prevention—were forced to censor their public advice on condoms. In contrast to their original, clear recommendation that condoms are "highly effective" against the spread of HIV and other sexually transmitted diseases, they now said that condoms "cannot guarantee absolute protection," a misrepresentation calculated to sow doubt and fear.

Groups worldwide receiving US government funding were barred from discussing condom use with young people and even most adults. It was permitted only "for those who practice high-risk behaviors," defined as "prostitutes, sexually active discordant couples, substance abusers, and others." ("Discordant" refers to a couple in which only one partner is HIV-positive.)

To deny people accurate information about the efficacy of condoms was reprehensible at any time, but in the age of AIDS it was criminal, arguably no different from culpable homicide. In much of sub-Saharan Africa, with often one in ten and in some places one in three adults already infected, every adolescent and adult faced a frighteningly high lifetime risk of contracting HIV. Tellingly, more than half of all new infections were occurring in young women and men by the time they reached their mid-twenties. They needed every bit of useful information about how best to navigate that terrible danger, not to be cruelly denied knowledge about the only effective and affordable barrier protection that existed.

And then, more concerted still, were the Bush AIDS team's strategies on HIV prevention specifically among drug users and sex workers.

One of its first efforts was a global campaign to ban "needle exchange" programs, in which injecting drug users are given free sterile needles and syringes in exchange for used ones so that they do not share injecting equipment potentially infected with HIV or hepatitis. The World Health Organization, UNAIDS, and other leading health institutions ranked needle exchange as one of the most vital steps in preventing the spread of HIV through injecting drug use. Numerous Western European countries and Australia had contained epidemics of HIV among drug users by giving out millions of free syringes and needles and providing other elements of harm reduction.

In sharp contrast, the United States' "war on drugs" approach of criminalizing drug addiction and repressive antidrug strategies meant that every administration since Ronald Reagan's had banned the use of federal funds for domestic needle exchange programs. Now senior Bush officials summarily told UNAIDS, the UN Office on Drugs and Crime (UNODC), and other UN organizations to stop recommending needle exchange in their policies and remove all references to such efforts from their websites and public materials. It began to cut off funds to service organizations on that pretext. With half a million people worldwide contracting HIV every year from contaminated injecting drug equipment—the world's fastest-growing HIV epidemics were fueled by intravenous drug use in Asia and the former Soviet Union—the Bush campaign had deadly human costs.

Sex work was the other, larger target. The United States Leadership Against HIV/AIDS, Tuberculosis, and Malaria Act of 2003, the legislation that created PEPFAR, portrayed sex work as indistinguishable from sex trafficking of women—a breathtakingly mala fide conflation between willing sex workers and actual victims but the basis by which it sought the "eradication of prostitution." (Tellingly, this position was no different to that of the archaic and confused 1949 UN Suppression of the Traffic in Persons Convention—itself springing from the early 1900s hysteria over "White Slave Traffic"—that had demonstrably done grave harm to sex workers the world over. With very few exceptions, modern sex-trafficking laws have actually been framed to punish sex workers as well as other "undesirables," particularly sexually active single women, mixed-race couples, people having pre- or extramarital relationships, and even consumers of pornography.) Henceforth, all recipients of US foreign assistance were required to sign a pledge "explicitly opposing prostitution and sex trafficking" or lose funding. The Bush administration could now openly dictate how organizations worked with sex workers around the globe.

Efforts that "promote or advocate the legalization or practice of prostitution and sex trafficking" were explicitly banned. That sweeping clause proscribed sex workers from mobilizing or advocating for the rights they felt they needed, at one stroke undoing the arduous years of efforts that had won sex workers some say in policies affecting them. It was another example of the age-old pattern of the powerful disempowering the weak while claiming to have their best interests—or the greater good and moral purity of society—at heart.

A signature on the antiprostitution pledge entitled US government officials to vet projects for compliance. Because the wording of the provisions was vague and open-ended, almost anything could be considered a violation, giving them unlimited room to deny or withdraw funding from groups that opposed or displeased them. Even the use of the terms "sex work" and "sex worker" could be taken to imply support for prostitution. The Bush administration wanted the old pejorative of "prostitutes" or preferably "trafficking victims."

It was an astonishing turn of events: The pioneering grassroots groups that had long worked effectively with sex workers in India and elsewhere were suddenly being told by an alien government that they had to prove that they were not promoting prostitution. And to prove that, they had to accede to a pledge that deceitfully conflated willing sex work with sex trafficking—specifically defined under international law as criminal abuses involving abduction, violence, fraud, debt bondage, and coercion stemming from traditional social status. That was a death knell for any rational discussion about sex work around the world.

But the assault on sex workers' lives only intensified. Just some months after launching PEPFAR, Bush declared in an address to the UN General Assembly that, besides its "war on terror," the United States would lead the world in a global war against sex trafficking. As with the language of PEPFAR's prostitution gag rule, sex work was intentionally confused with both child prostitution and trafficking. Asserting that "hundreds of thousands of teenage girls, and others as young as five" are trafficked into the sex trade every year, Bush called the sex "industry" a "special evil" amounting to "modern-day slavery."

Countries that failed a unilateral, annual US assessment of their performance on combating trafficking, chiefly sex trafficking and sex work, faced US-imposed sanctions, affecting US foreign assistance and even billions from the World Bank and International Monetary Fund—losses that could devastate vulnerable nations—under the Trafficking Victims Protection Act (TVPA) that had been pushed through by the Republican-controlled Congress in the last months of the Clinton administration and was now given destructive muscle by Bush. (In telling contrast, President Clinton had staunchly opposed the TVPA, arguing that unilateral sanctions imposing contentious US-defined norms were counter-productive and that lasting gains could be achieved through multilateral cooperation using the new antitrafficking treaty—the UN Protocol to Prevent, Suppress and Punish Trafficking in Persons, Especially Women and Children—that the US had spearheaded. Clinton's refusal to conflate voluntary sex work and consensual migration for sex work with sex trafficking drew the fire of religious conservatives and prohibitionist feminists, who charged him and Hillary Rodham Clinton of being "pro-prostitution.")

It was a barefaced bid to claw back some moral high ground after the catastrophic damage being done to the United States' reputation by the Bush administration—among other things, news of the horrific abuses at Iraq's Abu Ghraib prison was just emerging, with evidence that the US military and the CIA were using torture, physical and sexual abuse, rape, and sodomy against the men, women, and even children detained there, severe violations of the Geneva Conventions that amount to war crimes.

The bizarre outcome was that, within the space of a few months, the eradication of sex work had become a key focus of US foreign aid. Even the Republican, Christian-right crusade to deny the world's women safe abortions had never been anywhere so concerted or so well funded. In place of the broad, empowering policies for the well-being of sex workers carefully developed by the United Nations, as well as the parallel global effort to tackle human trafficking through the recent UN treaty, the Bush administration was using its superpower might and financial billions to push a malign nostrum, acting as an imperial moral policeman in the fashion of Great Britain in its era of empire.

In April 2004, just a year into Bush's discovery of AIDS as his global charitable cause, I testified against those destructive changes before the bipartisan US Congressional Human Rights Caucus. I was speaking in my personal capacity—I had just left UNICEF to join Yale University's Center for Interdisciplinary Research on AIDS as a scholar in residence—and did not have to modulate my disapproval. "Official American support has recently become—to speak frankly—misdirected, unhelpful and indeed damaging," I told them. "These positions have marred the US government's reputation amongst Indian civil society, so much so that many leading people are loathe to be associated with official US assistance on HIV/AIDS."

It was honest criticism. It would have been immeasurably harsher if I could have looked into the future and seen the full, disastrous extent of the harm the Bush administration's policies would soon cause sex workers, gay men, drug users, and the many others who desperately needed help in protecting themselves from HIV.

NINETEEN

A WORLD WAR UNFOLDS

On January 1, 2005, I left New York City again, this time to move to Geneva. It was a wrenching decision. There was simply no other place where I had such a deep sense of belonging. But the world had changed seismically—it was no longer the optimistic place it had seemed at the new millennium. Just two months earlier, Bush and Dick Cheney had been reelected, something that sickened me to see. I wanted to be actively engaged in doing whatever I could to oppose Bush's destructive policies. At the UN-AIDS Secretariat in Geneva, I would be working closely with the long-standing executive director, Peter Piot, as a senior adviser and speechwriter, and that promised a level of engagement with global policy making on AIDS that I would not have if I stayed on at the Yale AIDS center.

And so, late in the afternoon of that New Year's Day, I caught an overnight Swissair flight from JFK to Geneva. Lorca was tucked away in the hold of the plane. He had been characteristically trusting and uncomplaining when the airline handler had wheeled him away in his crate. But on the flight I spent a sleepless night worrying about him, my mind replaying the horror stories I had read about pets that died on long flights. On arriving in Geneva, I rushed to the area where he was to come out and minutes later he arrived, kicking up a shindy on seeing me, looking none the worse for his first plane ride. I was flooded with love for him and remembered Pablo Neruda's lovely insight: "With a traveling companion the road is never long."

I settled into a completely impractical attic apartment in the Pâquis. The ceiling came down sharply at unexpected places, the windows were set at an inconvenient slant, and a row of pillars divided the living room into two odd lengths. But it was airy and full of light, and I instantly felt at home. From one set of windows, I could glimpse the blue expanse of Lake Geneva and the snowy massif of Mont Blanc; from another set the magical column of the Jet d'Eau. The fluting song of blackbirds rose up from the unkempt garden below. The lake and its surrounding parks, dotted with magnificent Atlas cedars, were a short walk away, perfect for walks and swims with Lorca. I bought myself an old bicycle as well as a car so that I could get to the countryside on the weekends, resolved to embrace whatever good there was about this new life of mine to make up for losing New York City.

I came to love my neighborhood. It was on the unfashionable bank of the Rhône, an area of narrow lanes, graffiti-marred walls, and characterless modern buildings, worlds away from the monied primness of mainstream Geneva. Its invigorating, inclusive spirit reminded me of New York City, but it was an immeasurably safer, kinder environment. Young children played, unsupervised, on the streets or in the neighborhood parks. Late at night, single women nonchalantly walked through deserted streets.

All of Switzerland's bohemians and immigrants seemed to have found refuge among the Pâquis's cheap restaurants, down-market shops, and porn stores. Sex workers plied their trade with openness day and night, walking or carrying their toy-sized dogs, decked out in miniskirts and bright tops and chatting with neighbors. The local children and teenagers wandered past, paying them no mind. Near the train station, a drop-in center for injecting drug users had a stream of men and women going to and fro: there the cantonal government provided clean injection equipment as well as a fix for those who needed it. I was struck that none of the passersby avoided the center or the users, even the few who looked visibly ill or drawn. I had never seen anything like that before, not in India, the United Kingdom, or the United States—that peacefulness, safety, and respect for everyone. I longed to show Bush and his reactionary crew the Pâquis, so that they would realize that the problem did not lie in sex workers or in drug users but in their destructive war on prostitution and war on drugs.

❖

I was swept up in work from the very day I began. In just a month, Piot was to give a plenary speech at the London School of Economics. He wanted to lay out the case that AIDS was an exceptional threat to humanity and demanded an exceptional first call on finances and public priorities. That speech would be the launching pad for a series of think pieces, in both speeches and policy articles, in which Piot would lay out his reflections on the pandemic—it would soon be a quarter century since the disease had first been recognized—and the global response.

I relished everything, including the daunting responsibility of divining another person's views, tone, and declamation, about my first months at work. With its nondescript offices and informal dress code, the UNAIDS secretariat looked like a grassroots organization, and—just like the best of them—the commitment of its staff members was palpable. I greatly respected a number of my colleagues, several of whom I knew from my consulting assignments. Many had begun working on AIDS when it was still direly stigmatized. Several lived with HIV or had lost loved ones to the epidemic—among them women and men who had been pioneers in their countries when it came to confronting the persecution of people with HIV. Openly gay or lesbian staff held senior positions, still rarely if ever seen anywhere else across the United Nations.

I admired Piot for combining scientific skills with extensive experience in policy making, having led the secretariat since its founding in 1995. He had just begun his third and final five-year term. In 2005, he was an energetic fifty-six-year-old who cut a dashing figure in the dull world of international diplomacy. His finely tailored suits and geeky spectacles marked him out as a policy powerhouse, while his trademark "condom" ties advertised his iconoclasm.

I relished also the fact that the secretariat was the rare UN institution that had not fallen into irrelevance. I admired the things that it had helped achieve against all the odds—the advocacy that had won attention and funds from the world's political leaders, the painstaking putting together of a knowledge base of what worked, the guidance that balanced the imperative of tackling HIV with that of protecting human rights, and the courageous advocacy for stigmatized groups and people with HIV. It was the only body that commanded the global legitimacy needed to halt the Bush administration's destructive policies on HIV prevention, injection drug use, and sex work. I thought it could not but live up to that responsibility.

I was disillusioned with astonishing speed—not because of my colleagues but because of Piot's abeyance of his leadership responsibilities as the Bush assault on global AIDS policies gathered strength.

In late April, four months after I started work, I read the penultimate draft of a crucial prevention strategy that was coming up for negotiation in June before the UNAIDS governing board and wondered, astounded, if it was someone's raw copy that had been sent around mistakenly. Global strategy frameworks and AIDS summit declarations from previous years—some of which I had helped prepare—had done far more forward-thinking work, even under fire from the Bush administration's attack on their priorities, than what I saw in that draft. The vital role played by condoms in HIV prevention was minimized; so was the need for lifesaving adolescent sex education and sexual health services. There was hardly any mention of the fact that respecting the principles of human rights was key to HIV prevention. In short, every single thing the Bush administration opposed in

HIV prevention, and more broadly concerning human rights, had been censored out of the draft prevention strategy.

Though puzzled, I did nothing. At the back of my mind was the thought that Piot would tear apart the draft when it reached him for review. Piot read every sentence of every important document, from talking points to major reports, giving detailed feedback in his precise handwriting—and, given their importance, the materials sent to the board were signed off by Piot himself. At a working lunch, when I diplomatically brought up the poor draft, he commented that the prevention strategy needed to be "more explicit and businesslike."

I was flabbergasted to read the final version of the prevention strategy several weeks later, on the day it was sent off to the board members after Piot's approval. It was even weaker than the April draft, the language carefully censored and key sections either deleted entirely or moved to where they would be less noticeable. If the April draft had reeked of self-censorship, this one stank of active collusion with the Bush administration's AIDS team.

In the ten-thousand-word document, condoms were mentioned just three times in the body text. Previous global strategies had detailed recommendations running into several pages on the priority needed to be placed on key vulnerable populations—especially in prevention efforts. Inexcusably, this one reserved two woolly sentences for sex workers and drug users—an unmistakable rupture with the agreed direction of global, UN-led strategy ever since it had been laid out during Jonathan Mann's time at the World Health Organization in the late 1980s.

No less astonishing, it gave even shorter shrift to human rights than the April draft had. There was no mystery to it: Bush was, by then, leading a full-scale assault on human rights and international laws that he found inconvenient, even challenging the application of the Geneva Conventions' ban on torture to prisoners of war held in Abu Ghraib and Guantánamo.

Reading that strategy marked the end of my smooth working

relationship with Piot. Then and later, I saw that Piot's abdication of his leadership responsibilities was such that on every matter of ideological importance to the Bush administration—whether it was sex work, drug use, or abstinence-only education—he caved in rather than using diplomacy and confrontation to challenge the administration's destructive views. Though we maintained an appearance of civility, the strain and the antagonism between us were evident to others in his office. Only my usefulness kept him from doing what he did to others who questioned him: shunting me off to a distant corner of the headquarters or to an unpleasant posting. A working solution was soon found by his deputy acting as intermediary between us, a process that kept interaction between Piot and me to a minimum.

The tense three-day board meeting in June, dominated by discussions over the prevention strategy, revealed just how far Piot had taken the secretariat from the long-established fundamentals of global policy on AIDS. Within hours of the meeting's opening, the corridor talk was that many governments—including those of Canada, the United Kingdom, and quite a few major developing nations—were upset by the weakness of the draft strategy. Their representatives on the drafting committee were going to revise it together, an unprecedented occurrence in UNAIDS history. It amounted to a sharp rebuke of the secretariat, that its draft had fallen short of minimum standards.

The revised draft was enormously stronger, but even that last-minute salvage job could not meet the standards of earlier strategy documents. To bring it to that quality would have required trashing the secretariat draft entirely and writing a stronger one from scratch.

I made it a point to attend the session of the meeting at which the governing board tabled the prevention strategy. It left me with an overwhelming rush of depression—and gave me an insight into some of the factors that had allowed Piot to become so complicit with the Bush administration's demands without being held to account by either progressive governments or activist groups.

Whereas I had seen the venue, the elegant main meeting hall of WHO headquarters, packed during the annual World Health Assembly discussions, today no more than a third of the five hundred seats were occupied, mainly by national delegations. A life-and-death debate was under way, and all we had was this almost empty hall and a civil, emotionless debate among bureaucrats and the sprinkling of NGO representatives. Was this the sum total of how much the world's governments cared about a global crisis that had already killed more than 20 million people?

I sat through the entire session, even though the conclusion was known to everyone by now: the US delegation would not force a vote on the prevention strategy, given the vocal opposition it had faced from so many countries. A face-saving compromise was reached on the United States' opposition to needle exchange programs for injecting drug users—that was to note, in the minutes of the board meeting, that the strategy did not require donor countries to fund "activities that are contrary to the donor's national laws or policies." But, all in all, even though the board process had kept the Bush administration from wreaking even more damage on HIV prevention policies, it had failed to do much more. UNAIDS, under Piot's leadership, had failed the people who needed it most.

⸙

At any other point, I would have resigned, given the strength of my disagreements with Piot over fundamental matters. I forced myself to stay put. In part, I urged myself to be mature and to take stock of the fact that I had had disputes over matters of principle at every job I had ever had. I lectured myself that I needed to learn the compromised ways of bureaucrats now that I was in my forties. But the real thing that held me back was a matter of the heart.

Soon after arriving in Geneva, I had started dating a German man, Arndt, whom I had met the previous summer in New York City, introduced by a common friend. Arndt lived in Düsseldorf, and for several months we had a long-distance relationship during which, for all the stress of the situation, our affections strengthened. We were kindred souls on many counts. He loved dogs and particularly Lorca, so much so that I teased him that he dated me only because of Lorca. (For his part, my dog was shamelessly smitten with him.) He loved animals, trees, the lakes, and the mountains—and so the three of us spent every possible minute of our time outdoors. He did yoga and meditated and needed his solitude. He loved India. My initial apprehension about his being a decade younger faded, and I came to feel for him in ways that I had not with anyone since my relationship with Tandavan.

Arndt found a job and relocated to Geneva, so that, for the first time in over a decade, I had the joys of sharing a home with a lover, rushing home because he was there, eating potato chips while watching TV in bed, cuddling through the night (with Lorca taking up most of the bed), making love, being surprised on my birthday—all those seemingly innocuous things that are suffused with unforgettable sweetness when you're in love. The three of us were a happy family. I did not want my disputes with Piot to ruin that happiness, so painfully absent from my life for so long until now.

❖

Piot's acquiescence to the Bush administration's destructive positions on AIDS puzzled many observers.

For an article I was writing for Piot in the *Economist*'s "Viewpoint" section, I asked a handful of people to suggest issues that the article should tackle. Peter Gill, a former BBC journalist who was completing his book *Body Count: How They Turned AIDS into a Catastrophe*, on the leaders and institutions that were to blame for the tens of millions infected or dead, wrote back, "I cannot see how Peter and you can write the piece without wielding an iron-bar bluntness about the Vatican and condoms, the Americans on drugs, the Americans on prostitutes, the Americans on abstinence, the Americans on pretty well anything sensible in the prevention field! I keep being told how much the Americans admire your boss, and then these people scratch their heads a bit about why that should be!"

As the Bush onslaught against sex workers gathered force, incident after incident spotlighted Piot's failure to challenge him. That gave me some insight into the deeper reasons for his failure, beyond the simple fact that the United States was by far UNAIDS's largest donor.

In 2004, the US State Department put India on its "watch list," one of the worst tiers in its unilateral annual ranking of nations according to their performance in combating human trafficking, especially that relating to sex trafficking. India's new Congress-led government moved to placate the Bush administration. In May 2005, it proposed far-reaching amendments to the Immoral Traffic (Prevention) Act—the primary Indian law governing sex work and trafficking—that incorporated every point that the Bush administration was pushing globally. The amendments would transform the law from ambivalent, confused criminalization of sex work to outright, heavy-handed prohibition as in the United States.

Modeled on US state antiprostitution laws, the amendments would criminalize paying for sexual services even if the woman insisted she was selling sex voluntarily. Anyone found to even be visiting a brothel faced up to six months in jail and a fine equivalent to roughly $1,000, a vast fortune for most Indians. (In the US states with the harshest antiprostitution laws, clients can be jailed for up to five years for repeat convictions and fined up to $150,000.)

And, as in the US, all kinds of retrograde provisions were being introduced to inflict blatantly cruel punishments on the sex workers. One astonishing clause would increase the length of time—to an astounding seven years—that a sex worker could be imprisoned in corrective institutions. (I was astounded that the minister advocating for these changes was a woman—the long-standing politician Renuka Chowdhury, now holding the Ministry of Women & Child Development portfolio—and yet could be party to such cruel treatment of other women.) Another would sanction raids to forcibly remove and incarcerate even adult sex workers who expressly stated that they were selling sex entirely of their own accord; in the past, only minors or adults who declared that they were victims of abuse or trafficking could be legally removed through raids and given shelter by government institutions. Those provisions made a mockery of women's rights to self-determination. "This is typical of the patriarchal Indian state, which believes that women never achieve adulthood," Bharati Dey, the Durbar's secretary, commented. The intent was clearly to force sex workers out of their work by punishing them harshly.

Emboldened by the Indian government's compliance, the Bush administration turned to targeting the pathbreaking sex workers' collectives. Those groups posed the most potent counterevidence to the Bush assertion that prostitution was synonymous with sex trafficking and sex slavery. They were also powerful critics of the administration's views, returning or forgoing US government grants rather than signing the prostitution gag rule, and joining prominent human rights and AIDS groups around the world in releasing an open letter that criticized the Bush administration for its cynical conflation of sex work with sex trafficking. (Embarrassingly for the Bush administration, after a widely reported dispute, Brazil's government had recently refused nearly $50 million in US grants because the prostitution gag rule amounted to "interference that harms the Brazilian policy regarding diversity, ethical principles and human rights.")

Audaciously, the Bush administration set about accusing those groups of being complicit in child prostitution and trafficking of women. The sex workers' collective VAMP and its parent organization, Sangram, became its first targets.

Late on the afternoon of May 20, 2005, Gokul Nagar, a shantytown of narrow rustic houses on the outskirts of Sangli in southern Maharashtra, was raided by a contingent of nearly a hundred Indian policemen and policewomen. Bizarrely, leading the police action was a white American man—later identified as Greg Malstead, an American with a hard-line Christian organization, Restore International, bent on "rescuing" women from prostitution. Hearing of it, I thought angrily that if I had tried such Indiana Jones–esque shenanigans in the United States—perhaps rescuing some of the countless African American men unjustly jailed in brutal conditions—I would have ended up shot or locked away in prison. The police kicked in doors, abused the women, and thrashed several of them. Nearly fifty women were then locked up in Sangli's reformatory—most of them on the grounds that they were minors and had been trafficked into sex work, others accused of being brothel managers abetting trafficking.

There was an outpouring of support for Sangram/VAMP (as the group is commonly known) from many quarters. Many raised the obvious question why the area where Sangram/VAMP had worked painstakingly for years to fight sex trafficking—bringing it down to a fraction of past levels—had been targeted rather than crime-beset Mumbai, just three hundred miles away, where trafficking remained intractable and unaddressed. Eventually, a prolonged judicial investigation concluded that not one of the women had been trafficked and none of the brothel managers was involved in trafficking.

A second, equally violent and abortive raid on the collective's sex workers followed that summer. But the breathtaking culmination was that at the end of September the Bush administration accused Meena Seshu—the feminist and social worker who had founded Sangram in 1992—of trafficking children and women into prostitution and opposing their rescue from brothels.

"US Accuses NGO of Trafficking," blared a *Hindustan Times* headline. The report quoted US ambassador John R. Miller, the conservative former congressman appointed by Bush to lead the Office to Monitor and Combat Trafficking in Persons, as saying "I want to believe this is an exception, an anomaly. But we are reviewing other programmes and if there is any specific information that an organization is trying to keep people from being rescued from any kind of trafficking, we will be looking into it. . . . If the US is going to play a leadership role in abolishing this modern-day slavery in the 21st century, then we need to ensure that US funds go to support that effort and not frustrate it."

It was a surreal charge. Seshu, whom I knew well, was a member of UNAIDS's Reference Group on HIV and Human Rights. Sangram/VAMP's work had long been praised by UN agencies as well as USAID.

Seshu and her husband, Vasant, a prominent newspaper editor who belonged to the area, had adopted several children of sex workers.

The very next day after Seshu had been accused of being a "trafficker" by the US government, I found myself seated next to Mark Dybul, the second-ranking official in the Office of the US Global AIDS Coordinator and Health Diplomacy, at the opening session of a small strategy retreat hosted by UNAIDS. I couldn't restrain myself from telling Dybul how disappointed I was by the US government's actions against Seshu and Sangram/VAMP, that this was a historic low point in the United States' AIDS-related efforts in India.

Dybul looked astonished, no doubt taken aback that anyone from UNAIDS would speak so critically to a top official from a leading donor government. He recovered and replied, caustically, that the Indian government had confirmed Sangram's involvement in child trafficking. I retorted that all of us working on AIDS knew well that governments rarely if ever stood up for sex workers and other reviled citizens and so my government's views were hardly likely to be accurate. (As it was, breaking ranks with the Bush administration because of criticism within India, the Indian government insisted a few days later that the US embassy in Delhi publicly retract its charges against Seshu and Sangram.)

My disappointment with Dybul was the sharper for seeing that in spite of having himself faced the difficulties of being openly gay, he was so lacking in empathy for sex workers and so willing to be complicit with a bigoted president who had long attacked gays and other underdogs in his own country and was now doing so abroad. Not so long ago, being gay had been no less damning to a public career in the US than being a sex worker.

Dybul was soon promoted to the post of US global AIDS coordinator and became ever more clearly an apologist for the Bush administration's brutalizing policies, calling them a "compassionate response" to prostitution. That was one of my first moments of realization that there was little certainty that the gay men and women now taking seats at the tables of power would have notable empathy for other disadvantaged people. As some thoughtful feminists had already noted about women in power, most such people were likely to readily participate in oppressing and exploiting others.

Apart from the confrontation with Dybul, that meeting served only to reveal to me yet another depressing cause of Piot's decline: he had developed the *Lords of Poverty* syndrome, the chronic addiction of many in the international development set to enjoying high luxury at public expense. The venue of the two-day meeting was the grand palace-hotel of Le Mirador Kempinski at the Swiss resort town of Mont Pèlerin. UNAIDS was hosting dozens at that châteaulike building with its unrivaled views of Lake Geneva and paying for sumptuous Michelin-starred feasts at baronial dining tables. The bills for the pointless talkfest—which Piot had touted as an "envisioning exercise" for the long-term response to AIDS—would have covered a small country's annual supply of anti-AIDS drugs. The excess was on a par with the worst that I had seen at the World Bank. To see it coming from the UNAIDS Secretariat, a place that not long ago I had thought was run like a barebones nongovernmental organization, was devastating. I was relieved that I had been assigned to a cheap place nearby, rather than being implicated unknowingly in that shameless waste.

It was obvious to me that a decade of being a top UN official handling the era's global cause célèbre—Piot was now in an unbroken third term as the secretariat's boss, thanks to a loophole in administrative rules, had left him divorced from reality. Endless hobnobbing with billionaires, royalty, and celebrities may have led Piot to forget the hoi polloi whose survival he was supposed to be fighting for, the tens of millions struggling to survive despite their HIV infections as well as the many millions of marginalized people at risk of contracting HIV. And the top-level misgovernance that is the bane of the UN system, a key reason why it is perennially a shadow of its laudable ideals, meant that he was never held to account.

Piot should have either lived up to his responsibilities or, if he felt he no longer had the dedication to combat the Bush administration, handed the job to someone who could do it justice. Instead, he frittered his formidable energy on vanity projects akin to the Mont Pèlerin meeting that contributed nothing to fulfilling the secretariat's core responsibilities.

There was endless money to burn, with the secretariat's biennial budget now touching $200 million. Half a million or one million dollars, or even vastly more, was wasted on worthless reports and initiatives. There was *AIDS in Africa: Three Scenarios to 2025*, a coffee-table tome on the future of the continent's epidemic, told through folksy illustrated stories, as if Africans could not grasp anything more complex. There was a 250-page chronicle on the first decade of UNAIDS's work, which itself took three years to be written and published. There was aids2031, touted as planning the long-term response to the pandemic, looking ahead to the fiftieth year after the disease's first medical reports in 1981. All those fed the gravy train for highly paid staff and consultants in the multibillion-dollar AIDS industry; neither any money nor any good trickled down to the people who needed to be helped. And all the while, the quality of the secretariat's essential policy and technical reports plummeted—the *2006 Report on the Global AIDS Epidemic*, marking twenty-five years of the pandemic, embarrassingly needed an entire page of corrigenda.

When the UNAIDS Secretariat moved at the end of 2006 from its nondescript offices to the latest addition to the United Nations' gleaming modern buildings in Geneva, boasting sky-high atriums and acres of tinted glass, Piot told the assembled staff that we should be proud to have the nicest building and the best art collection of the city's international organizations. Quite a few of my colleagues seemed as baffled as I was to hear that, no doubt wondering where the once committed scientist had disappeared to. The glacial new building symbolized how much the secretariat had changed in recent years under Piot; like countless other UN organizations, it had become a self-serving bureaucracy for fat cats.

TWENTY

UNIVERSAL RIGHTS AND SCANDALOUS WRONGS

O ver the Christmas break of 2005, Arndt and I joined my father for a brief holiday in Goa. I then went to Baba ka Gaon
to visit Ram Dass, Prayaga Devi, and the people I considered
my family in that village. On the return leg of that journey, I stayed
overnight in Lucknow with Saleem Kidwai, a close friend from the
1980s, when we had both been drawn together in Delhi's tightly knit
gay community of that time. Saleem, a historian of medieval India,
and another friend, Ruth Vanita, a noted feminist scholar, were the co-
editors of *Same-Sex Love in India*, published in 2000, a meticulously
researched work that brought together extracts from literature about
same-sex love in the subcontinent from ancient times to the current.

Our conversation returned time and again to the frustration we
both felt over the lack of headway made by a second legal suit challenging Section 377 of the Indian Penal Code. The case had been filed
in December 2001 in the Delhi High Court. The first challenge, filed
in 1994 by ABVA, the activist group in which my friend Siddhartha
had been a driving force, had petered out, a victim of the deadening
pace of India's appallingly underresourced judicial system. We had all
hoped that that second challenge would make faster headway than the

1994 case. The two civil society groups driving the challenge—the Naz Foundation (India) Trust, one of the country's first groups to begin HIV prevention efforts for gay men and transgender individuals, and the Lawyers Collective, which undertook public interest litigation— had better resources than the ABVA collective and were better placed to deal with the judiciary's institutionalized weaknesses.

But the case had been obstructed not only by the judiciary's slow pace but also by what seemed to be the reluctance of the judges to grapple with the matter. Then, in December 2004, when the petition belatedly came up for hearing, the court dismissed Naz India's case on the questionable grounds that its chief executive and listed appellant, Anjali Gopalan, was not gay, had not been personally harmed by Section 377, and therefore had no legal standing to file a public interest challenge. (Indian courts had long established that public interest litigation could be moved by anyone, and the involvement of an affected individual or community—an aggrieved "test case," as in *Roe v. Wade* or *Lawrence v. Texas* in the United States—was not necessary.) It had taken another year before the efforts of Anand Grover, the human rights lawyer who had played a unique role in challenging HIV-related discrimination since representing Dominic D'Souza in 1989, made the Supreme Court instruct the Delhi court to hear the case promptly, saying it had erred in dismissing it. Yet another year had passed without action by the Delhi court. It now seemed that that case would also die from attrition.

Somehow, in a whirl of animated conversation, by the time I left Lucknow the following day, Saleem and I had chalked out a detailed plan for getting the most thoughtful and highly respected Indians to make a collective public statement in favor of striking down Section 377. As a model we had in mind the 1897 petition signed by prominent Germans—including Albert Einstein, Hermann Hesse, Magnus Hirschfeld, Thomas Mann, and Rainer Maria Rilke—asking the government to overturn Paragraph 175, the section of the German penal code that criminalized homosexuality. We hoped we might push the courts to stop ignoring the matter, as well as influence public opinion and possibly even the government's stand.

Everything fell into place rapidly. Anjali Gopalan and Anand Grover agreed that that would help summon the court's attention. Within minutes of my emailing him, Vikram Seth, my senior at Doon School and now a close friend, wrote back to say that he would be willing to lead the campaign.

Addressed to the government, the judiciary, and India's citizens, our open letter, drafted by Vikram, Saleem, and me, began by stating "To build a truly democratic and plural India, we must collectively fight against laws and policies that abuse human rights and limit fundamental freedoms. This is why we, concerned Indian citizens and people of Indian origin, support the overturning of Section 377 of the Indian Penal Code, a colonial-era law dating to 1861, which punitively criminalizes romantic love and private, consensual sexual acts between adults of the same sex.

"In independent India, as earlier, this archaic and brutal law has served no good purpose. It has been used to systematically persecute, blackmail, arrest and terrorize sexual minorities. It has spawned public intolerance and abuse, forcing tens of millions of gay and bisexual men and women to live in fear and secrecy, at tragic cost to themselves and their families."

Vikram, with his poet's unerring eye, added at the letter's end, "In the name of humanity and our Constitution, this cruel and discriminatory law should be struck down."

We sent the letter off to canvass signatures—and every day our hearts swelled with joy to see how many thoughtful, eminent Indians were writing back to say that they would add their signatures to it. Soon the lead signatories included legendary freedom fighters, progressive Hindu leaders, retired top UN officials, even a former attorney general of India. It spoke volumes about our cause being a matter of fundamental human rights that all the lead signatories, apart from Vikram and me, were straight.

More than 150 eminent Indians signed the open letter. Not only were many great thinkers, journalists, filmmakers, artists, and writers on the list, but also some of the country's most respected leaders in business, education, the civil service, and the armed forces, demonstrating the strength of support even in traditionally conservative quarters of the establishment. All of India's secular, democratic, forward-thinking promise was represented in what had become a citizens' movement.

In August, a month before the campaign was to be launched, Amartya Sen, the Nobel Prize–winning economist, said he would join us but would write a complementary letter as he wanted to convey points that he felt strongly about. That was a godsend: Sen is lionized in India, with a broad appeal in virtually every section of society. I had never forgotten the compassion with which Sen had responded when, as a young Harvard graduate student, I had told him I was gay. No doubt realizing that it had taken all my courage to be open with him, he told me at length about the fear his gay friends in England had lived in during their college years in the 1950s and then, in an quintessentially Indian act of reassurance, had put his arm around my shoulders as we had left the faculty dining room.

His concluding paragraph took away my breath when I first read it. Sen wrote, "It is surprising that independent India has not yet been able to rescind the colonial era monstrosity in the shape of Section 377, dating from 1861. That, as it happens, was the year in which the American Civil War began, which would ultimately abolish the unfreedom of slavery in America. Today, 145 years later, we surely have urgent reason to abolish in India, with our commitment to democracy and human rights, the unfreedom of arbitrary and unjust criminalization."

The two open letters were launched in Delhi on September 16, 2006, just a few weeks before the Delhi court was scheduled to begin hearing the Naz challenge. Across India, in every language, the campaign dominated headlines, columns, and TV shows for days. Media outlets the world over reported on the campaign. India's judiciary and government could not ignore those letters.

For me as well as for many other gay Indians, those open letters marked a watershed in our conflicted, fearful feelings about life in our country. I realized that the India of 2006 was not the same country I had encountered as a twenty-five-year-old in 1986, exactly two decades before, when I had returned from college in the United States. It filled me with boundless hope to see the open letters overwhelmingly elicit supportive comments from the public and media; the homophobic hatred that had swelled under the BJP's recent rule was not representative of Indians. For the first time ever, I felt I could return to live in India as an openly gay man without feeling constantly wary or threatened. I wished my beloved friend Siddhartha had been alive to see this thrilling turning point—many of the people who hadn't even replied when he had asked them for statements of support for "Less than Gay" in 1991 were now backing this campaign.

⬦

Just two days after the launch of the open-letter campaign, I informed Piot and his deputy that I was resigning from the secretariat, though I would stay on for a few months so that the executive office's work was not disrupted.

I had signed an agreement to stay on at the secretariat for two more years just that summer. But I had reached an irrevocable tipping point on realizing that Piot's personal and professional lives were entangled in the workplace, having a romantic relationship with a highly paid consultant to UNAIDS. (At the World Bank, where ethics rules are clearer cut and better enforced than at the UN, Bush appointee Paul Wolfowitz was at that time being charged by the institution's anticorruption branch of arranging a massive pay increase and promotion for his companion; Wolfowitz was eventually forced to resign, despite the White House's efforts to defend him.)

I told Arndt I couldn't bear to work for Piot anymore and that I would resign. Arndt supported my decision and lovingly pooh-poohed my worries about being possibly jobless in expensive Switzerland.

⬦

"There is no shame among the shameless," I thought to myself, when, in April 2007—within a few months of my leaving UNAIDS—the

American press reported that former US global AIDS coordinator Randall Tobias, the close Bush friend who had recently been promoted to deputy secretary of state in charge of all US foreign aid, was a regular user of high-end call girls. "Ex-AIDS Chief in Escort Flap Called Hypocritical: Backed US Policy That Forbids Aid to Help Prostitutes," the *Boston Globe* headlined.

The hypocrisy beggered belief. Tobias's attempts at defending himself included the tragicomic claim that he had not had sex with the women from the Pamela Martin & Associates escort service but had merely had the "gals come over to the condo to give me a massage." Why Tobias had not called the Beltway's mainstream massage experts rather than an escort service famed for providing attractive young women was a question he evaded. A year later, undermining Tobias's claims, a US district court in Washington, DC, ruled that the escort service was charging clients $250 to $300 an hour plus tips for full-fledged sexual encounters, not for massage or erotic role-playing.

Within months, Republican senator David Vitter, one of the proudest proponents of "family values" conservatism and opponents of abortion and gay rights, was implicated in the same scandal. And soon thereafter, New York governor Eliot Spitzer, a Democrat, resigned after a federal investigation showed that he had spent as much as $80,000 in recent years on high-end sex workers. Not only had Spitzer vigorously prosecuted escort services—of precisely the kind he later secretly patronized—in his previous post as New York State's attorney general, he had also inked one of the most extreme anti–sex work laws in the United States during his first days in the governor's office, parroting Bush in calling prostitution "modern-day slavery."

The scandals involving Tobias, Vitter, and Spitzer, following one another in quick succession, led to the worldwide ridiculing of the Bush administration's antiprostitution crusade. They showed the moral bankruptcy of its advocates, doing more to discredit their views than all that had been achieved by our appeals to logic, evidence, and human rights principles.

There was more evidence still, in those years, to demonstrate that it was precisely those who most loudly condemned the supposed immorality of others who were themselves the most immoral abusers. The Catholic Church was battered by revelations that for decades it had enabled the rape and sexual assault of tens of thousands of children by pedophile priests worldwide, systematically shielding serial abusers and continuing to let them prey on youngsters. Republican congressman Mark Foley, the author of the sexual predator provisions of the Adam Walsh Child Protection and Safety Act of 2006, was forced to resign after ABC News uncovered his long history of sending congressional pages, some still minors, texts and emails with repeated references to sexual organs and acts.

But, as always in history, it was rare for the powerful men in even the most blatant scandals to be punished, escaping by virtue of their wealth and stature as well as the rigged standard of justice by which the laws that apply to ordinary folks are not enforced on the powerful. Thus, under US federal and state laws on prostitution and sex trafficking, Spitzer, Tobias, and Vitter should have faced criminal charges and the possibility of jail terms. But nothing of the sort happened. Though the scandal forced Tobias to resign from his top-level Bush administration post, he immediately became the head of the Indianapolis Airport Authority. Vitter continued as senator after apologizing for having committed a "very serious sin." Spitzer became a political pundit, with a column in *Slate* and a nightly TV show.

In depressing contrast, as always, the women who catered to those powerful men were cruelly persecuted. On January 30, 2007, Brandy Britton, a forty-three-year-old single mother of two and former professor of sociology and women's studies at the University of Maryland but recently facing bankruptcy, hanged herself rather than face trial for prostitution. (Britton had been an employee of Pamela Martin & Associates, the escort service used by Tobias and Vitter.) On May 1, 2008, Deborah Jeane Palfrey, the fifty-two-year-old former escort and onetime paralegal who had run Pamela Martin & Associates, hung herself shortly before her sentencing, rather than suffer years in jail. In a handwritten note, she described her predicament as a "modern-day lynching."

Within months of leaving UNAIDS, I realized that frustration with Piot's abeyance of leadership had mounted to such an extent that—for the first time in its short decade of existence—UNAIDS was embattled rather than praised. It faced a barrage of criticism from policy makers, public health experts, activists, and nongovernmental organizations around the world, its reputation reaching such a nadir that there were calls for the program to be disbanded altogether.

One of the major charges against the secretariat was that for several years it had consciously exaggerated the global estimates of the number of people living with HIV, refusing to accept convincing evidence from outside experts that the epidemic had peaked even in sub-Saharan Africa and was not expanding relentlessly elsewhere, including in China and India. Eventually, in its 2007 epidemiological report, the secretariat cut its estimates of the worldwide number of people living with HIV from 40 million to 33 million and the number of new HIV infections from nearly 5 million a year in the previous year's estimate to 2.5 million. For India alone, the estimates of people living with HIV were more than halved, falling from 5.7 million to 2.5 million. In one sweep, it transformed India from being a country with a runaway HIV epidemic to one that had seen it grow only sluggishly over the past twenty years.

The stunning scale of those revisions did enormous harm to the secretariat's reputation for technical excellence. To many, it was evidence that the secretariat had been motivated by the desire to keep AIDS high on the global political agenda—or by the self-serving goal of ensuring that AIDS continued to command the lion's share of global donor funds.

Another storm was triggered by a "UNAIDS Guidance Note on HIV and Sex Work" posted on the secretariat website for consideration at the summer 2007 meeting of the governing board, coincidentally right at the time of the sex scandal engulfing erstwhile US

AIDS commissioner Tobias. It was the first major UNAIDS publication on sex workers in years, following the pall of self-censorship that had fallen over it thanks to the Bush administration's policies. Astonishingly, the guidance note parroted that government's prohibitionist views, sparking outraged criticism from sex workers' rights networks and other human rights groups. The secretariat pulled the document from the website, and the governing board eventually instructed UNAIDS to revise the guidance note in consultation with sex workers' rights groups.

I was not surprised by either the outraged reactions or the demand for revision. The document was shoddily argued and had an abysmally weak evidentiary base. Most odd, its argumentation and recommendations broke completely with UNAIDS's past understanding of sex work, which had been detailed in numerous documents, such as the *International Guidelines on HIV/AIDS and Human Rights* that I so admired. There was no explanation given for why UNAIDS had turned its back on the closely considered guidance of the past. In a bizarre but revealing omission, the guidance note did not list any of those reports in its footnotes or bibliography.

The grubby fingerprints of the Bush administration were visible all over the guidance note. The kowtowing to the administration's duplicitous equating of sex work with sex trafficking began in the opening section, which read, "The increasing feminization of migration and the involvement of families, kin networks and local communities in the movement of women and girls, blurs the difference between trafficking and sex work." Yet not a single footnote or reference was provided to back this stunning claim.

In telling contrast, an evidence-based review of sex work by UNAIDS had concluded just five years earlier that the "forces that drive people into sex work . . . can vary—sometimes widely . . . Many people enter sex work for economic reasons; that is, it may be the only, or the best-paying, employment option. Others are coerced into sex work through violence, trafficking or debt bondage. Some, particularly adults, freely choose sex work as their occupation."

And so it went—one unfounded claim after another, one inexplicable break with past UN guidance after another. Whereas UNAIDS, the Office of the UN High Commissioner for Human Rights, and the Inter-Parliamentary Union had previously clearly advised governments to review "with the aim of repeal" criminal legislation and other laws that criminalize "adult sex work that involves no victimization," there was not a hint of that in the guidance note. Nor was there any echo of the recommendation that "where sex work has legal standing, laws against abuse and exploitation are more likely to be enforced, thus reducing the incidence of violence against sex workers, especially as perpetrated by corrupt enforcement authorities." The acquiescence to the Bush administration was so extreme that no mention was made that the worldwide evidence reviewed by UNAIDS over the past decade had showed that collectives run by empowered sex workers, such as the Durbar and Sangram/VAMP in India, consistently had the greatest impact not just in stemming HIV rates and improving overall conditions for sex workers but also in tackling sex trafficking and child prostitution.

TWENTY-ONE

A HOME IN INDIA

At the end of August 2007, I moved back to India from Geneva. My relationship with Arndt had not survived the turmoil thrown up in our lives by my resignation from UNAIDS.

I had feared the relationship was too new to be tested so sorely—we had lived together for less than a year at the point that I had resigned—and sure enough that proved true, jolted by the premature questions it raised about the certainty of our commitment to each other. For me, the question was to know whether Arndt already cared for me so deeply that I should stay on in Geneva only to be with him. For Arndt, the question was whether he could tell me with confidence that what he felt for me was so strong that I had ample reason to stay.

The months that had followed had seesawed endlessly—from blessed highs because there was so much evidence that we loved each other and couldn't bear to part to tortured lows brought on by Arndt's doubts and then my anguished awareness of them. We were both soon worn out.

By the end of that wrecked summer, things were clear: Arndt couldn't commit to me, and I wouldn't stay on without having that certainty. It had taken us ten months to arrive at that decision—precisely as long as we had lived together before my decision to quit UNAIDS, a bittersweet testimony to the genuineness of our loss.

On August 30 that year, Lorca and I caught a flight to Bengalūru. Looking out from the window as we flew eastward and the sun began to set, I was filled with numbing sadness and regret. The end of my relationship with Tandavan had left me even more grief-stricken, but at least I had known that the relationship had run a full course. This one had come to an unnatural, premature end. I was filled with disquiet over whether, even in my mid-forties, I was making headstrong decisions that would do terrible harm to my prospects for happiness.

❖

Yet my grief was lightened because there were things to look forward to in my life ahead in India.

Soon after my resignation from UNAIDS, I had been awarded a grant by the Ford Foundation to write about the AIDS pandemic's impact on sexual outlaws and was elated at the prospect of the years of rewarding, independent work that lay ahead. Being a free agent again, I could speak up about the devastating harm being done by the Bush administration to global HIV prevention policies and to the well-being of sex workers and other excluded individuals. I began to dream, too, of writing a sequel to my book on rural poverty, already a decade old, and decided to apply for a research grant for that as well, as I could work on both books simultaneously.

Never during my several previous sojourns had I felt at ease about the prospect of living here—but seeing how warmly people had embraced the open-letter campaign to decriminalize same-sex relations a year before, those apprehensions had fallen away. I thought, to my own surprise, that I could enjoy India fully now, in a carefree way that I never had before.

Uppermost in my thoughts was that I was moving back at a point when my father really needed my support. (Through the tortured last months with Arndt, I had invariably turned to him for advice and support, even more than I had to my closest friends or my brothers, a telling testimony to the closeness of our bonds.) He had turned seventy-five at the beginning of the year, and though he was as uncomplaining as ever, I could see that he was tiring of coping alone. Two years earlier, he had finally given in to his sons' urging that he should shut down his struggling tea garden, retire, and move out of Kolkata. He had hesitated out of concern for my mother—who continued to live in isolation at our family home in the city, disabled by her mental illness—but eventually my brothers and I had prevailed by insisting that it was our turn to take care of her. My father had set out on an adventurous road trip in his SUV to discover where he wanted to settle. I could tell that he longed for mountains and wilderness, and sure enough, he finally decided on the Nilgiri mountains of Tamil Nadu, a tea-growing area at India's southern tip that he knew well and where he had many friends from his years in the industry.

The first goal I set for myself on arriving was to build him a home. Having settled him, I would move to Goa. That would be the perfect arrangement: my father could spend the winters with me when the mountains grew cold, and I could escape to his home during Goa's hot summers.

There was so much to look forward to.

✤

We soon decided on a site that touched my father in a way that no other place had. It had an equally singular effect on me, too.

It was a long, gentle plateau between two six-thousand-foot-high mountains. Both mountains were equally untamed, the tea bushes quickly fading out to be replaced by massive rocks and dense clumps of forests. The only other place where I had felt this quality of infinitude, the sense that the world both began and ended here, was the Grand Canyon.

There were no neighbors at all—not one. Getting to the nearest of our friends would be a half-hour drive on a good day; on stormy days, it would be impossible, as the only access was a rutted track of earth and rock that quickly turned treacherous. The closest village was several valleys distant. Coonoor town was nearly an hour away. There were no electricity or water connections.

It was teeming with wild animals. On every visit we spotted herds of *gaur*, one magnificent, solitary old *gaur* bull in particular. There were barking deer, black eagles, and Malabar giant squirrels, which resemble fleet-footed red pandas. We spotted a pair of otters in the stream below. The friend who had taken us there told us that sloth bears and leopards were common—and that a tigress had sometimes been spotted on the facing hill.

The minute my father visited that untamed spot, he wanted to live there, drawn to it as if by an insuperable force. I was not surprised, as I felt exactly the same way. Somehow it felt like home even though there were just rocks, trees, and wild animals there—nothing that suggested human habitation was possible. My father had never felt like that about a place, he told me: as though he wanted to stay put, put down roots, and not leave, ever, for even a day. I knew without being told that he was longing to retreat to that isolated forest to find solitude and peace after the difficulties of his life; it was a time-honored step in the Hindu view of life, *vanaprastha*, retiring to the forest after a life well lived.

My father said he wanted to see the waterfall across the valley while lying in bed. His voice ringing with excitement. Indeed, he wanted to see it even from his bathroom. Would that be possible? He wanted a skylight above his bed so that he could gaze up at the stars and the moon. He wanted a terrace outside his bedroom—just in case he felt like wandering outside at night. Whatever he wanted, I happily agreed to (*sans* the open bathroom). The home was going to be my gift to him—a small, inadequate thanks for all the love that he'd given me.

I bought the land all the way from the plateau stretching down to the *panchayat* road, because eventually we would have to construct our own road up to the house. (For the moment, the management of the neighboring tea estate—which owned the rocky road abutting the property—generously allowed us to use theirs.) I found an architect and a contractor willing to construct the house at record speed despite the difficult site. They began to build a home that matched my father's wishes, the expanses of glass outweighing the concrete. The forest authorities helped us design a formidable fence that would keep out the leopards, which have a particular fondness for eating dogs. We had Lorca and my father's mammoth German shepherd, Sher Khan, to protect, as well as Puppy, a stray waif my father had adopted after Sher Khan had found her, lost in the tea bushes, miraculously alive in spite of the leopards.

A few days after the purchase was finalized, my father and I went for a walk around the higher of the two mountains. At its very top, from which there was a breathtaking 360-degree view stretching to the horizon on every side, I spotted a small painted sign with the mountain's name in both Tamil and English—Pana Para Mattam, "the sacred place of treasure" in Tamil. We had seen the sign many times together. On that day my heart leaped, as I spotted in the name an anagram of "Papa" and "Rana," my nickname.

A sacred, treasured place for Papa and Rana! I excitedly pointed out the coincidence to my father. He looked at the sign, wordless, and then turned to me with a smile of delight and enveloped me in the most loving hug. We stood there together on that wild mountaintop, father and son, our hearts filled with wonder.

TWENTY-TWO

THE MOST DANGEROUS OF TIMES

From 2007 through 2009, I traveled widely across India and Southeast Asia. Everywhere I went, in all the many places where US aid and might wielded outsize clout, the scale of the harm done to sex workers by the Bush antiprostitution campaign mounted each year. There was the imposition of ever-harsher laws, intensifying persecution of sex workers, and disastrous cuts in HIV prevention funding for any groups that stood up for sex workers. The progress that had seemed imminent in India and elsewhere just a few years earlier had instead turned into terrible reversal.

In Cambodia, I witnessed firsthand the unleashed storm of abuse. At the beginning of 2008, to avoid losing direly needed US foreign aid and World Bank loans, the Cambodian government issued a draconian law—the Law on Suppression of Human Trafficking and Sexual Exploitation—that toed the line of the United States' diktats conflating sex work with sex trafficking of women and children. The Bush administration commended Cambodia for the new law and promptly moved it off its list of countries that were at risk of US-imposed sanctions.

But within Cambodia, the new antiprostitution law unleashed a campaign of arrests against sex workers by the police. It was very different from the random periodic sweeps of the past. The police had been given untrammeled power because the new law criminalized soliciting, which had not been an offense until then. A large but unknown number of female and transgender sex workers were imprisoned in jails and so-called rehabilitation centers—and even by the time of my documentation visit in April 2008, several months after the raids had begun, the whereabouts of hundreds remained unknown, domestic human rights groups, such as the Women's Network for Unity, told me.

The fear was palpable in the sex workers I met. It was a strange contrast to the indolent French colonial atmosphere of Phnom Penh, with its colonnaded houses, the promenades along the slow-moving Mekong, and the elegantly attired Cambodians and expatriates. Not one sex worker was willing to be quoted or even to meet anywhere that could put her at risk of being spotted with me, an outsider with a notepad. (That brought home to me afresh how different India was from many other developing countries—in India, barring the most extreme conditions, even marginalized, powerless people typically felt emboldened to speak openly, certain that there would be some kind of attenuating support from the media, civil society, or decent officials.)

I interviewed sex workers in crowded cafés, pretending that we were friends meeting. I kept to my promise of not taking written notes or taping the conversations. The women I met had sold sex off the street or from porn video shacks and small brothels located in the poorer parts of Phnom Penh. It was clear from what they told me that even more than in India, sex work was one of the few options to earn money open to impoverished women in Cambodia. The small, agrarian country had been ravaged by French colonialism and American political meddling, years of covert US carpet bombing during the Vietnam War, and then the genocidal Khmer Rouge regime. It was poorer even than Myanmar now. Fewer than one in three girls even began secondary school. The hundreds of thousands of young men and women fleeing desperate rural conditions competed for a handful of low-paid jobs in tourism and sweatshop garment manufacturing. Sex work typically paid twice as much as what women could earn in the sweatshop factories, so it was little surprise that it seemed an attractive economic option.

The women told me that ever since the police crackdown had begun some months before, they had been subjected to extortion, beatings, and rape by policemen. Until then, the police had never acted in such a concerted, harsh fashion. Most had stopped working because the police now demanded bribes of fifty or more US dollars, ten times more than what they had extorted before the enactment of the antiprostitution law. Their children and parents were destitute, they told me, as they depended on the women's daily earnings to eat and live.

Two of the women I interviewed had been held against their will for several months in a rehabilitation center, prevented from contacting their relatives despite having IDs proving that they were in their thirties. Even frantic pleas to be allowed to phone their children had been denied. Each had friends who were still missing—they had no idea where they were and were too scared to look for them.

Later I hired a local motorcyclist to drive me through the neighborhoods where they had worked earlier—whole stretches of eerily empty bamboo huts that had once housed low-price karaoke bars and brothels but were now sealed off. The only living creatures in sight were stray dogs and cats.

Just as astounding as the all-pervading sense of fear was the conspiracy of denial. Barring sex workers, human rights groups, and a few journalists, everyone else in Phnom Penh acted as if not one sex worker had been beaten, raped, or made to disappear in recent months. Human rights abuses were so commonplace in Cambodia and so intertwined with the corrupting overreliance on the charity of foreign governments that the United Nations habitually looked the other way. UNAIDS's Cambodia office, despite being the first place that Cambodian and international sex workers' rights groups had turned to for support, joined in the public silence, as did its Bangkok regional headquarters.

As it happened, at the time of my research in Cambodia, UNAIDS's governing board was meeting in Chiang Mai, in neighboring Thailand. Would Peter Piot criticize the horrific abuses being inflicted on Cambodia's sex workers—and the Bush administration's manifest responsibility for that persecution—in his opening speech to the board? I doubted it, given Piot's complicity with the Bush administration and because US AIDS commissioner Mark Dybul was chairing the UNAIDS governing board at the time. And so it was: there was not even a single word about the dire situation of Cambodia's sex workers in Piot's speech or in any of the discussions in the days of the board meeting. UNAIDS's fall to being an accomplice in Bush's war on sex workers was absolute.

It took many months of protests before the Cambodian government suspended its violent campaign against sex workers. The UN Office of the High Commissioner for Human Rights and Human Rights Watch both investigated the abuses, revealing that hundreds of sex workers—as well as drug users, beggars, street children, and homeless people—had been held in inhuman conditions in so-called rehabilitation centers, including the government's infamous Prey Speu and Koh Kor detention centers. The evidence testified to daily beatings, torture, rapes (even of children), and custodial deaths, and suicides to bring an end to the torment. The *Economist*'s correspondent wrote from Phnom Penh in the summer of 2009, "Barely legible on [Prey Speu's] grimy walls a few weeks ago were cries for help and whispers of despair from the tormented souls once crammed into its grimy cells. 'This is to mark that I lived in terror under oppression,' read one such message."

⚜

As in Cambodia and India, governments the world over began to accede to the United States' antiprostitution demands. They increased criminal sanctions against sex workers in already existing laws—copying the punitive US model that punishes sex workers with years in jail and prohibitive fines—or weighed new antiprostitution laws that equated sex work with sex trafficking and child sexual exploitation, in this case criminalizing clients as well as sex workers. The list soon included, in addition to Cambodia and India, countries as far-flung and disparate as Bangladesh, the Czech Republic, Guatemala, Lithuania, Mexico, Nepal, Papua New Guinea, South Africa, South Korea, Thailand, and Zambia. It was the rare government, such as Brazil's, that had the courage to reject the Bush administration's diktats.

In those countries and many others, the antiprostitution sentiment fueled by the Bush campaign led to government and public violence against sex workers of a deadly purposiveness that had rarely ever been known before. Participating in those campaigns were not just reactionary political parties, the police, and right-wing vigilantes, but also, astonishingly, American-financed and even American-led prohibitionist groups.

In Cambodia, Laos, and Thailand, at an increasing pace from 2001 onward, hundreds of sex workers were arrested in violent police raids orchestrated by American-financed prohibitionist organizations and sensationally filmed for prime-time Western TV. The most notorious of those were the International Justice Mission, a Virginia-based group of far-right Christian lawyers and former police officers, and AFESIP (Agir Pour les Femmes en Situation Précaire), headquartered in Cambodia. Both received millions in funding from USAID and other US government bodies, as well as from a vast network of right-wing Christian groups. Even adults who insisted that they were working voluntarily and did not want to be rescued were detained and held forcibly in governmental detention centers or private shelters, in some cases for several weeks, on the pretext that they were victims and needed to be guarded. In case after case, the women escaped the minute they could, often at grave physical danger to themselves, letting themselves down multistory buildings and scaling high walls. An even crueler fate awaited the hundreds of women and older teenagers who were illegal immigrants from Myanmar or Vietnam, who were typically jailed for a year and then deported back to the crisis areas that they had fled in desperation.

In sub-Saharan Africa, where violence against female, trans, and male sex workers by police and thugs is endemic—a consequence of the colonial-era laws that punitively criminalize sex work as well as the stigma that they are AIDS "carriers"—the Bush administration's anti-prostitution campaign intensified their persecution. Zambia launched a mass incarceration of young women suspected of selling sex, with the police publicly whipping sex workers while calling them "bitches who are killing the nation" for spreading AIDS. In the Democratic Republic of Congo, twenty-nine cases of sexual violence against female sex workers by police or military, including rape, kidnapping, and torture, were documented in just three months of 2007. In 2006, a Botswanan judge who sentenced ten Zimbabwean prostitutes to a year in jail justified his decision by saying, "It was time the courts took serious action against these people who are responsible for the spread of HIV/AIDS."

American-funded evangelical Christian clergy—and often visiting American preachers themselves—led those witch hunts, urging their governments and followers to execute sex workers, lesbians, gay men, and trans women, as they were to blame them for those countries' AIDS epidemics. The inflaming of state-led and popular homophobia—in Kenya, Namibia, Zimbabwe, and Uganda, ruling dictators (some allied closely with successive US administrations) pushed for laws to execute gay men—was another signal lesson about the folly of involving right-wing Christians or other zealots in anything to do with AIDS or sexuality, as the Bush administration had done as a main plank of its AIDS policies.

❖

In India, too, the Bush campaign ignited a storm of violence against sex workers. Revealingly, the violence was concentrated in the half-dozen states where the Hindu supremacist parties held sway: in the BJP and Shiv Sena, the Bush administration had found truly receptive allies for its hypocritical and violent views about sex work.

Indeed, regarding all women, there was a vivid similarity between the views of the right-wing Christians allied to Bush and Hindu extremists: a core belief of both was that the proper role for women was to be faithful and submissive to patriarchal men and to forgo rights and autonomy, as men were their God-anointed protectors. The commonality in their views was ironic, as the Hindu supremacists vilified India's Christians, maintaining that Christianity and Islam were inherently violent religions that had been imposed on peaceable Hindus by marauding colonizers. Hindu-supremacist violence against Christians had escalated during the eight years of BJP national rule (ending in 2004 when the Congress Party was voted in), the savagery including the torching to death of the Australian missionary Graham Staines—who had long worked with leprosy sufferers in Orissa's villages—and his two young children.

In the view of the Hindu supremacists, Indian women had to embody Bharat Mata, "Mother India," the revanchist Hindu motherland they dreamed of establishing. They had to be goddesslike, to be chaste until marriage, and then to have dutiful sex with their husbands to create sons—daughters wouldn't do—who would become foot soldiers for the Hindutva ("Hinduness") cause.

There was no place in the misogynistic "motherland" for women who insisted that they had equal rights with men, particularly the right to refuse sex and childbearing or to have it freely or for money with individuals of their own choosing. It said everything that the two sets of women routinely targeted for violence by Hindu-supremacist men and women were those known to be sex workers or those they considered Westernized and immoral—which they equated with even merely wearing jeans or owning a cell phone or for wishing to marry someone of their own choosing.

The Hindu-supremacist groups had begun persecuting sex workers even before President Bush's campaign further fanned their animus. In 2002, in Nippani, a small town in Karnataka's Belgaum district, years of HIV prevention efforts by Sangram/VAMP were destroyed by the Shiv Sena Party and its vigilantes, who attacked the collective's local office, beat sex workers, and barred them from returning to their homes. The local Shiv Sena leader pronounced, "Under the garb of the HIV/AIDS prevention programme, these women are promoting prostitution." Far from defending the women, the local police chief refused to act on their complaint, calling them "bloody *veshya*s [whores] and not normal citizens," threatening to "strip all the sex workers in the public square and beat them black and blue" and to arrest them under antiprostitution laws.

With their views legitimized by President Bush, the Hindu-supremacist forces launched a sustained campaign against sex workers. (On matters relating to AIDS and sexuality, the BJP's leaders routinely looked to Bush—thus, Sushma Swaraj, minister of health and family welfare in the BJP federal government until 2004, had approvingly cited Bush's "ABC" model in insisting that India's AIDS efforts should move away from promoting condom use to advocating abstinence and faithfulness.) What unfolded was far more devastating than even the terrible abuses sex workers had suffered in the first decade of India's AIDS epidemic. While the earlier mass raids and imprisonment had been episodic, knee-jerk actions fueled by hysteria about the disease, the efforts this time appeared almost aimed at eradicating the women themselves, as if they were foul blots on Indian culture that had to be obliterated.

In late 2003, with the BJP still in power at the federal level, the Gujarat government of Narendra Modi invoked the national antitrafficking act and other laws to evict nearly seven hundred sex workers and their children from Surat's Chakla Bazar, even though the area had been home to sex workers for countless years. The following year the BJP government in Goa demolished the vast Baina slum and red-light area, which I had visited a decade earlier while with the World Bank. Bulldozers razed more than a thousand brick-and-tin shanties, leaving hundreds of sex workers and their children, as well as thousands of other migrant squatters who were not connected to sex work, homeless and defenseless in the midst of the ferocious monsoon storms.

The government then moved to deport the sex workers to their home states, even though many had lived in Baina for years and had no other home.

Baina, demolished

In Uttar Pradesh, the homes and workplaces of sex workers in cities such as Allahabad, Lucknow, and Meerut were torched or razed by Hindu extremists. Then there was the series of American abolitionist-led raids in 2005 and 2006 in the small towns of Maharashtra where Sangram/VAMP worked. That year, dance bars—featuring Bollywood-style *mujra*s by fully clad women whom the men could admire but not touch or proposition—were banned throughout Maharashtra for allegedly being a front for trafficking and prostitution. More than a hundred thousand women lost highly paid jobs, forcing many to turn to sex work—many of them went to Middle Eastern countries to sell sex, facing an even higher risk of abuse and exploitation. In 2007, in Karnataka's Channapatana, with a BJP government in the offing, goons and the police brutally attacked sex workers who had gathered to demonstrate peacefully against police brutality. In Bihar, ruled by the BJP-allied Janata Dal United, mobs attacked sex workers in Sitamarhi town and burned down 250 homes while the police stood by.

The conflagration would have been fiercer still were it not that the Congress Party and its allies controlled the federal government after national elections in 2004 as well as most state governments. For all their many failings—not simply rapacious corruption but also the outright criminality of some of its leaders—the Congress Party was immeasurably more progressive on every important front, and most certainly on the rights of women, than the Hindu-supremacist parties. Importantly, they also largely honored electoral democracy, the rule of law, and constitutional checks on executive power, in telling contrast to the Hindu-supremacist parties, which cynically employed mob violence and gang-style executions to subvert the judiciary, the press, human rights defenders, unions, and other legitimate forms of opposition. Tellingly, even as Congress Party minister Renuka Chowdhury was attempting to secure the draconian amendments to India's antiprostitution law that the Bush administration was pushing on the country, she had to do battle with progressive leaders within her own party who opposed those changes as being patently harmful to the rights and well-being of women who sold sex.

The National AIDS Control Organization of the Ministry of Health and Family Welfare was now headed by a committed bureaucrat with a specialization in public health, Kanuru Sujatha Rao (we had overlapped at Harvard), and had the backing of an unusually committed health and family welfare minister, Dr. Anbumani Ramadoss. NACO lambasted the amendments for the destructive impact they would have on HIV prevention efforts.

"The criminalization of clients would force both clients and sex workers underground, worsening the already high obstacles to promoting safer sex in the commercial sex trade," NACO stated in an interministerial memo. "Moreover, with fewer clients and diminishing earnings, sex workers would find it harder to insist on condom use, resulting in escalation of STIs and HIV."

And, crucially, the powerful Ministry of Home Affairs—with specific responsibility for the police and for enforcing criminal laws—stated that the amendments would worsen the confusion between trafficking and voluntary sex work, distracting attention and resources from aiding genuine victims of trafficking and abuse. The ministry candidly noted that the harshness of the amendments was likely to encourage low-ranking police to abuse sex workers even more brutally than they had so far. The cabinet could not ignore that advice, coming as it did from the most staunchly conservative of ministries.

The opposition to Chowdhury's position strengthened. In 2006, thousands of sex workers from across the country gathered in Delhi to protest outside Parliament. Chowdhury argued that her ministry, which was responsible for women and children's welfare, cared foremost about women's empowerment, but press and commentators noted acerbically that she was brushing off the explicitly stated concerns of the women who would be directly impacted by the amendments. AIDS service organizations and human rights groups warned that the police would now turn to harassing and blackmailing sex workers' clients, in addition to exploiting the sex workers themselves. This was India, they noted, with the Indian reality prevailing that the police abused and exploited everyone but the powerful, and the likely impact of the amendments had to be viewed in that context.

The fact that the sex workers had won support from such a wide set of groups underscored just how much the well-known achievements of the sex-work collectives in stemming HIV and improving the women's lives had influenced public understanding far beyond public health circles. Leading TV shows ran prime-time debates about whether sex work should be decriminalized. Newspapers featured detailed op-eds discussing the pros and cons of decriminalization and other policy measures.

Even the first published autobiography by an Indian sex worker was a runaway success. It was the work of fifty-year-old Nalini Jameela of Kerala, a barely literate mother of two, produced first in her native Malayalam in 2005 and then subsequently in English. Both editions had been bestsellers, making Jameela a household name. Jameela, who began to sell sex when her husband died and her factory job didn't pay enough to care for her children, was proud and unapologetic about her profession, saying "I have written this book for other sex workers. I wanted to talk about it to remove the stigma." She had lived successfully on her own terms, marrying twice more. With in-dependent-minded candor, Jameela said she would not have opposed her daughters—both of whom were now housewives—becoming sex workers if they had wanted to.

All this was testimony to the vigor of public discourse in India. The fact that most commentators were sympathetic to the women also testified that the pervasiveness of poverty led even well-off people to understand that marginalized or impoverished individuals had to make hard choices to fend for themselves and their families.

And contrary to the ignorance of the 1980s, when sex workers had first come to public attention because of the panic over AIDS, there was now a wealth of data and knowledge on Indian sex work condi-tions. The two decades in which sex work had been in the spotlight because of AIDS had led a range of researchers to produce thousands of papers and dozens of books on contemporary sex-work patterns in India. The Bill & Melinda Gates Foundation's $300 million HIV pre-vention effort in India, begun in 2003, systematically commissioned rigorous countrywide surveys as well as microresearch on sexual be-haviors to guide its planning and projects.

That research, undertaken by some of the world's leading public health and gender experts, studied everything from the diverse moti-vations that led women, trans women, and men to sell sex, the age of entry, and the number of partners and daily earnings, all the way to explaining the wide variation in sex-work patterns across India, as well as the striking new dynamic of high-end sex work in the booming cities by middle- and upper-class women and men. (I was taken aback to see that even mainstream newspapers were full of classified ads for massage parlors and "friendship clubs" that offered the services of both women and men—and a quick web search for "escorts" and "call girls" produced thousands of sites, ranging from independent one-woman operations to large agencies featuring every gender.) This rich empirical data meant that arguably more was now known about sex work in contemporary India than in any other comparable country. It was finally possible to reach conclusions based on hard evidence and an understanding of dynamic trends, rather than on ideology or imagination. All of that evidence contradicted the main arguments put forward for the amendments: namely, that India's sex workers were universally or largely victims of trafficking.

The net result of that opposition was that though Chowdhury repeatedly brought the amended bill to the union cabinet and Parliament for approval, the bill stalled, with parliamentarians urging Chowdhury to reconsider the two amendments to criminalize clients of sex workers and to allow for the lengthy imprisonment of sex workers. Whether Chowdhury would eventually prevail—perhaps because the Indian government's top leaders would be forced to act because of US pressure—or fail still hung in the balance.

❖

The fact that the destructive amendments being pushed by the Bush administration via Chowdhury had for years failed to be passed into law testified that India's democracy was robust enough to keep the worst of outcomes from being realized into public policy. But the impact on India's sex workers and their fight for justice was nonetheless disastrous. The first decade of the twenty-first century became an increasingly dangerous time for India's sex workers, instead of being an era of great progress as had seemed likely just a few years earlier.

Over everything hung the threat that the draconian amendments would one day be passed into law. The leading sex workers' collectives were constantly under threat of having to fight raids or campaigns accusing them of being traffickers, blatantly engineered by the Bush administration and its domestic prohibitionist allies. In addition to the United States' efforts in 2005 to tar Sangram's Meena Seshu as a "trafficker," in 2008 a number of US Republican senators wrote widely publicized statements accusing the Durbar's iconic founder, Dr. Smarajit Jana, globally respected for his public health and human rights work, of being a "sex trafficker." Sex-worker groups lost vital funds from USAID, derailing their efforts and worsening the myriad risks faced by sex workers. (It was a stroke of good fortune that the Bill & Melinda Gates Foundation's HIV prevention project covered those funding gaps in the states where the AIDS epidemic had reached its worst levels. Tellingly, the foundation invested in replicating and expanding exactly the model of mobilization, empowerment. and nonstigmatizing support that had been pioneered by the sex-worker collectives and that the Bush administration condemned.) In all the places where the Hindu supremacist parties were a strong force, sex workers lived in fear of violence, of being evicted from their homes, or of their entire neighborhoods being torn down.

Watching all that, I thought that if this was the scale of destruction that could be unleashed by the Bush administration in a country as large, democratic, and self-reliant as India, then it signaled how many times more destructive the impact was in the countless countries where the United States wielded even greater clout.

❖

I was not surprised that such destructive and wrongheaded policies would flow from President Bush and his right-wing backers. I expected no better of them; they represented the worst aspects of the United States, a mirror image of India's Hindu supremacists. But I was troubled to see a number of otherwise thoughtful Americans embracing the Bush administration's canards that conflated sex work and sex trafficking as well as backing his use of unilateral sanctions to bully India and other countries on that front. It was another depressing display of the tendency in American do-gooding abroad to, in fact, do worsened harm, a tendency that intensified as the US became the world's only superpower and was blinded by triumphalism and hubris.

The earliest of those figures, and the key, were *New York Times* columnist Nicholas Kristof and the feminist icon Gloria Steinem. They were soon joined by a constellation of Hollywood stars, including

Ashley Judd, Ashton Kutcher, and Meryl Streep, such business titans as Sheryl Sandberg, and billionaire donors such as Peter Buffett. They had an outsized impact in convincing many Americans and other Westerners—woefully unconversant with these complex matters—that sex work was indistinguishable from sex trafficking and child prostitution and that the only acceptable solution was to stamp out sex work.

To an outsider like me, it was bewildering that those avowed humanists would not be wary of joining a crusade dominated by some of the bitterest foes of women's sexual and reproductive rights as well as gay rights. As a case in point, the architect of both the destructive TVPA and the global prostitution gag rule was New Jersey's Republican congressman Chris Smith, an archenemy of *Roe v. Wade* and one of the harshest antigay voices, views driven by his fervent Catholic beliefs. Calling abortion "child slaughter," Smith fought to deny abortion except to victims of "forcible rape" and to prevent women from using birth control pills. In 1995, in that era of mass death among gay men, he cosponsored a bill, the entire text of which was the following sentence: "No Federal funds may be used directly or indirectly to promote, condone, accept, or celebrate homosexuality, lesbianism, or bisexuality." Yet, to my astonishment, Kristof wrote of Smith in his bestselling 2009 book *Half the Sky,* "He is a good man."

Kristof's efforts to draw attention to human trafficking, beginning in 2004 (by which time the Bush antiprostitution campaign was in full force), could have been a useful public service given his journalistic prominence. But it went dangerously awry because instead of disinterested analysis of the complex and still poorly understood realities of human trafficking—which spans coercion and deception of men, women, and children into forced labor or slaverylike practices within and between countries, including in agriculture, construction, factories, domestic work, criminal trade in human organs, and sexual exploitation—he took doctrinaire positions indistinguishable from those of the Bush administration, functioning as a zealous campaigner. Embarrassing disaster was bound to follow, and it did.

Thus, in Cambodia, from which Kristof filed several harrowing

New York Times reports of young girls brutalized in sex slavery, the bulk of them were later revealed to be cases of outright fraud. They were ordinary girls whom Kristof's antitrafficking partner, the Cambodian Somaly Mam, though she denied it, had allegedly recruited, carefully trained, and paid to lie about being sex slaves. In one of the goriest of Kristof's trafficking pieces, hyperbolically titled "If This Isn't Slavery, What Is?," Long Pross, a young Cambodian, recounted that she had been enslaved in a brothel at the age of thirteen and subjected to rapes, brutal abortions, daily electric shocks, and being "painfully stitched up" so that her "virginity" could be sold again and again. The litany of savagery was capped by Kristof's description of how Pross's right eye had been gouged out by an angry pimp, soon growing "infected and monstrous, spraying blood and pus on customers." Pross went on to repeat her gory story on *The Oprah Winfrey Show* and the PBS documentary version of *Half the Sky*.

The truth, revealed by a meticulous 2014 *Newsweek* investigation, was that the teenager had never been in a brothel and had lost her eye in a childhood operation due to a tumor, facts corroborated by her eye surgeon and family. The *Newsweek* investigation reported that the slew of deceits by Mam included her own backstory, laid out poignantly in her 2005 memoir, *The Road of Lost Innocence*. A "heroine from the brothels," Kristof called Mam—and his glowing foreword to the book had helped it become an international bestseller, published in more than a dozen languages.

In it, Mam wrote that as a young orphan she had been sold into a brothel, where she was imprisoned in a cage, raped, and tortured. In actuality, *Newsweek* reported, Mam had led a conventional rural childhood with her middle-class parents, later training to be a teacher. And Mam's heartbreaking claim that, in retaliation for her work, traffickers had kidnapped her fourteen-year-old daughter in 2006, videotaped her being gang-raped, and locked her up in a brothel—all of which Kristof had catalogued in his *New York Times* column—was repudiated by the girl's father and other sources, who confirmed that she had eloped with her boyfriend.

While such massive journalistic failures would have derailed the career of most journalists or writers, Kristof is the media equivalent of JPMorgan Chase, "too big" to suffer. He got off with the weakest mea culpa. He wrote plaintively that he wished he had never met Mam. She had "hoodwinked" him. The developing world presents unique journalistic challenges because "ages, names and histories are sometimes elastic," he now asserted, a claim that sat oddly with his continuing punditry on those nations. Rather than revisit his views, Kristof preachily urged his readers to not let Mam's lies—"this is about more than one woman," he argued—undermine the noble cause of fighting sex slavery.

Kristof should have treaded even more carefully in India than in Cambodia, given the complexities posed by its billion-plus population, equal to writing about the populace of North America and the European Union combined. But instead, as in Cambodia, he sallied forth with a catalogue of breathtakingly confident generalizations—with a shocking lack of supporting data or historical context and, resoundingly incorrectly.

Thus he wrote in his *New York Times* blog in 2007 that although in other developing countries "many women genuinely choose to be prostitutes because of economic pressures or opportunities . . . in India, I have yet to find a single woman who made that choice—every single one of them first entered after being forced by a trafficker, her parents, or her husband." In a related column, sensationally titled "The 21st-Century Slave Trade," he charged, "The brothels of India are the slave plantations of the 21st century." About a woman whom the controversial prohibitionist group Apne Aap Women Worldwide had reportedly rescued from a brothel, Kristof wrote, "Meena's owners also wanted to breed her, as is common in Indian brothels. One purpose is to have boys to be laborers and girls to be prostitutes, and a second is to have hostages to force the mother to cooperate." Some years later, he pronounced, "India probably has more modern slaves than any country in the world. It has millions of women and girls in its brothels, often held captive for their first few years until they grow resigned to their fate."

Even as an outspoken critic of India's myriad brutalities and failures, I couldn't recognize the country Kristof was writing about. Was this India or an imaginary heart of darkness awash in American-style chattel slavery? His rants reminded me of an elite American of an earlier generation, Katherine Mayo, a prominent white supremacist and imperialist, whose 1927 book *Mother India* had variously castigated Indians for inhumane treatment of women, Dalits, and animals, the men's "sex-ridden" character—responsible for everything from rampant homosexuality to rape and prostitution, she charged—and not least the moral flaws of Indians who dared demand freedom from "benevolent" Britain. Mahatma Gandhi had tellingly called it "the report of a drain-inspector."

Revealingly, nowhere in his writing did Kristof refer to the wealth of empirical knowledge about contemporary sex-work patterns in India undertaken by internationally respected researchers and published in leading peer-reviewed journals. Those studies showed an entirely different picture from Kristof's speculative claims. The average age of entry into sex work was between eighteen and twenty-one. The overwhelming majority of women selling sex had turned to it out of a mix of financial need, limited choices, and the far higher earnings offered, typically after they had worked as manual laborers or in other poorly paid jobs. A smaller number, coming from diverse class backgrounds, said they had freely chosen it for being lucrative. Trafficking and "hereditary prostitution" were reported by a small percentage of women. Only a tiny proportion of sex work took place in brothels, which were by now rare in most parts of the country Omitting such empirical information prevented Kristof from being a truthful observer. If he had written the same way about domestic US issues, not referring to available data and scholarship, he would have been excoriated for dealing in Kellyanne Conway–style "alternative facts."

Gloria Steinem's opposition to sex work dated back to the 1980s, when she had led a major movement within American feminism condemning pornography and prostitution as the most extreme manifestations of male exploitation, amounting to "commercial rape." "Prostitution involves body invasion and so it is not like any other work," she wrote. "So how can you call it sex work? Prostitution is the only word you should use."

From all that I had seen, read, and studied over the decades regarding sex work by women, men, and trans women, I disagreed with Steinem's absolutist position. It denied a wealth of empirical evidence as well as the expressed views and decisions of adults regarding their best interests within the particular circumstances they faced or even how they wished to live their lives. Opponents of reproductive rights have long employed similar strategies against women, and homophobes against gays and transgenders.

Tellingly, in the late 1990s, Western feminist prohibitionists allied with evangelical groups in an effort to erase the traditional legal distinction between forced and voluntary prostitution by cracking down on all of it as sex trafficking and "modern-day slavery," which would expand and stiffen criminal punishment. In contrast, developing-country antitrafficking feminists and human rights campaigners, such as the numerous nongovernmental groups that established the Global Alliance Against Traffic in Women in 1994, have steadily emphasized the need for decriminalizing sex work and other aspects of sex workers' rights so as not to stigmatize or suppress sex work.

While Steinem and other feminist prohibitionists have recently claimed that they are proponents of the so-called Nordic model—clients are punished with jail terms and monetary fines, and sex workers are, at least in theory, not overtly punished—they have actually unreservedly allied with efforts that promote the US model (including the plethora of worldwide efforts driven by the US government), in which both clients and sex workers themselves face jail terms. Knowing full well her own government's unflinching insistence on criminalizing sex workers both domestically and abroad, Steinem bizarrely claimed, in a 2016 letter in the *New York Times*, "There is no one this side of the Taliban who isn't trying to get rid of archaic laws that arrest and imprison prostituted people." Distant barbarians are always convenient whipping boys.

Nor have feminist prohibitionists done anything noteworthy to combat the jail terms and other punishments inflicted each year on tens of thousands of American women, trans women, and men convicted of selling sex, an omission so glaring that it can only be interpreted as being driven by condemnation of those individuals. This spotlights the tense and even antagonistic relationship between some Western feminists and sex workers that has persisted across eras and continents, reflecting an invidious undercurrent in feminism about "decent" versus "indecent" women.

I was struck, too, by how the inflammatory language used by Steinem and other prohibitionists was so similar to the tactics employed by antiabortionists. Steinem's description of sex work as "commercial rape" was cut from the same cloth as Congressman Chris Smith calling abortion "child slaughter." In no other part of the world that I knew well—whether Western Europe or India (at least until recently)—were such rabid denunciations and staking out of fanatical positions considered an acceptable part of public debate as in the United States.

But what troubled me most was that Steinem would insist that a position that she had reached vis-à-vis women in Western industrialized countries represented the only possible solution in a setting as different as India or other developing countries. Those worlds were simply not comparable. Most Indians, men and women alike, still struggled to survive against terrible deprivation and were battered by one economic dislocation after another as the country was opened up to globalization. India was not going to become the United States—let alone a Nordic welfare state—anytime soon, perhaps not even in fifty years. Surely Steinem's focus—like mine—should unwaveringly be on the best interests of sex workers in the here and now, not in an imaginary utopian India?

Instead, on a visit to India, Steinem railed at the sex-work collectives—all they had "done is to enhance the ability of the sex industry to attract millions of dollars from the Gates Foundation for the distri-bution on [*sic*] condoms," she charged, and "created a big new source of income for brothel owners, pimps and traffickers who are called 'peer educators.'" In rubbishing the explicit choices and demands of the hundreds of thousands of impoverished women running these col-lectives, Steinem showed that "imperial feminism" still flourished long after the ending of the British Raj.

I wondered to myself what explained the chasm between the views of Steinem and those of other American feminists whom I admired, particularly those who placed debates about sex work within a broader context of social injustice and the harsh actual conditions prevailing in much of the world. "The stigma tradition-ally attached to prostitution is based on a collage of beliefs most of which are not rationally defensible, and which should be especially vehemently rejected by feminists," the University of Chicago philos-opher Martha Nussbaum wrote. ". . . [T]he correct response to this problem seems to be . . . not to rule off limits an option that may be the only livelihood for many poor women and to further stigma-tize women who already make their living this way." (At another point, Nussbaum commented sharply, "The idea that we ought to penalize women with few choices by removing one of the ones they do have is grotesque, the unmistakable fruit of the all-too-American thought that women who choose to have sex with many men are tainted vile things who must be punished.") Noting that it is a "dead end to consider prostitution in isolation from other realities of working life," she urged feminists to "talk more about getting loans, learning to read, and so forth if they want to be rel-evant to the choices that are actually faced by working women, and to the programs that are actually doing a lot to improve such women's options."

Doubtless one factor is that Steinem, Kristof, and other celebrity sex-work prohibitionists avoided grappling with any of the realities of sex work in low-income countries that challenged their views. They instead valorized local prohibitionists as authoritative interlocutors, even though those figures merely played to their preconceived views in a self-serving, symbiotic relationship. In Cambodia, that role was played by Somaly Mam, and in India it was and continues to be played by Ruchira Gupta, a former journalist who, in 2002, founded the prohibitionist group Apne Aap Women Worldwide. With Kristof and Steinem's backing, Gupta, who has lived largely in the United States for the past twenty-plus years, was soon feted by exactly the same circles as those who were hero-worshipping Somaly Mam—ranging from the Bush administration and evangelical groups to the Clinton Global Initiative and the Buffett-financed NoVo Foundation.

Gupta, like Mam, sensationalizes the scale of sex trafficking. In a 2009 *Wall Street Journal* op-ed, Gupta claimed that in India "the average age for beginning sex work is between 9 and 10." (Mam, in a similar vein, thereafter claimed that girls as young as three were being sold in Cambodia's brothels, an accusation that even other hard-line prohibitionist groups criticized her for.) I emailed Gupta repeatedly to ask for the source and robustness of that statistic, but neither she nor her colleagues ever replied. Still, Steinem and others repeated the canard endlessly. A similar canard that the average age of entry into sex work in the United States is "between twelve and thirteen" continues to be aired by them, though it has been debunked by leading scholars.

Among the other dubious claims made by Gupta are that in the industrialized countries where sex work is either decriminalized or legalized, the sex workers' "children are held hostage so that they will do different kinds of sex with the customers rather than just the regular," and "the sex industry has been able to get away with bringing in little girls with impunity . . . [I]n front is a legal documented forty-year-old person and behind, if you give a little bit more of extra money, you get the little girl at the back." It speaks volumes that, none of the claims made about the gargantuan scale of sex trafficking into the United States has withstood scrutiny—in practice, US officials have year after year found just a few hundred cases of trafficking into the country, and those mainly for agricultural labor, not

the fifty thousand to one hundred thousand sex-trafficking victims that the CIA and Justice Department hyperbolically projected when congressman Chris Smith and other prohibitionists were ramming through the 2000 Trafficking Victims Protection Act. (This inconvenient counterfact didn't stop Kristof from claiming in a 2015 *New York Times* column that "some 100,000 minors are trafficked into the sex trade each year in America.") The prohibitionists' reliance on sensationalistic claims—much like their use of inflamed language and angry vituperation against critics—inescapably suggests that they know their arguments are hollow and will not prevail in an honest, fact-checked debate.

Much as with Mam, the celebrities invested in Gupta have not seemed to ask questions about the quality and impact of her work, though Gupta has been dogged by controversy. In 2010, two Harvard undergraduates, Niharika S. Jain and Tara Suri, who had raised $20,000 for Gupta's Apne Aap group—inspired by Kristof's adulatory praise for her—and then spent several weeks volunteering at a Delhi site where Gupta had long promised to deliver "holistic income generation programmes, education for children and . . . a residential hostel for the children to prevent trafficking and second generation prostitution," wrote an excoriating article in the *Harvard Crimson*, saying that "Apne Aap had nearly no presence there" and that "the women are completely disillusioned and continue to work in the sex trade." Writing that they were "devastated by this farce of an initiative," they insisted that Gupta return the funds they had raised.

Though Gupta's lawyer threatened to sue the *Harvard Crimson* for publishing an "article replete with false, defamatory statements," even sharper criticisms surfaced just three years later when a group of former American and European interns and Indian staff members of Apne Aap wrote to Apne Aap's board and major donors criticizing Gupta's leadership of the organization.

The exhaustive seven-page report from the interns was a barrage of criticisms—all the more poignant because it came from individuals

who shared Gupta's prohibitionist views. Reiterating the concerns of the Harvard undergraduates, the former interns pointed to the "large gap we saw between AAWW's vision of providing prostituted women with alternative livelihoods and its actual operations," accusing Gupta and the organization of "inflated" and "highly misleading" claims about the numbers of beneficiaries.

Their criticisms also focused on "top-down mispresentation" and exploitation in Apne Aap's public relations strategy. At an event in Delhi, girls from a community where Apne Aap works were presented as "inter-generationally prostituted girls, wherein this was not the case," they noted, calling it "another PR tactic in very poor taste as it completely exploited the girls for their unawareness and vulnerability." And Apne Aap's portrayal of entire neighborhoods as "red-light districts," when "intergenerational prostitution" is in fact limited to only some of those households, had angered these communities, leading to several girls and women being beaten by their families and a damaging rupture with the organization's field staff. Criticizing Apne Aap for claiming to have closed down dozens of brothels, the interns noted that while "the term 'brothel' connotes a large house with many prostituted women," these "are home-based brothels in Bihar with perhaps one prostituted woman per brothel."

Gupta dismissed the Harvard undergraduates and the interns as being young and inexperienced. But key aspects of their assessment were borne out by one of India's leading public health and gender experts, Dr. Ravi Verma, the Asia regional director of the International Center for Research on Women (ICRW), who visited Apne Aap's longest-running project site in Bihar, at Gupta's invitation, in the very same year as the Harvard students. Verma told me he was dismayed by what he had seen. On the first day of his visit, several of the women castigated Gupta for misrepresenting them as being "hereditary prostitutes" when they were landless agricultural laborers and had been lured to the project by Gupta's promises of government-provided housing. Another pleaded piteously with Gupta to be allowed to see

her young daughter, whom Gupta had placed years earlier in a boarding school, barring the mother from visits. Verma said he saw no evidence that even the women who sold sex were controlled by others, as Gupta claimed and Kristof had vividly reported from the area—rather, as is commonly the pattern in rural India, selling sex was one of several things the women did to earn for their families. He told me acerbically that Gupta's work is "entirely focused on catering to international donors."

In the wake of the protest letters by the former interns and staff, it emerged that Gupta, in true *Lords of Poverty* excess, had spent hundreds of thousands of dollars on the rent for Apne Aap's Delhi office in the city's most exclusive area, as well as an upscale guesthouse. Not only is this sum a staggering fortune in India, if it had been merely invested in mutual funds—returns on which reach 15 percent annually in India—that alone would have ensured that a great number of the women and girls Gupta claims to protect could have been economically independent, with no need for the further infusions of hundreds of thousands of dollars that Gupta has sought out and received. (After a 2016 *New York Times Magazine* article reported on these expenses, Apne Aap barred access to financial reports on its global website—while continuing to actively solicit donations—a practice that I have never seen elsewhere in all my decades of work in development.)

Kristof, Steinem, Ashley Judd, and other Western celebrity prohibitionists turned an equally blind eye to whether Gupta's policy positions were substantiated and meritorious. Indeed, more often than not they held her up as the sole voice of authoritative advice on India, rather than carefully canvassing insights from a range of expert and local sources. That invariably resulted in their urging policy approaches that were outlandish and destructive and helped neither sex workers nor genuine victims of sex trafficking.

Thus Kristof urged that India utilize sweeping police raids in red-light areas, saying that raids had caused a major decline in the fortunes of Mumbai's criminal-controlled central red-light areas. Gupta appeared to be his sole source of information. But the truth is that the decline in sex work in these localities has been driven by a constellation of systemic factors, most of all intense gentrification pressures in an area that commands some of the world's highest real estate prices as well as the dispersal of the blue-collar clientele to far-flung neighborhoods as the area's textile mills and other industries closed or relocated. And in urging expanded raids, Kristof seemed to be unaware of the advice of leading human rights experts, including the UN's Special Rapporteur on Violence Against Women, who have repeatedly condemned indiscriminate raids for intensifying police brutality against sex workers, sanctioning invasive medical examinations and enforced incarceration of sex workers, and other grave human rights abuses.

Another of Gupta's main policy recommendations, modeled on laws prevailing in several US states, is that clients of sex workers—even when there is no evidence of trafficking—be punished with up to five years of rigorous imprisonment, many times the length sought by the Ministry of Women & Child Development in the contested amendments to the antiprostitution law, a surefire recipe for arming the notoriously corrupt police with a potent tool for targeting impoverished and powerless men. Though India's criminal justice system does not come close to the United States' for injustice and brutality, it is a travesty nonetheless, which should have held Gupta back from urging laws that would multiply human rights abuses and set India on the path to being a prison state like the US.

For countless reasons, I had long disliked the mainstream of American do-gooding. There were the obscenely wasteful galas. There was the know-it-all smugness and self-congratulatory PR of the celebrities, "experts," and philanthropists. There was the peculiar inability to think of low-income countries in conventional terms, as societies much like the US, with similar, chronic challenges that needed to be addressed by political, economic and social change. There was invariably instead the caricatured portrayal of these nations as overpopulated, malarial, failed states teeming with piteous women and children exploited by fiendish men and evil rulers. There was the inexplicable myopia on display that though the do-gooders had visibly failed in remedying the US's gargantuan domestic injustices they could solve intractable problems in remote countries they barely understood. There was their imperialistic habit of foisting American notions on other societies, however obscurantist and damaging these views. And running through all this was the do-gooders' blindness to their own and their country's complicity in creating and perpetuating the world's miseries, the causes ranging all the way from the US' ingrained trigger-happy militarism and consumerist entitlement to the propulsive rise of predatory capitalism.

Just as off-putting was the vacuous faith in American exceptionalism that propelled Nicholas Kristof and many others—in such depressing contrast to the perceptive worldview of earlier American thinkers from James Baldwin to Howard Zinn, who saw that the US was so often on the wrong side of justice and history. Despite the US' record of failure and harm at home and abroad today's elite do-gooders somehow still believed that the United States had a unique commitment to advancing social justice and that progress seen anywhere in developing countries was somehow owed to the example or magnanimity of the United States. The "White-Savior Industrial Complex," the Nigerian American writer Teju Cole called this juggernaut.

Watching the collective damage being done by Kristof, Steinem, and other celebrity foes of sex workers' rights intensified my revulsion. It was one thing for President Bush, Congressman Smith, Christian zealots, and neocons to insist that the United States play global moral policeman; it was quite another for individuals who imagined themselves to be feminists and humanists to help lead the shambolic, bullying crusade.

TWENTY-THREE

WORDS LIKE FREEDOM

Once the construction of my father's home in the Nilgiris was in full swing, I moved to Goa. It was early in 2008. Just over half a year had passed since I had left Geneva.

One of my lifelong dreams had been to live right by the sea, and I rented a spacious sea-facing home in a quiet enclave on the outskirts of Panjim. From the veranda, it was just a hundred meters down to the Arabian Sea. At sunset, the calm waters turned roseate and the tugboats became inky spots against the orange sun. When the monsoon set in some months later, the pouring rain and pounding breakers seemed to merge, so that I felt, thrillingly, that I was living on some untamed tropical island alone with faithful Lorca.

I unpacked my paintings and books from Geneva. I had live-in help in Shanta Kumar, a Nepalese waiter at a Goa hotel whom I had become friends with many years back and who now joined me as a jack-of-all-trades, from cooking and handling practical matters to caring for Lorca when I was away on my long research trips. Shanta knew I was gay and paid it no heed; I didn't inquire about his sexuality or off-hours life, knowing only that his wife and young children lived with his parents in Nepal.

That full life, full of novelty but comfortingly full of constants, too, was precisely what I needed to begin to heal from my grief about losing Arndt and my once joyous life in Geneva. Slowly, I began to look ahead rather than backward.

✤

Once again, I was wonder-struck at seeing how life for well-off and upwardly mobile gay women and men, at least in the half-dozen major cities, had been transformed in the near decade I had been away. It was an entirely different world from 1986, when I had first returned to India. I sometimes had to shake myself to remember that this was indeed the same country that I had known all my life.

Nothing summed up those changes as vividly for me as the fact that in my first months back, my friends set me up with nearly a dozen men in the various cities I was traveling to. I had never known such a cornucopia of matchmaking, not even in New York City. It was so very different from 1986, when my Bombay friends had not known of one gay man that they could introduce me to.

And though nothing romantic came of those introductions—leading only to friendships, in good part because I was still too raw from the breakup with Arndt—they showed me how many out gay men and women there now were in the major cities. They led full lives. They had dealt with the inevitable difficulties of coming out to their families. They knew large numbers of other gay men and women of their own background. Some were in relationships. They didn't commonly face homophobia in their social circles. If they worked in the creative arts, they were usually out to their colleagues; so were some of those in the media or who worked with multinationals. They were discreet around their homes and neighborhoods without quite hiding themselves.

Every day there seemed to be a landmark new advance in those globalized urban enclaves. *Time Out Delhi* ran listings of LGBT-themed events, while Mumbai's edition went further still, with a regular column about LGBT life and issues. Gay support groups ran help lines and weekly support meetings—and hosted sold-out parties. A handful of bars had weekend gay nights, advertised as "private" parties to hide them from the police or censorious groups. Online dating and sex sites, from Planet Romeo to Grindr, were bursting with countless profiles of gay men, many of them showing full-face shots.

Annual gay pride marches began in city after city, the hundreds of marchers including gay men, women, trans women, and even one or two trans men; many wore carnival masks, but many others publicly announced their orientation. They were joined not only by their friends and families but also by women's and human rights groups and even by trade unions.

A stream of English-language books with gay, lesbian, and queer themes appeared each year, published both by major mainstream imprints and by feminist and human rights presses, spanning the gamut from novels to scholarly works. A profusion of groups and think tanks worked on LGBT issues and rights; some of them were as heterodox as the most radical queer groups in New York City. Leading TV shows held debates on LGBT rights, with moderators and audiences invariably in favor not just of decriminalization but also of equal rights in marriage, inheritance, and other areas. To my astonishment, LGBTQ university campus groups had begun to spring up.

A Tamil-language TV channel, with a viewership of 64 million, began a talk show hosted by a trans woman, Rose, a poised twenty-eight-year-old former website designer who covered everything from sex to divorce and sexual harassment. At a Goa multiplex, friends and I watched the Bollywood rom-com *Dostana—Bromance*—in which two young men, played by A-list stars, pretend to be gay so that they can share an apartment with a pretty woman they are both attracted to. Every one of us was struck by how the audience (which included parents with children of all ages) was caught up in the story, laughing at the flirtation between the men and whistling loudly when they kissed on the lips; it spoke volumes that the movie was one of the year's largest box-office earners.

Even outside the major cities and the relatively small numbers of Westernized, globe-trotting individuals, I saw astonishing evidence of how comfortable people I met socially or professionally now were with matters of same-sex orientation. This held true whatever their political leanings—thus, even among people who would not consider themselves either politically or socially liberal. Almost without exception, no one ever remarked on my orientation, even though it was well known. I noticed that they treated it, correctly, as a matter without bearing on our particular interactions. In the rare cases that anyone broached the topic, it was only in a sympathetic spirit, to learn more about the difficulties I or the others they knew had faced. Others spontaneously embraced the fact of my orientation. One of my most precious recollections is of my father's immediate neighbors in the Nilgiris, a couple a few years younger than I, who told me that they were happy that I had moved there, as their teenage children would now have a real role model in case they were gay.

Even the few signs of bigotry I spotted outside the Westernized enclaves now seemed to rapidly resolve themselves, almost as though they were the last gasps of habit. Thus, in 2006, Manvendra Singh Gohil, the forty-year-old scion of the former maharaja of Rajpipla in conservative Gujarat, was disowned by his parents after he came out publicly. His mother threatened legal proceedings against anyone who referred to him as her son. Local protesters made a bonfire of Manvendra's photographs and jeered him when he appeared in public. Even so, the times had changed so enormously that Manvendra's father soon reconciled with him, and Manvendra became a LGBT activist, appearing on *The Oprah Winfrey Show* and establishing a local AIDS prevention charity for gay men and trans women.

All that convinced me that what I had long thought but never been certain of was indeed true: that there was a strong element of easygoing tolerance and even nonjudgmental acceptance in Indian culture regarding many matters, which emerged readily when people had reason to think through any of the issues, a paradoxical counterpoint to the divisions of caste, class, gender, and religion. Correspondingly, I realized, outside particularly oppressive settings, bigotry did not spread readily unless it was consciously fueled by propaganda, as in the recent efforts of the violence-prone Hindu-supremacist groups to demonize gays or emancipated women or their long-standing victimization of India's Christians and Muslims.

⊹

Even outside the relatively small numbers of the urban upper and middle classes, there were striking changes under way in the lives of gay men and trans women from lower-income and impoverished backgrounds, sometimes even in far-flung small towns. That had not been visible less than a decade back when I was researching my book on AIDS. At that point, the prospects were promising for women sex workers but not for gay men and trans women. But now, I found, the opposite held true: the cause of sex workers was almost defeated, while the emancipation of gay men and transgender individuals was advancing.

That turnaround held an indelible lesson for me about the power of class. It was very clear that because rights relating to sexual orientation and gender identity mattered personally to well-off individuals in India and around the world, that cause had an inexorable staying power that tragically did not exist for sex workers, however just their cause and however clear the steps that would dramatically improve their situation. In contrast, people power, as in the powerful mobilization of sex workers that had happened in India, was not sufficient to guarantee changes in and of itself—especially because of the risk that groups of powerful people would oppose those changes for any number of motivations, as had so vividly happened in the case of sex workers with the Bush administration, Western prohibitionists, and conservative Indians themselves.

I came to understand the power of those changes through Mahavir, a gay sex worker in Sangli, a small agricultural town 250 miles southeast of Mumbai. By now, twenty-five years from the time I had first set out into villages and slums, I had seen how even the most brutally op-pressed individuals—once given the slightest cause for hope—would begin to fight fiercely for their freedom, even though to any outsider it would seem that their chances remained hopeless and their efforts were foolhardy and even irrational. I had realized that they would fight and sacrifice even if it was patently impossible to improve their material circumstances: what they were fighting for, first and foremost, was to free themselves psychologically—to feel less shame and fear and more self-respect themselves and to force their oppressors to show them some grudging respect or even merely wariness. Mahavir showed me those truths in ways that I was never to forget.

There was so much about Mahavir's life in Sangli that could have destroyed his capacity for hope.

The poverty he had grown up in would have been reason enough. His parents' home was the poorest of the hutlike structures in an im-poverished area, the brick-and-tin structure seemingly on the verge of disintegrating. There were just two small rooms, virtually bare of possessions.

His parents were probably my age, no more than in their mid-to late forties, but both looked aged in a way that is commonplace among the impoverished in India. Mahavir, too, looked many years older than twenty-nine, his frame small and bony, the delicacy of his facial features nearly obliterated by gauntness.

Ever since Mahavir could remember, the history of his family had been one disaster after another. He had been a toddler when his father, an alcohol addict, had been thrown out of his job as a supervisor at the adjacent factory, which manufactured cement drains. His father had soon squandered the family's meager savings on *matka*, a popular form of gambling. It was only the endless hours that his mother had worked as a housemaid that had saved Mahavir and his sister, some years younger than he, from begging or starvation. They had gone hungry routinely, he told me.

And Mahavir had had his own particular source of childhood tor-ment: he was a "girly-boy." "When I was seven years old, I first felt something is lacking in me," he said. "I used to play with small girls and wanted to help around the house. I'd be teased at school, so I'd often stay at home."

By his teens, Mahavir's family faced destitution, with his mother permanently incapacitated by a life-threatening seizure. Mahavir dropped out of school and begun to work as a cook, trying desperately to provide for his parents and sister—so that they had enough to eat, so that his sister could continue in school, so that his mother had the medicines she needed.

"But then, later, I started doing *dhandha*," said Mahavir. *Dhandha* literally means "business" but in Hindi-speaking areas is a code for selling sex. "I still do this. Every night I have two or three customers. I charge them fifty or a hundred rupees each. If I spend the full night with a customer, I charge much more, five hundred or even a thousand." The earnings were many times greater than he could ever make as a cook or in any other job within his reach. It was only that trade, he said, that ensured he could look after his parents, his sister, and himself.

Life as a gay man in small-town India would have itself been sufficient cause for despair. I had seen enough of it to know how soul-destroying it was—a lifelong sentence of secrecy and loneliness, of being trapped in a loveless marriage, settling for furtive sex instead of love and intimacy, and fearing violence, blackmail, and ostracism at every turn. Every risk was magnified for feminine gay men like Mahavir, rather than straight-acting men who could hide their orientation and claim that they had sex with men or trans women because women were unavailable. I saw that bleakness afresh in the days I spent with Mahavir.

He took me to all the places that amounted to life in Sangli for gay men. There was the busy area around the train and central bus station, the crowds providing anonymity and cover to strike up a flirtation. There was the park as well as the riverfront along the Krishna, both with dark groves and corners to have sex in. There was the Shivaji Sports Stadium, where college boys stayed on to find sex. There was the Padma Truck Rest Stop, unending, dusty, tire-worn, diesel-choked fields with countless long-distance trucks pulling in and out for a few hours of rest, the truckers longing for alcohol, food, and sex after risking their lives on India's lethal roads.

It said everything about the lack of alternatives that just in this small town there were so many cruising spots, with dozens of men searching for sex in each place. From what I saw on the ground and Mahavir's estimates, several hundred men were seeking out other men or trans women for sex and love every night in Sangli. And they were of every income level, background, and age—owners of businesses, middle-class professionals and officials, college students, truckers, and laborers—their differences obliterated by desire and loneliness.

Those furtive, dangerous meeting places that came to life only in the dark had long been the only places in Sangli for gay men or trans women to find some faint sense of community with others like them. "I first came to these places with a friend," Mahavir told me. "I felt much better knowing there were so many others like me. We had sex, of course, but even more these were places to meet others and to become friends, almost like community clubs."

All that was shadowed by the constant threat of exposure, blackmail, and persecution, as well as violence, sexual and otherwise. "We could never meet the eyes of anyone speaking to us," Mahavir told me. "When local boys spoke to us, we'd lower our eyes and walk on."

Then there was the impunity with which the police and thugs could act against men found out to be homosexual, particularly feminine *kothi* men such as Mahavir. "The police and the *goondas* were the worst problem," Mahavir told me in anger. "They have thrashed us, stripped us, and paraded us naked. They'd come at night, not alone but in a group of four or five and have sex with us. They'd do this to all the *kothis*. In fact, there was one policeman who demanded free sex from me regularly at two a.m., when he got off duty."

Bitterly, he said, "We *kothis* are always scared of society because we feel there is something inferior in us, something weak or bad. But when we see such behavior from heterosexuals, we feel there is something inferior in them, too, that you forcibly demand sex from us, that you don't care about injustices that are done to us, that you are so full of hate for us!"

Then there was the threat of AIDS, present even before Mahavir became sexually active. It was more serious in this area of India than in almost any other.

He had started to lose friends to the disease in 2000, and about "fourteen or fifteen close friends" had died, he said. "One friend who had HIV hung himself at home." Mahavir had started out selling sex without protection, and two of the friends who had died had been his sexual partners. Mahavir had gone for his first HIV test in 2007. He felt like fainting at the thought of the test results. "I thought to myself that I should just not go back to the testing center at the hospital to collect the report! When I tested HIV-negative, I was very happy. But I have always felt so bad that I couldn't save the others."

In spite of all the bleakness that Mahavir recounted, I was buoyed by his palpable sense of self-worth, even of happiness and fulfillment. No less remarkable, I saw that Mahavir had become a key figure in gradually transforming life for other gay men and trans women in Sangli and its environs. All those changes, personal as well as larger, Mahavir said he owed to Muskaan, a support group for Sangli's gay men and trans women started in 1999 by the activist Meena Seshu, the founder of the HIV prevention organization Sangram and the sex workers' collective VAMP. *Muskaan* means "cheerfulness," and the support group was the one subject that Mahavir spoke of with excitement rather than his characteristic watchful reserve.

Years back, a chance meeting at a cruising area with a Sangram staffer—who was estimating the number of gay and bisexual men and trans women in the town—led Mahavir to Muskaan. During his first visit to the nascent group, a condom demonstration was under way. "It felt very dirty!" he said with a laugh. "I didn't know about AIDS then or what a condom was or how to use one." In those early years, the group had no more than a dozen members. They met every Saturday to spend time together, but just that in itself was "a big help psychologically to all of us," Mahavir recalled. "If someone wanted to wear a sari and dance, he could—we could do whatever we couldn't do outside. Until then, all of us were so nervous and fearful."

Mahavir joined the group as a peer educator and field coordinator. There was no looking back. Within a decade, Muskaan had seven hundred registered members, seventeen staffers, and a drop-in counseling center and covered not just Sangli but the neighboring districts as well. The group's presence had led to major changes in the lives of local gay men as well as trans women, Mahavir said. The foundational changes began with confronting the prejudice and violence they had faced so far. "Earlier, if we went to the Civil Hospital for any problem, it was a real problem. The doctor would call four or five other staff and announce, 'Look at these homosexuals. They have anal sex, and then look what has happened to them!' We used to weep in anger and shame, but there was nothing we could do then. There were many of us who even died, usually of AIDS but sometimes of suicide, rather than go to the hospital and be humiliated. But now we have changed so much that we now go boldly to the Civil Hospital! If any of our members are ever rudely treated there, we go to help them out."

The most important change, he said, was in tackling abuse by police and thugs. "Us *kothi*s and others are scared because we don't live together in a group. Not like the women sex workers, who live together and now that VAMP has given them courage, if there is a problem, they feel they are in it all together. But among *kothi*s, at least earlier, if the policeman or a *goonda* was thrashing me, the others wouldn't intervene, they would watch from afar. But now that we have come together because of Muskaan, we fight back against anyone, whether it is the police or thugs!"

He told me, with obvious relish, of incident after incident that showed how far-reaching their revolt has been.

"Recently, one of my colleagues and I were waiting at the bus stop, on our way to outreach work, when two thugs began to fight with us. They were drunk and insisted that we have sex with them. We refused to go. They were rickshaw drivers, and they drove their rickshaw into us! When we fell down, they began to thrash us. We fought back. When the police came, I told them what had happened, that these men are harassing and beating us, that I want to file a written complaint so that they will be arrested. The policeman said, 'No, whatever it is, just settle it here peacefully.' I said, 'No, I insist on a written, official complaint.' So, for the first time, the police were forced to write a complaint, and the rickshaw drivers were arrested and kept in the jail for three days. It gave courage to others not to be silent, either! I've been working with Muskaan for years, so I must take the first step, no?

"Another time, when some of us *kothis* were beaten by the police, all the VAMP women came to support us at the police station. That really worried the police." From Mahavir's frequent, admiring references to VAMP, it is clear that the sister collective of women sex workers is a model of solidarity and collective action that the area's gay men and trans women aspired to.

Mahavir added, "Now we visit the police, show our Muskaan identity card, educate them about HIV prevention methods, and then have a dialogue with them about why they should not trouble us. We tell them we are saving lives by preventing HIV, not promoting sex. But it will take a long while to build relations. They still think of us as criminals. It will really help if Section 377 is removed."

I was struck to see Mahavir single out the egregious effect of Section 377 on the police's view of gay men and trans women, that it cast us as criminals. Despite Mahavir's and my coming from the antipodes of Indian society, Section 377 was the common root cause of the homophobia we faced. That is why the movement for gay and trans rights in India had organically developed into a nationwide one that bridged the vast class and urban-rural divides. (I noticed that in settings such as Sangli there were few divisions between gay men and trans women, especially in activist groups. That was strikingly different from activism among better-off urban gays, where gay men and lesbians came together but trans women were excluded. It was rare to find out or self-identified lesbians anywhere outside the larger cities and middle- and upper-income groups, reflecting the even greater constraints and risks that face women.)

Mahavir said, "So I feel very satisfied and happy with this job. I don't get much of a salary, but I scrimp and save. Altogether, I feel as if I get paid to have job happiness—and I get sex as well!" He grinned.

He was even, he told me, in a long-term relationship. Aditya was shy, tall, lanky, and with a thick head of wavy hair—in every visible way the diametric opposite of Mahavir. Like Mahavir, he was a sex worker and had also recently joined Muskaan as a peer educator.

Mahavir spent most nights at Aditya's home: one in a row of box-like brick huts in an area that seemed newly settled and poor, yet was clean and pleasant by India's degraded urban standards. Inside, there was a single small room with pink walls.

They had been together for three years, and the love between them was obvious and moving. They eagerly told me about the history of each one of their few possessions. Pointing to two bright green nylon parrots intertwined on a wall, Mahavir said, "One *tota* is Aditya, and the other is me. We are a pair, a couple!"

Aditya then produced the gifts that Mahavir had bought him for his recent birthday—a sari as well as trousers. "Only for a *kothi* can you buy both a sari and a pant," Mahavir quipped.

They showed me the jewelry that they had bought for each other over the course of their relationship. To solemnize their vows, Mahavir had given Aditya a *mangalsutra*—a pendant worn by married Hindu women—and Aditya had given him a gold-tinted ring. Aditya placed them in my hands, telling me that if I closed my eyes I could feel the love they had for each other.

On escorting me from their home later that night, Mahavir and Aditya greeted with puppylike enthusiasm the middle-aged woman who was filling a metal *ghara* at the hand pump outside, calling her Mausi, aunt. They told me that she looked after both of them. Mausi smiled shyly. It was clear that the affection was mutual. I was filled with joy to see such real acceptance rather than the homophobia I always expected. Against all the odds, those two feminine gay men in a small town had managed to carve out a full, happy life.

As Mahavir told me his story during my days in Sangli, there was one special point of emphasis: this was the pride Mahavir took in how he had fended for his family. I had seen the mutual affection between him and his parents, and how clearly they relied on him. He had put his sister through school and a nursing course. She now worked as a nurse in the affluent city of Pune, where her husband lived. For her marriage, Mahavir had bought her jewelry, furniture, and everything else that the couple needed to start off.

"Later, when my sister needed fifteen thousand rupees for the down payment on the house they were buying, I had to ask my regular customers for a loan," he said, fixing an intent gaze upon me. "Actually, I had just had a piles operation and the doctor had told me not to take customers for a year. But I could not say no to my sister when she asked for money, and I suffered many health problems, as I had to take many customers. I can barely sit properly now."

Mahavir had his eyes fixed on mine, clearly waiting to see how I would react to that last comment of his. I knew he had pointedly put everything in such graphic terms—the hemorrhoid operation, the risks to his health from being fucked, the fact that even so he'd sold so much anal sex. He wanted me to understand how deeply he had sacrificed himself to fend for his family, and he wanted me to understand that he had secured his sense of self-worth and dignity from providing the very sexual act that men inevitably consider most debasing: being fucked.

⬥

My grief at losing Arndt and my life in Geneva didn't ease for many months, despite my being in an utterly different world and the incessant pace of my new life.

But then, on my research trip to Cambodia in early 2008, I had a romance with a gay activist. It had that headlong connection, emotional and sexual, that occurs between people who are both hungering in the same way. It was what I needed to begin curing me completely of my grief, by making me realize that I could fall in love again.

A few months later, at a meeting in Delhi of gay and transgender activists from around India, I found myself drawn to one of the men. We hadn't spoken directly to each other, but watching him speak from the podium and in discussions, I was struck by his gravitas, a quality that was all the more surprising as he was clearly young, probably in his early thirties. I was also deeply impressed to see that he took pains to translate for participants who didn't speak English, treating them with a respect that was rare at the meeting, where the well-off Westernized individuals grouped together clubbishly and dominated the proceedings.

Unexpectedly, a friend of mine came up to me later that day and said, "Hey, I really want to introduce you to Anand. I keep thinking you'd be perfect for each other!"

Anand and I did meet and began a relationship. It developed slowly. We met for dinner each time I visited Delhi, but that was rarely more than once every month or second month. We talked endlessly when we met. I was wonder-struck to see how deeply he felt and had thought about every kind of social injustice, whether poverty, caste-based discrimination, or persecution of sexual minorities. He had given up a career in corporate law on realizing that he found satisfaction only in work on human rights and social justice. He was a practicing Buddhist. He was fiercely independent and principled. And he was funny, kind, and loving.

The more than ten-year difference in our ages—a gap that I had often felt with Arndt—seemed irrelevant. I felt secure with Anand in an absolute way that I had never felt in any of my previous relationships, even with Tandavan. I had finally found a soul mate. Long before we even kissed—sex was still months away—I felt real love for him.

Anand came to visit me that winter in Goa. My father was staying with me. To my surprise, I found them forever engrossed in conversations. I had never seen my father warm so readily to anyone I had dated. On January 1, 2009, on a perfect Goa winter morning, when the three of us were having breakfast together on the sunlit veranda, Lorca stretched out on the cool floor next to us, my father looked intently at both of us and, addressing us jointly, said, "Sons, you can make this a special year for this old man by getting married. How about it?"

⚜

Some months after my moving encounter with Mahavir in Sangli and my momentous meeting with Anand, the Delhi High Court began a dozen daylong hearings on the legal challenge to the sodomy law, Section 377 of the Indian Penal Code, in *Naz Foundation v. Govt. of NCT of Delhi and Others*. The hearings began in September 2008 and were expected to take several months to complete.

Seven interminable years had passed since the case had been filed by Anjali Gopalan of Naz Foundation (India) Trust and Anand Grover of the Lawyers Collective—and a decade and a half had passed since ABVA, the grassroots group that my friend Siddhartha had been with, filed the first challenge at this very court. Indeed, it had been two years since the open-letter campaign had shown unambiguously that thoughtful Indians from all walks of life felt that the courts should urgently address this wrong. I wished there had been some way of showing to these judges what I knew from my recent research—that millions of gay men, women, and trans women were looking to them for justice, irrespective of whether their homes were in rural shanties, urban *chawl*s, or mansions.

But, however long the delay, at least in the judges hearing the case we were guaranteed an intelligent and unbiased review. The two-person bench comprised the Delhi court's chief justice, Ajit Prakash Shah, who had authored numerous progressive verdicts, and S. Muralidhar, a former human rights lawyer. Ever since Independence, every oppressed community in India had despairingly turned to the higher courts in its search for justice. Perhaps inevitably, as with courts even in other liberal democracies, the Indian courts' record of advancing justice for the oppressed was mixed.

On innumerable thrilling occasions, the courts had corrected old wrongs on constitutional grounds, empowered by a strongly emancipatory Constitution, improving the course of India's history and sometimes even raising the global bar for human rights jurisprudence. But sometimes, even in the most unconscionable cases of injustice, the courts had sided with the oppressors or with bad laws, motivated by conservatism, prejudice, and literalist readings of the law or simply because they acceded to the demands of the state. Fortunately, those two judges were widely considered to represent the most stellar qualities of India's judiciary.

On November 7, 2008, I went with Anand for the final day of the hearings, held in Courtroom Number 1 of the Delhi court, an impressive colonnaded building at the eastern end of Rajpath, the magnificent ceremonial boulevard along which are set the presidential palace, Parliament, and other landmarks of state. On that day, and in earlier reports from the hearings that I had followed attentively, the justness of our position shone through—the evidence of the terrible damage done by the unjust law; the force of universal human rights principles; the past half century's global trajectory of decriminalization and of moving toward equal rights (countries as diverse as the United States, South Africa, Russia, almost all of Latin America, and neighboring Nepal had decriminalized same-sex relations by now); and, not least, the proof from the open letters that the most respected Indians urged an end to the archaic, alien law.

That morning, Anand Grover argued that the criminalization of adult, consensual same-sex relations violated constitutionally guaranteed rights on numerous overlapping counts. By imperiling HIV prevention efforts, criminalization left gay and bisexual men and trans women far more vulnerable to contracting this fatal disease, hence violating their rights to health and to life. (It was testimony to the unexpected positive changes catalyzed by the AIDS pandemic that both this legal challenge and the earlier one moved by the ABVA group had taken the depredations of AIDS on gay men as their starting point.) Criminalization also deprived those Indian citizens of the right to liberty, privacy, and dignity. The government had failed to prove any compelling grounds for selectively denying those rights only to those who had same-sex desires, Grover argued. And the disproportionately harsh punishments prescribed under Section 377 for "private sexual activity between consenting adults" merely because they were of the same sex also flagrantly violated the right to equality before the law, he stressed.

Supporting the Naz challenge was a friend-of-the-court intervention by Voices Against Section 377, a coalition of civil society groups ranging from those working on women's and children's rights to those focused on HIV prevention and yet others directly on gay and transgender rights, showing that the demand for decriminalization now had wide backing across Indian society. The lawyer representing the coalition, Shyam Divan, drew the court's attention to the harrowing personal affidavits filed by gay men and women, which showed that Section 377 "subjects male and female homosexuals as well as transgenders to repressive, cruel and disparaging treatment . . . [and] degrades such individuals into sub-human, second-class citizens." The harm done to them by Section 377 was all the more unconscionable for being provoked "simply because they seek to engage in sexual conduct, which is part of their experience of being human," Divan pointed out. In a moving closing speech, Divan, who has an openly gay brother, said, "Public morality is not a valid or sufficient justification to deny a person his dignity . . . Indeed, in this context, it is the fundamental rights enshrined to protect minorities, including sexual minorities, that ought to prevail. Morality, by itself, in the absence of any other harm, cannot be a ground to restrict the right to live with dignity."

I had closely followed the arguments of the three opposing parties—comprising the Indian government's Ministry of Home Affairs, a Hindu-supremacist politician, and a fringe AIDS denial group—in reports of the hearings. If there was any merit or even basic logic to their views, I could not grasp it, reinforcing my growing conviction over the years that the "moral majority" everywhere consists of aggressively opinionated cranks.

The senior lawyer representing the Home Affairs Ministry, P. P. Malhotra, argued that homosexuality must remain criminalized because it was "neither known to nature, nor known to law." He claimed that decriminalizing "unnatural sex" would "open floodgates of delinquent behaviour and be misconstrued as providing unbridled licence for the same." Those, as well as other outlandish statements by Malhotra—in an earlier hearing, he had insisted that consensual adult homosexuality was indistinguishable from pedophilia—earned him sharp rebukes from the judges, who scolded him to "take this issue seriously." While I was relieved that Malhotra's arguments were so weak that even the judges could not hide their irritation, I was also aghast that such a visibly incompetent person could become additional solicitor-general, the third-highest-ranking lawyer for the Indian government.

The Home Affairs Ministry's stand had also been dealt a body blow by a counterintervention filed by the NACO, the Health and Family Welfare Ministry's AIDS control agency. In direct opposition to the Home Affairs Ministry, the Health and Family Welfare Ministry pressed for the decriminalization of homosexuality as an imperative step to checking the spread of AIDS, emphasizing that IPC Section 377 was crippling HIV prevention efforts among India's large populations of gay and bisexual men and trans women, and consequently among their wives and other women partners. The judges noted in surprise, "A rather peculiar feature of this case is that completely contradictory affidavits have been filed by two wings of Union of India." The upshot was that when the Home Affairs Ministry's lawyer argued that homosexuality should remain criminalized on public health imperatives, too—saying that gays have "sex with hundreds of persons, two hundred, five hundred, even more, [so that] it's more likely to transmit disease"—the judges noted that the NACO's affidavit "points to the contrary."

Then there was B. P. Singhal, a prominent Bharatiya Janata Party politician and former member of Parliament, a heavyset, forceful man in his seventies who seemed to be brimming with a generalized rage. In an angry intervention, Singhal vented, "The mother of all harms to the human body comes from homosexuality." He insisted that a majority of Indians found gay sex "inherently immoral, grossly unnatural . . . the very antithesis of the lofty ideals, lofty values and lofty objectives" of Indian civilization. It was astonishing to see how utterly ahistorical Hindu supremacists were in defense of their bigotry: they were arguing that a colonial, British-imposed law dating back a hundred and fifty years was an integral part of Indian civilization!

The arguments made by Singhal's lawyer were more unhinged still. "Anus is not designed by nature for any intercourse, and if the penis enters the rectum, victim is found to get injury," he pronounced. By their suspect sexual behavior, gays had forgone the right to justice, he stated, saying gay men who "didn't use condoms do not deserve sympathy or mercy." He put forward an endless number of mystifying arguments for why the sodomy law had to remain in place. Decriminalization of same-sex relations would lead to a flood of divorces. It would "shatter" every member of the family. It would change the country's sex ratio. If the court were to decriminalize homosexuality on the grounds that it was the choice of two consenting adults, then why not also allow incest and the selling and buying of kidneys?

Rounding off the opposition was the bizarre AIDS denial group known as Joint Action Council, Kannur (JACK). As far back as 2002, that fringe group had filed an intervention against the Naz petition on the incomprehensible grounds that although HIV was not the cause of AIDS—it didn't explain what the real cause was—Section 377 helped control the AIDS epidemic by discouraging "rampant homosexuality." It had since accused the prominent lawyers representing the Naz Foundation and Voices Against 377 of financial corruption as well as other wrongdoing. Those wild charges earned the ire of Chief Justice Shah, who acerbically noted that he had never seen "such low levels" of argument in court.

Month after month after that final hearing, we waited impatiently for a verdict. Eventually it was listed for the morning of Thursday,

July 2, 2009. There were throngs outside the court, and the courtroom was packed to capacity.

Anand was in the courtroom, and soon my phone pinged with a message from him that said, "We won!"

Justices Shah and Muralidhar had ruled, "Section 377 IPC, insofar it criminalizes consensual sexual acts of adults in private, is violative of Articles 21, 14, and 15 of the Constitution . . . Moral indignation, howsoever strong, is not a valid basis for overriding individuals' fundamental rights of dignity and privacy. In our scheme of things, Constitutional morality must outweigh the argument of public morality . . . A provision of law branding one section of people as criminal based wholly on the State's moral disapproval of that class goes counter to the equality guaranteed under Articles 14 and 15 . . . The criminalization of homosexuality condemns in perpetuity a sizable section of society and forces them to live their lives in the shadow of harassment, exploitation, humiliation, cruel and degrading treatment at the hands of the law enforcement machinery . . . [Thus] Section 377 IPC grossly violates their right to privacy and liberty embodied in Article 21."

Anand told me that he and many others had wept unabashedly in the courtroom when they heard the judges rule in our favor. Days of celebration followed across India. People danced in the streets. Countless crisscrossing emails shared the judgment's inspiring hundred-page text. There were impromptu open-door parties. For days, the newspapers and TV shows carried editorials, op-eds, and speakers praising the decision.

I was free. We were free. We were no longer criminals.

❖

I couldn't join in the celebrations, however. I was with my father that day at his home in the Nilgiri mountains. Just a month earlier, after complaining of unbearable headaches and disorientation, he had been diagnosed with glioblastoma, the most aggressive form of brain cancer. The headaches had disappeared after surgery to drain the cerebrospinal fluid that had dammed up in the brain—but he didn't have long to live, perhaps as little as another three to six months.

His voice breaking with emotion, my father told me he was over-joyed that he had lived to celebrate this day with me, to know I could no longer be persecuted because of this hateful law. He would no lon-ger fear for me as he had when I had first returned to India from the United States twenty-five years before. He could pass away peacefully now, he told me, knowing that I would be safe even if I continued living in India. He said he would now pray that one day soon I would win the right to officially marry Anand.

With Dad, on one of his last walks

I was too choked with tears to say anything of consequence in response—let alone to say all that I wanted to say, which was that I was filled with such gratitude to have had him for a parent, that just this far outweighed the share of hardships I'd faced, that had it not been for him I would probably never have had the courage to fight, that I would probably not have made it through my dark years of early adulthood, and indeed that I didn't know how I was going to make it through the rest of my life without him.

I had been constantly choked with tears since rushing here in May, after Ketaki, his *ayah*, had called me in anxiety in Goa, when the terrible headaches had first begun. When I had arrived, worn-out after driving seventeen hours straight with Lorca, my father had stared at me blankly, as though I were a stranger. Some minutes later, he had reached out and touched my face, saying "Rana," a look of relief washing over him, telling me that his head was bursting with pain.

Within minutes of seeing him the doctor at the hospital in Coimbatore, a three-hour drive away on the plains, told me the signs were distinctly of a brain tumor, a diagnosis soon confirmed by a scan. They had operated on him the next day, fortunately able to drain the accumulated spinal fluid surgically rather than having to implant a shunt with all its attendant risks.

I had barely left him for more than an hour or two at a stretch since. All the plans dreamed up just over a year earlier and just beginning to be realized—that I would live in Goa and he here in the Nilgiris and I would see him through a happy old age—had been destroyed. The most beloved person in the world to me, the most reliable constant I had or would ever have, was dying. I had experienced loss and suffering and even heartbreak before, but all those now seemed insignificant, preparatory losses—this was the real loss, the unbearable loss, the life-changing loss. So alone with my dying father at his solitary hillside home was where I wanted to be on that day of celebration.

TWENTY-FOUR

A DEATH

Among the many unlikely and singular things that our father taught us brothers while we were still children was fearlessness about death.

None of us can remember exactly how young we were when he first sat the three of us down together, in an orderly row, to talk about death, but we all know it was one of our early memories, so well before even Pratap reached his teens, which would mean that I was probably age eight or nine. The gist of what we remember is that he told us that if he was ever severely disabled or in any way not able to enjoy his life, we boys were to ensure that he could pass away. That was, of course, many decades before discussions about assisted suicide or "death with dignity" became at all common. We children had asked him what he meant. He explained that he didn't want to live if he was in grievous pain or bed-bound, that he would rather be sent on his way to God happily and willingly.

We didn't dwell on the conversation, but all three of us recall that from that moment on each of us decided that dying willingly was the right way to die, and consequently, for each of us, death became not a fearsome thing to be avoided but something that we ourselves would choose to embrace at some point. It affected all of us in similar ways in our adult lives. Though we worried over careers or finances or our love lives, we had never worried about our own deaths. (Losing others was a different matter.) As adults, we were always genuinely puzzled that others were so fearful about dying—and we remarked to one another what a difference it had made to have our father's guidance. There was no bravado involved; it was simply just an old familiarity with the notion of dying, that we would embrace it willingly when the time came.

Even so, I could not bring myself to tell my father about his tumor and grim prognosis. My brothers had left this decision to me as his main caregiver. Week after week went by as I constantly found one excuse or another not to do so. When he asked me about the odd golf ball–sized indentation on his forehead—left by the surgery to drain the hydrocephalus—I lied and told him he had hit his head on the washbasin after slipping and didn't remember because he had passed out from the blow.

But then, characteristically, my father asked me point-blank, just as he had all those years ago during that unforgettable car ride on which he had pushed me to tell him I was gay. He was in bed one morning, looking out at the waterfall in the distance, in thrilling force from the monsoon rains. He looked at me with that direct gaze and said, "Son, how come you're hovering around me all the time and not going back to Goa? There is something you need to tell me."

And just as with coming out to him all those years back, my heart missed many beats and I wished I were anywhere but there. I sat next to him on the bed cross-legged. He pulled himself up to a sitting position, his face now impassive. And I told him, in just so many words, about the tumor, how it had come to light, and the terrible prognosis.

He looked at me steadily throughout that minute or two. Knowing him as well as I did, I knew that the concern he was trying to hide had to do not with his death but at the volcanic grief that I was clearly doing my hardest to suppress. He then smiled broadly and said, "See, I was right, you were hiding something," humor that helped ease the tension I was under.

He asked me a handful of questions and nodded in approval when I told him that my brothers and I had jointly decided that he wouldn't want to suffer through chemotherapy, as it would give him only a few extra months. After about fifteen minutes of conversation, he said, smiling and calm, "Son, thank you so much. Will you give me some time alone."

An hour later, my dad came down to the living room, where I was doing yoga in an effort to control my emotions. For the first time since the problem with the tumor had emerged, he had back his old serenity rather than seeming bewildered. I was instantly glad that he had pried the truth out of me. He sat on the sofa near me and told me that he'd spent the time sitting in front of his gods and he was now at peace. Though he didn't say anything directly, his eyes were full of compassion for me.

❖

Remarkably, defying the odds, for nearly a year after I told my father about the tumor, he carried on much as before. He did everything with that attentive, lived-in-the-moment relish that had struck me from my childhood—whether it was something as routine as splashing cold water on his face when he began his morning ablutions, his impregnable absorption during his morning yoga and prayers, or the transparent joy with which he played with the dogs or gazed at a passing herd of *gaur*.

He retained that quality even though he was not the youthfully vigorous and alert person he had been before the tumor had emerged. Though he walked six miles up- and downhill every day with me, he was visibly frail, his shoulders bowed, using a stick or my arm for support when he tired and taking frequent breaks. There was no question of him going alone on walks any longer—quite apart from the risk of falls, he would often lose his bearings, whereas earlier he had had the trained hunter's unswerving sense of recall and direction.

At home, both Ketaki and I made sure he was never alone once awake, given the real risk that he would fall in the bathroom or while taking a shower or walk out one of the floor-to-ceiling windows on his second-floor bedroom. We did so as unobtrusively as possible, and if it irritated him, he never let on. The one source of daily friction with my father was over my attempts to limit his drinks to one or two a night—a battle that I gave up when my brothers or his friends were visiting, as there was no stopping him then in his convivial mood.

My father barely ever mentioned the tumor again. It was not that he had forgotten. One day, when he must have sensed that I was particularly struggling with the prospect of losing him, he said, "Son, how about I go only after we celebrate my eightieth birthday? And we have a real ball until then, for the next two years! Agreed?" And once in a while he would rub the indentation on his forehead left by the recent surgery and remark that it was amazing that such a simple procedure could leave such a large, permanent mark.

Momentously, in December 2009, six months after his diagnosis, when I had moved him to Goa for the winter, he and a friend of mine who was visiting from Geneva fell deeply in love. I was there when Marguerite and he first set eyes on each other—as I returned from the airport from fetching her—and they were smitten with each other at first glance.

From that minute, they spent every moment with each other like besotted teenagers embarking on their first love. Long after I had turned in for the night, I could hear them chatting away on the veranda. It made my heart sing to see that they had both found love and were living every moment with headlong relish, unmindful of what lay ahead.

My father told me, beaming, "Son, you've been the best son one could ever dream of—you've even arranged the last relationship of my life!"

✤

Through all that, I was floundering myself.

It was not that I had an emotional breakdown, but I found I was consumed with the thought that nothing in my life seemed to have any lasting stability—indeed, everything seemed to be built on quicksand. Just when I had pieced it together from the rupture with Arndt, happy with this new life where I got to be with my father and a boyfriend I cared for deeply, work that was extraordinarily fulfilling and productive, it had all come apart again. All my courage and resourcefulness seemed pointless. I was constantly losing everything I cherished, I thought. It filled me with despair.

The worst impact was on my relationship with Anand. He had been faultless in caring for and supporting me, rushing up to my father's home to help when the crisis first began, and then regularly taking time off from work to visit us. But I truthfully had no emotional capacity to give him anything in return. All my thoughts were about my father—and all I wanted to do was to care for him. (There was no doubt that my desperate subconscious reasoning ran that if I cared for him with single-minded devotion I could somehow keep him alive—or even that perhaps my devotion would somehow impress the gods into being charitable to me and letting him live.)

I ended our relationship early in 2010, all the while angry at myself for hurting Anand so. If I could have been more logical, I would have explained my feelings and sensibly asked for just a pause in our relationship. My father continued to ask often about him: about when Anand would next visit, when he could speak to him on the phone. I took advantage of his fading concentration and short-term memory loss. I didn't have the courage to tell him the truth—that I had been unable to sustain that wonderful relationship, that the marriage he had wished for me would not happen, and that I'd be alone after he passed away.

❖

In June 2010, shortly after Marguerite had left for Switzerland after several months with my father at his mountain home, promising to be back soon, I moved there to be with him. Then the normality ended with heart-stopping sharpness.

On his usual evening walk, which by now had shortened to about three miles, on the final steep incline a half mile from home, my father's face went gray and he sat down abruptly in the middle of the road of rock and earth. He looked exhausted, in a desperate way, almost as though he knew he was now losing control over his body forever. I could have left him there and returned with the SUV, but I was afraid of what might happen in that time; there was a steep fall where we had stopped. I never carried my mobile phone, as there was no coverage on that walk around the mountainside. Half an hour later, with him apologizing constantly, we struggled up together, me carrying his weight as best I could.

My father seemed shaken but otherwise better at dinner. But when I went to check on him the next morning, I felt a wave of apprehension, as he was lying stiffly in exactly the same position as when I had left his room late at night. I could see he was breathing, so I let him sleep, imagining he was exhausted and would recover. But when Ketaki and I tried to wake him at noon, we realized he was unconscious.

The doctor arrived from a kindly friend's nearby tea-garden hospital. He put my father on a drip but told me honestly that he wasn't sure he would recover, that complications related to brain tumors proceeded in inexplicable ways. I called my brothers.

It was only when Pratap walked into my father's darkened bedroom late the following night, entering from the walkway at the far end of the bedroom, walking softly so that his caliper did not scrape the floor, that my father stirred for the first time in forty-eight hours and, still unable to see him, said, his voice tender in the darkness, "Son, I was hoping you would come."

What a strange period followed—an indefinite sentence of fear, of knowing I would lose my beloved father today or tomorrow or this week or next week, this month or next month. The end would come soon. There were no miracle interregnums possible.

It was the most anguished period of my life—and the most precious. I suffered constantly, day after day, but I would not have escaped for anything, even if I had been given a guarantee of having forever every other joy I wished for.

Whatever progress my father made in the coming days, with Pratap and the nurses caring for him ceaselessly, there was no denying that the tumor was now inexorably shutting off his capacities. There is no knowing what brain tumors will do. What my father's did to him was, on the whole, given the horrific possibilities, a blessing: it shut off all pain. Brain tumors do this sometimes, I learned, though usually they cause the most excruciating, ever-changing repertoire of agony. So in the manner of his dying my father was given the peace that had been denied to him throughout his life, a peace that he so singularly deserved.

Inevitably, however, the tumor caused terrible losses in his well-being. He lost much of his mobility. And then, week after week, the tumor shut down his ability to speak. It was heartbreaking to see him go mute, knowing that his mind worked as sharply as always, knowing that he was aware that he couldn't speak despite every effort. Whenever he summoned up a sentence or word, I hung on to them, knowing that they were the last things he would ever tell me.

One night, as I was helping the nurses change him into his pajamas, his arms propped up stiffly on my shoulders, he looked straight into my eyes and said, speaking unusually in Hindi, "*Bacche, maaf karna mujhe, is bimari ka koi thikana nahin hain.*" ("Child, forgive me, it's not possible for me to win against this disease.")

One morning, one of the nurses rushed down the stairs to say my father was calling me. Seeing my disbelieving look, he said, "Sahib is saying 'WanaPana, WanaPana.'" WanaPana was what my father had called me most times since my childhood, a play on my nickname, Rana. I rushed up, and there was my father propped up in bed, beaming at me, repeating softly, "WanaPana, WanaPana, WanaPana!" He looked like a toddler astonished at his ability to speak.

My brother Bharat, on one of his vists, decided to read out Rudyard Kipling's "If," our father's favorite poem. It was afternoon and we were sitting out in the sun, my father immobile in his wheelchair. Bharat read out those wise sentences, sentences that, like our father, each of us brothers knew by heart: "'If you can keep your head when all about you / Are losing theirs and blaming it on you . . . If you can meet with Triumph and Disaster / And treat those two impostors just the same. . .'" He read beautifully and slowly. "'Or watch the things you gave your life to, broken, / And stoop and build 'em up with worn-out tools . . .'"

My father sat there, his face looking stony, almost as if he had lost his hearing. But then, a minute after Bharat had ended, his face lit up and he said simply, "Vah!" (the Hindi equivalent of "Wow!" or "Encore!").

There came a time, eventually, when there were no more sentences, not even after weeks. His expression became unchanging, brought on by his waning muscular control. I knew he still understood everything perfectly. I could see his body relax every morning when I played his favorite *bhajan*s. At sunset, when I knew he began to crave a drink, I would play Nusrat Fateh Ali Khan's *qawaali*s or Begum Akhtar's *ghazal*s and his face would light up soundlessly. His face glowed on the night I showed him the old male leopard sitting quietly outside the gate, its dappled coat ethereal in the yellow lamplight. It shone every time I pointed out the *gaur* herd or the solitary bull foraging on the vines on the fence. It was imperceptible, but I could see it.

He began to waste away. He lost weight rapidly, even though we tempted him with all his favorite things—mutton curry, *kaali daal*, *saag paneer*, *allo ka paratha*, *kheer*, and caramel custard. Yet, like the cadaverous, fasting Buddha, an image of serenity in suffering that had moved me so profoundly ever since I was a child, he lost more and more weight till he was reduced to skin and bones.

I suffered to see all that, even as I knew that I was being given gifts that I would treasure forever, that would be more precious to me than any other memories. One gift, of course, was to know that I could look back with a clear conscience, knowing that I had cared for my father with something approaching the selfless love he had always bestowed on me.

There was another, less obvious gift. I saw that as my father lost his capacities, his external personality was falling away, too, the personality spun together by class and upbringing as well as self-preservation. What was left was his essence, the real, true him, and it filled my heart with joy to see what a shining goodness, kindness, and sweetness there was to that essential him. Perhaps nothing gave me so much joy as to have the privilege of seeing my father as the person he truly was, and to know that I was so fortunate as to be the child of that lovely person.

A time came, five long months later, when I began to realize that I would have to live up to my promise to my father that I would help him pass away if he became bedridden. I told my brothers. I called a beloved friend of mine, a doctor, to ask for advice. I began to plan to arrange for a large supply of morphine.

Not more than a few days had passed when, one morning, with Pratap back for another visit, my father seemed to practically light up, his face incandescent and beaming. Sitting in his wheelchair on the patio in his favorite spot, overlooking the valley below, Pana Para's peak on the left and the other wild peak on the right, he ate an entire small bowl of caramel custard, fed slowly by the nurse. When the nurse bent to wipe his mouth, he said softly, "Thank you. God bless you, son."

Those were his last meal and his last words.

When Pratap accompanied him upstairs to his bedroom for his prayers, he took one shuffling step forward toward his gods, smiled with bliss as if he were with a great love, and died.

TWENTY-FIVE

AN INDEFINITE SENTENCE

I desperately wanted to make sense of my life. In less than a year, I would turn fifty. Since I had encountered Jiddu Krishnamurti's philosophical works back in my undergraduate years, I had never consciously shied away from confronting my inner struggles. But now my struggles had intensified in a way that I couldn't make sense of— the one person who had cared constantly and watchfully and lovingly for me was gone, and I felt orphaned. All of my life seemed full of failure and impermanence—with no children, no lasting relationship, no place or cause where I was desperately needed, not even a conventional steady job. For all that I had convinced myself along the way that I was brave and principled and successful, I now felt I had been fooling myself. I had failed to overcome my handicaps, failed to make the right decisions. Whatever the truth or balance, I wanted to make clear sense of my life now, without flinching. For that, I needed to be utterly alone and to have no crutches and no support.

There was no other place that I could imagine myself in at that point, while dealing with those struggles, but Pana Para. Just as that sign on the mountaintop, that anagram of Pana Para—"Papa Rana"—had promised, it was a place of destiny for my father and me. It had given us incomparable treasures—even if they were not the treasures we had hoped for, even if it took all our wisdom to realize that they were treasures, not tragedies. Pana Para had given my father glorious last years and a blessedly peaceful death. It had given me what I wanted most deeply: a gift with which to honor him, a place in which to care for him, a mountaintop to cremate him, a place to give him a *samadhi* in the untamed wilderness that he loved so deeply.

It was our Ithaka. Cavafy, my beloved poet, was right about Ithakas—"And if you find her poor, Ithaka won't have fooled you. / Wise as you will have become, so full of experience, / you will have understood by then what these Ithakas mean." Pana Para was my home—and so I stayed put.

⬦

The years that followed were by far the most difficult of my adult life. Yet, paradoxically, they were also critical, changing me in lasting, positive ways. Every one of my experiences in Pana Para invariably had that dichotomous quality of pain and glory.

One cause of anguish was my father's absence. Virtually everything in the house was his—from the furniture and the books down to the photographs of our ancestors and love letters between my mother and him. And then, at the foot of the garden, right by the second set of gates leading into the forest, was his *samadhi*—the flat rocks on which his funeral pyre had been placed, the flowering shrubs and ground creepers that I had planted only now beginning to cover the ashes and other remains—to which I was drawn constantly to talk to him or to just stand there sobbing.

Now, routinely a full week or even a fortnight or more would go past without my seeing or speaking to anyone but the staff who remained to manage the house as well as the land under tea. The only other people I saw occasionally were the workers on the neighboring tea plantations—I would call out "*Vannakam,*" a respectful Tamil greeting, to them, met by a chorus of greetings and smiles. The home was so isolated that if a vehicle passed anywhere nearby, it came as a surprise. I rarely even spotted planes.

I had never been one for chatting on the phone, and though I tried to make an effort to speak to my siblings and close friends regularly, I found that the prolonged silence had a snowballing effect, making me ever less comfortable with phone conversations. Year in and year out, for an eternity, every day stretched ahead just like the ones that had passed.

It required all my resourcefulness, built up over my life and learned from my father, not to be overcome by loneliness and instead to maintain an equilibrium and work productively. The discipline of work itself provided solace. Half the day went in my writing hours, from 8:00 a.m. to 2:00 p.m., to which I kept religiously. I typically put in another two hours before dinner. By my desk in my home office, I kept a printout in thirty-six-point type of what one sex worker had told me many years back: "I was arrested in a raid on the brothel . . . Earlier, many times these same policemen would come to the brothel and have sex with us for free. In the lockup that night the policemen beat me on my genitals with sticks. I was naked. They said it was for talking back to them!" If my concentration flagged or I felt sorry for myself, I reread those piercing words, which never failed to goad me back to work with the knowledge that I owed it to her and to the countless impoverished and outlawed people who had spent hours confiding in me to do whatever I could to improve things.

Lorca was my greatest solace. His need to be with me every minute of the day, from waking to sleeping, and his depth of love made me feel privileged. I felt as though I had a child as well as the most constant and loving of friends. And it was impossible not to feel cheered up by that furry face, with those surprisingly steady, thoughtful eyes, looking like some daemon conjured up by J. K. Rowling's wondrous imagination. I realized how lucky I had been to have him as a companion across three continents and through all the dislocations of these strange years. I also came to realize that I was perhaps more suited to this particular kind of relationship than to being in a romantic relationship with all its potential for trauma.

I found consolation, too, in the incredible natural beauty of Pana Para. Late in life, I had found the refuge of forests and wild animals I had constantly dreamed of as a child. On my long daily hikes, which typically began at 3:00 p.m. and ended at dusk, it was a certainty that I would see barking deer, wild boar, and *gaur*—and, less frequently, leopard, sloth bear, huge *sambar* deer, and Chihuahua-sized chevrotain. Because I was virtually the only person living there—especially paying such rapt attention to them—I felt I had a personal relationship with each of those wild animals.

The *gaur* were one of my favorite animals there. Even though I saw them every day, I was freshly enchanted. They were stunningly beautiful—the bulls the glistening black of wet rock, the females a velvety chocolate. And despite their forbidding size—the males stood nearly seven feet at their humped shoulders—they were unaggressive. The matriarchs that led the nearby herds soon became used to me, setting the tone for the others by continuing their foraging or napping unafraid, so that I could stand or sit close by and watch them for as long as I wanted. Only the youngsters—as slim and doe-eyed as deer—playfully pretended that I was some exciting creature that they had to keep an eye on.

My other favorites were the leopards. I saw them often, even as often as six times in one special month. Yet each encounter was indelible. There was the late afternoon that Lorca barked in the most fearsome tone I had ever heard him produce and I realized it was directed at a leopard that was staring up at him hungrily from the path outside the fence. There was the day when a pair of near adults played with each other in the tea bushes outside the fence. There was the day when I watched a pair mating, irritably trying to fend off the two female *gaur* who kept mischievously attacking them. And then, most precious of all, there was the series of late afternoons when the old male would wait for me at the same spot near the rock where he lived as I wound my way back home, both of us sitting down to stare at each other, less than a hundred yards separating us, building that inexplicable, indescribable bond that can be struck up between wild things and humans.

My solace in the evenings was to whirl. I had learned that form of meditation from an extraordinarily perceptive Sufi teacher I had met in Goa, talking to whom had helped me grapple with the loss of my father as well as my old traumas. At the end of a visit to her, no doubt sensing my dread of returning to the loneliness of Pana Para, she had told me simply, "I envy you your whirling alone on your mountainside, under the stars," and then walked away without a word of explanation or comfort.

She was, of course, unerringly correct. The whirling in the infinite solitude of Pana Para was what I desperately needed.

I would turn off every light, open the living room to the outside, put a Maria Farantouri or Nusrat Fateh Ali Khan disc on repeat play, and whirl endlessly, beginning on the living room carpet and then out onto the patio. Every emotion that was coursing through me emerged in full force. There was endless grief at having lost my father. There was rage at the meaningless course of my life, which had left me here utterly alone on an isolated mountainside. There was self-pity. But I noticed that each of them alternated, almost automatically, with feelings of joy, of gratitude, of bliss, of laughter. And, strangely, not only did the whirling make me feel my emotions more clearly and strongly than ever, it also let me think more clearly than I ever had otherwise, as if I could study everything with distance. It was strange to find acuity and mental balance while whirling off balance!

Though I don't know exactly when or how, those many nights of whirling gave me psychological breakthroughs. I realized I could endure anything, even the worst losses and the worst grief. I realized, too, that grief was vital, that it tempered me in ways that no other emotion could—made me, oddly, more capable of living. I realized just how deeply I loved solitude. And seeing the pleasant and unpleasant emotions come and go naturally in turn, their power over me began to lessen, in that my longing to be "happy" rather than "troubled" diminished. The perpetual sense of apprehension and anxiety I had felt as long as I could remember, certainly since my school days, began to fall away. Gradually I felt that all my fractured pieces had fallen into place.

❖

I was in Pana Para when, in early 2012, India's Supreme Court began hearing the challenges to the 2009 ruling of the Delhi High Court decriminalizing same-sex relations.

For every reason, it was certain that the Supreme Court would speedily uphold the high court decision. Even more consistently than the state high courts, the Supreme Court was known for progressive judgments that defended the rights of the poor, disadvantaged, and marginalized. Moreover, it was rare for the apex court to overturn a rigorously argued ruling by any of the major state high courts. The Delhi court's ruling had subsequently also been embraced by other courts when faced with cases relating to same-sex matters. In early 2010, in response to the brutal victimization of an academic, S. R. Siras, who had been covertly videotaped in his bedroom while having sex with another man and then forced to quit his post by the university administration for "gross misconduct," the high court of Uttar Pradesh had cited the Delhi court's ruling to rebuke the university administration and reinstate Siras. (Tragically, Siras was found dead in his apartment just days after he won the case, the cause of death remaining unclear.)

Moreover, the Congress-led government was not a party to the challenge. In its written submission to the court the government had unequivocally said that it found no fault with the judgment. The law and justice minister, Veerappa Moily, a well-regarded lawyer himself, had publicly praised the judgment for being "well-researched, well-documented, well-argued . . . [T]his is one judgment which has really stood out in the judicial annals of this country." (I felt enormous relief that the extreme-right BJP was not in power—its track record of bigotry and its angry criticism of the high court's ruling meant that it would unfailingly have sought to overturn it.)

And not only did none of the fifteen petitioners have any standing in a constitutional matter, but—and the justices of the Supreme Court could not but be appalled by this—they were an embarrassment of cranks and nuts. The first petitioner in *Suresh Kumar Koushal v. Naz Foundation* was Suresh Kumar Koushal, an obscure astrologer who maintained that the decriminalization of homosexuality threatened India's national security because officers in the armed forces would now be emboldened to sexually abuse their troops. From the original Delhi High Court case, there was the fulminant BJP strongman B. P. Singhal as well as the fringe AIDS-denial group JACK. There was Baba Ramdev, a popular yoga teacher known for his bizarre views—in this case, he feared that India's population growth would be harmed by the spread of homosexuality. There were obscurantist faith organizations, including the All India Muslim Personal Law Board and the Apostolic Churches Alliance. I felt sympathy for the Supreme Court justices who would be subjected to their drivel.

In contrast, the individuals and groups defending the high court's decision were highly respected. In addition to the Naz Foundation, which had filed the original public interest challenge in the Delhi High Court and the activist coalition Voices Against 377, there were affidavits from leading mental health experts, legal scholars, prominent academics, and parents of gay, lesbian, or transgender children. Arguing pro bono on their behalf were some of India's most celebrated constitutional lawyers.

And, by now, global thinking about same-sex rights had advanced so much that if the justices looked abroad—at UN secretary-general Ban Ki-moon and US president Barack Obama emphasizing that sexual and gender orientation were basic human rights matters or at the hundred-plus countries where same-sex relations were now legal and the dozen that recognized same-sex marriage—they would only find support for the Delhi court's ruling that twenty-first-century India had to be a part of this march of progress.

The hearings ended in March 2012. I had expected a prompt

ruling, but none came. Months passed, and then a year. Inexplicably, there was still no indication from the Supreme Court about a date for the decision.

Eventually, it became clear that the ruling would have to be issued by the end of 2013 because Justice Ganpat Singh Singhvi—the senior member of the two-judge bench—would be retiring then. Justice Singhvi seemed to be delaying the judgment for his last day in court to forestall any controversy.

Though I paid close attention to the proceedings, reading the detailed daily reports from the courts as well as the legal briefs (all efficiently shared on an LGBT email list), I was not worried about the outcome. As long as the ruling was announced by summer 2014—when the forthcoming national elections threatened to bring back the bigoted BJP in an anti-Congress wave—there was no reason for worry, we observers told ourselves.

The judgment was finally listed for the morning of December 11, 2013, Justice Singhvi's very last day in court. The courtroom was packed to capacity by the time Justices Singhvi and S. J. Mukhopadhya arrived at 10:30 a.m. Outside, hundreds of supporters of same-sex rights had gathered. At home in Pana Para, I sat glued to my computer to check emails and online news briefs and kept the TV news on loud.

At 11:00 a.m., two terse emails from gay activists present in court appeared in my inbox:

"They have overthrown the High Court judgment."

"It seems they said Section 377 stands constitutionally. They have said Parliament must decide."

I read those emails again and again in disbelief.

I turned quickly to the TV news. There, a few minutes later, headlines confirmed that the Supreme Court had overruled the Delhi court's decision, with the judges saying "We hold that Section 377 does not suffer from . . . unconstitutionality and the declaration made by the Division Bench of the High Court is legally unsustainable."

Once again I was a presumptive criminal in my own country.

❖

India had progressed so much that criticism of the judgment far outweighed the few reactionary voices that welcomed it. In editorials, newspaper after newspaper called the judgment "disgraceful," "retrograde," and a "body blow to liberal values and human rights." India's attorney general, Goolam Vahanvati, published a critical op-ed in the *Times of India*, saying that he had decided to break with precedent to write publicly because of "the importance of the matter" and then going on to call the court's ruling a "tragedy." Sonia Gandhi, the president of the ruling Congress Party, condemned Section 377 as "an archaic, repressive and unjust law."

The most moving criticism came from Leila Seth, my friend Vikram Seth's mother and a distinguished jurist, who had retired recently after serving as the first woman to be the chief justice of a state high court. Through all the efforts Vikram and I had put in in the past, she had— as a matter of principle—refused to influence her colleagues in the judiciary in even the slightest manner possible. But now she wrote in the *Times of India*: "The judgment claimed that the fact that a minuscule fraction of the country's population was gay or transgender could not be considered a sound basis for reading down Section 377. In fact, the numbers are not small, but even if only very few people were in fact at threat, the Supreme Court could not abdicate its responsibilities to protect their fundamental rights, or shuffle them off to Parliament . . . The reasoning in the judgment that justice based on fundamental rights can only be granted if a large number of people are affected is constitutionally immoral and inhumane."

It was gratifying to see the Congress-led government's commitment to the matter. Within ten days of the judgment, the government had pressed for a review before a full bench, per Supreme Court procedure.

In visibly critical language, it detailed seventy-six grounds to underscore that the judgment authored by Justices Singhvi and Mukhopadhya had not fulfilled the apex court's responsibility for judging the constitutional validity of laws, "especially a pre-Constitutional law," and was "contrary to well-established principles of law laid down by this court enunciating the width and ambit of fundamental rights." The government's plea was joined by the Naz Foundation, Voices Against 377, and several other groups, each of them stressing that a larger bench should review the case.

However, on January 28, 2014, a Supreme Court bench rejected those petitions and decided that there was no reason to reexamine the original judgment. There was little hope that the decision would be reversed anytime soon. It would remain indefinitely, perhaps for my lifetime.

❖

It was in those years that I realized that independent India's particular national tragedy was that its governance perpetually betrayed the stunning opportunities for emancipation and progress thrown up by the democratic churning at the grassroots.

For sex workers, as for gay men, there was to be no justice. All the vast promise of change I had seen in India since the mid-1990s until the Bush assault began had not been translated into lasting gains. The extraordinary sex-worker groups that dotted the country continued to make a huge difference to the safety and well-being of those in the areas they worked in. But they were relatively few in number, and the vast majority of sex workers did not have sustained help of any kind, especially because the hundreds of millions in international funding for India's AIDS efforts had evaporated now that the epidemic was not escalating as long feared.

And though the sex-worker collectives and supportive human rights groups continued valiantly to turn to the courts and sympathetic politicians to challenge the laws criminalizing sex work, there was no sign of a breakthrough. Instead, with the laws never having been changed, the old abuses of the past—the raids on brothels and homes, the arrests and imprisonment of dozens of women at a time—recurred with depressing everyday regularity, reported in newspapers across the country. The new vocabulary of "antitrafficking" provided fresh cover for the old abuses, with the police now insisting they were breaking up traffickers' rings and rescuing "victimized" women; but, as in the past, the women were arrested, cursorily tried, imprisoned in reformatories, and all the while subjected to every kind of exploitation and abuse, making a mockery of the police and antitraffickers' claims of helping them. I often could not bear to read those newspaper reports, those constant reminders that sex workers remained as abused and wronged as decades earlier.

I saw that heartbreakingly everywhere I traveled in those years. In a remote rural area of Tamil Nadu, I was told by the district's chief of police, a thoughtful, competent official, that his juniors had reported to him that there were two brothel keepers in his area, reputedly also involved in trafficking of women, and that he was cracking down only on them but not on sex workers. With some trepidation, expecting two fearsome criminals, I went off to find them. But the truth was as far removed from what his zealous juniors had told him as could be imagined.

One was a middle-aged sex worker herself, Jayamala, a visibly exhausted woman, living in a ramshackle hut in the poorest part of the village. From a backward caste and widowed early, she had educated and raised her daughter by selling sex as well as working as a laborer; her daughter was now married and well settled in neighboring Kerala. Alone once again, she was desperately struggling to survive by selling sex herself as well as simply charging other women a small fee to use her hut to service their clients—but for that she had been accused by the local policewoman of being a pimp and a trafficker. Jayamala said angrily, "This policewoman is a terror. She wants to blame us sex workers for everything! She has even tried to implicate us in some random man's murder!" The other alleged pimp/traffickers proved to be an elderly couple whose only adult son had died in a mishap, and to survive they looked the other way when sex workers paid them to use the spare bedroom in their modest home.

My despair reached its nadir when I met Kamala in the summer of 2013. She had agreed, though reluctantly, to meet me outside the women's reformatory in Chennai's Mylapore area. That was where, in a sense, it had all begun nearly thirty years before—in 1986—when Selvi and the five other HIV-positive sex workers had been imprisoned there. It was also where Kamala had been imprisoned until recently, in a depressing parallel to Selvi's fate all those decades ago.

Kamala was waiting for me on the far side of the road from the reformatory's gates, the unbroken traffic clearly providing her with a reassuring sense of distance from the reformatory. She was thin, dark, middle-aged, dressed in a green-and-black sari of some shiny synthetic material, her hair braided neatly. There was a telltale strain of constant worry in Kamala's voice. "My years in the remand home were the worst of my life," she told me. "It was a prison. From the time I was arrested by the police in 2010, I kept saying to them that I was not a victim of trafficking or pimping, that I wanted to be free, that there was no reason to hold me. But no one listened. And they held me there for more than two years, till 2012."

She went on, "Perhaps I would have been released earlier, but when I was arrested, my husband was arrested, too—booked as a pimp. He is not a pimp! He works as a guard. All he did was come to the police station on hearing that I had been arrested. Of course he knows about my work, but he never pimped me. He was sent to Puzhal prison for a month.

"My boys were suddenly on the streets, because, hearing of our situation, our landlady had thrown them out. They slept on the pavement at [the] Broadway bus stand before a neighbor found them and took them into her house, even though she is as poor as us. She fed them every day. I will never be able to repay my debt to her. My boys had to leave school and start working at a mechanic's shop, even though they are so little.

"When I was freed, my husband said to me, 'We will manage with what we have. You must not do this work anymore.' But he now has to work both day and night shifts as a watchman. He is very tired. And the boys' education has come to an end. They are both working and bringing in a little money every week. I want to help. But I don't know how. All I can do is manage the household expenses as best I can."

I didn't tell Kamala about the emotions coursing through me as I heard her out.

I felt boiling anger that such disastrous harm was being done to impoverished, defenseless people because of the cynical misrepresentation by prohibitionists—Bush, his evangelical zealots, and misguided do-gooders such as Nick Kristof and Gloria Steinem—that all those involved in sex work were madams, pimps, and traffickers preying on victimized women and children.

And I felt despair. In the second decade of the twenty-first century, Kamala had suffered precisely what Selvi had suffered nearly three decades earlier—years of imprisonment and abuse because of the bad old laws that left sex workers at the mercy of bigoted policemen and judges.

That was the most damning proof of India's failure to provide justice to those sinned-against, outlawed women.

EPILOGUE

In June 2014, I left Pana Para to move back to New York City. I had lived in India for seven years, my longest stretch in my home country as an adult—and the first in which I had felt at ease living there.

Yet there were compelling reasons for me to leave. India was heading into a dark era, potentially more dangerous to the country's prospects than even the years in the mid-1970s when Indira Gandhi had ruled as dictator. The Hindu-supremacist BJP had come to power in national elections in May 2014. The party had won just 30 percent of the vote, but longstanding flaws in the electoral system meant that it controlled three-fourths of the parliamentary seats, a situation it was certain to exploit. The US, with Obama leading it, seemed in a halcyon era, and I ached to share in it.

The joy of being once again with my beloved friends and renewing my carefree life eased the pain of leaving my home in Pana Para. I knew also that I would eventually return there—I had come to love my solitude on this enchanted mountainside too deeply to be able to live anywhere else for long.

❖

My move back to the United States was made unforgettable a year later, on June 26, 2015.

I got to celebrate firsthand the US Supreme Court decision upholding marriage equality. It was as exhilarating a day as the one exactly twelve years earlier on which that court had struck down America's sodomy laws, and the day in July 2009 when the Delhi High Court had struck down India's IPC Section 377. For the first time in my life, just months short of my fifty-fourth birthday, I would be living in a society where gay men and women were legally assured an equal right to romantic love and to families of their own, even if equal protection and true justice remained very distant.

Though I exulted in seeing this progress, I found that my own longings for a relationship or even for sex were no longer as pressing as in the past. I went out on a few dates—with an old flame, with pleasant men I was set up with by friends, and another handful I met through dating sites—but in time these petered out. The recent years of loss and grief and solitude at Pana Para had fundamentally changed my expectations from life.

I savored the joys that I had—Lorca (now nearing sixteen and painfully frail, as dear to me as if he had been my child, whose passing I dreaded), my beloved friends and siblings, my work passions, and my peaceful existence. It was very different from my forties, where I had battled the dissatisfaction I had felt about the things missing in my life, romantic love most of all. I felt blessed to have lived long enough to make sense of my life, to be at peace with both the blows and the joys I had been given and what I had made of them.

❖

The beginnings of true gay liberation had been won with certainty, in the span of my life, in the US and in dozens of other countries worldwide. Yet in India things seemed hopeless, between the Supreme Court ruling in December 2013 upholding IPC Section 377 and the obscurantist BJP in power, who, by this time, had shown that the killing of Muslims, terrorizing of Dalits and *adivasi*s, and the suppressing and murdering of dissenters was integral to their assault on India's secular fabric. It was India's shame that it was the only major democracy of the seventy-plus countries that continued to criminalize same-sex relations.

Year after year, efforts to get the court to reconsider its 2013 ruling made no headway. The court's intransigence seemed all the more inexplicable after another set of Supreme Court judges made a pathbreaking ruling on transgender rights in April 2014—recognizing a "third gender" and ordering the government to provide them with affirmative action benefits in education and jobs.

Eventually, in February 2016, the court agreed to refer the judgment to a full bench of five justices. This was a breakthrough but still did not mean a favorable ruling was likely. And with this being the last stage of judicial appeals, the stakes were climactic.

Then, in August 2017, things turned around unexpectedly—and to such an astonishing degree as to instantly fill me with optimism that the indefinite sentence I had endured all my life would soon be lifted.

In a landmark 547-page ruling in an unrelated case that affirmed that each of India's billion-plus citizens have a "guaranteed fundamental right" to "individual privacy" as an indivisible part of the rights to life and personal liberty, the Supreme Court commented: "Equality demands that the sexual orientation of each individual in society must be protected on an even platform."

The justices stopped short of overturning the court's 2013 judgment—noting that another of the court's benches was already hearing the challenge to this matter, with final hearings scheduled for the summer of 2018. But they left no doubt of the direction in which India had to move, describing the court's 2013 judgment in *Koushal v. Naz Foundation* as "flawed" and "misplaced," and concluding that they "disagree with the manner in which Koushal has dealt with the privacy-dignity–based claims of LGBT persons."

And so, in the near future or perhaps even by the time this book is read, it is almost a certainty that my country, too, will overturn this historic injustice. On that day, for the first time in modern history, an overwhelming majority of the world's people will be living in societies where same-sex love is not criminalized.

❖

In the US and elsewhere in the Western world, in sharp contrast to the gay liberation that was being realized, there had been no parallel liberation for sex workers.

The US government's antiprostitution gag rule and unilateral antitrafficking crusade remained in place, testifying to the depressing fact that the most irrational, egregious policies are precisely the ones most difficult to end. When President Obama moved to weaken the gag rule, Congressman Chris Smith, the right-wing Republican who had authored that clause, accused him of "enabling sex trafficking and prostitution all over the world."

Within the US, the persecution of sex workers continued un-abated—as did the hype about sex trafficking. Year after year, tens of thousands of women, trans women, and men were arrested on prosti-tution charges. A government crackdown on online adult services and sex workers' ads—such as those advertised on Craigslist and Back-page—was couched as a move to combat the sex trafficking of minors, but more often than not it proved to be an attack on sex workers themselves, making it harder for them to find clients and worsening their risks of violence and exploitation.

Beggaring belief, in August 2016, federal agents from the Depart-ment of Homeland Security arrested the CEO and employees of Rent-boy.com in Manhattan, a website that had openly served countless male sex workers and their male clients for two decades, on the grounds that "this Internet brothel made millions of dollars from the promotion of illegal prostitution"—even though the service had made life safer for sex workers and there was no evidence of exploitation or other crimes.

The irrationality of American thinking on sex work came under the spotlight when Amnesty International announced that it was considering a global policy to urge governments to fully decriminalize sex work as a crucial step toward "the highest possible protection of the human rights of sex workers." Amnesty based its recommendation on years of research in diverse countries. The final say lay with Amnesty's eighty national chapters, five hundred delegates from which were to vote on the draft policy in August 2015.

If its delegates voted in favor, Amnesty would call on governments to "repeal existing laws and/or refrain from introducing new laws that criminalize or penalize directly or in practice the consensual exchange of sexual services between adults for remuneration," alongside stronger efforts to prevent trafficking and exploitation, on the grounds that criminalization forces sex workers to operate covertly in ways that compromise their safety and serve to deny them support or protection from government officials.

In the extensive materials posted on its website, along with the draft policy, it gave example after example of how even indirect criminalizing laws were invariably used to persecute sex workers, noting that "in many countries of the world, two sex workers working together for safety is considered a 'brothel,'" while "so-called 'pimping laws'" lead to sex workers being routinely evicted from their homes. Even the Nordic model being embraced by many Western nations—where clients are punished with heavy fines and prison terms and sex workers are in theory considered victims—resulted in extensive harm to sex workers, Amnesty noted, including worsening violence, police harassment, eviction from homes and workplaces, loss of custody of their children, and weakened HIV prevention—not surprisingly, as its goal is to force sex workers out of this work.

Just days before the vote, in a public letter that made headlines internationally, prohibitionist groups and a swath of American and European celebrities—including Tina Brown, Jennifer and Peter Buffett, Henry Louis Gates Jr., Gloria Steinem, and Meryl Streep—accused

Amnesty of "incomprehensibly proposing . . . the decriminalization of pimps, brothel owners and buyers of sex."

Women "whose lives are shaped by absence of choice" would be "set apart for consumption by men and for the profit of their pimps, traffickers and brothel owners," they charged.

I could not remember when the carefully thought-out position of a reputable organization had been so deliberately misrepresented as this. It was depressing to see intelligent, otherwise humanistic thinkers be party to this effort, seemingly as if they had not bothered to read the extensive draft policy and the wealth of research that lay behind it. Amnesty's long record of resolute support for human rights—even those that made them a lightning rod for criticism—was forgotten.

Despite this costly blow to Amnesty, which depends on donations for its work, the overwhelming majority of its national chapters voted in favor of full decriminalization of sex work, making it the organization's official position in its work with governments. But the face-off exposed a wide fault line between rich Western countries and many developing countries.

The signatories to the open letter denouncing Amnesty's position were overwhelmingly white women, disproportionately from the US, with very few signatories from developing countries. Within Amnesty, too, the opposition had come most strongly from its Norwegian and Swedish chapters—the Swedish chapter resigned en masse, while Norway's decided it would fall behind the democratically reached institutional position. It was impossible not to conclude that the mainstream of the rich world—including its mainstream feminists—was now hopelessly out of touch with the practicalities of how to advance the best interests and rights of sex workers, particularly of sex workers in developing countries.

Fortunately, public health and human rights defenders still understood what needed to be done. *The Lancet* and Human Rights Watch, for instance, had adopted this position several years ahead of Amnesty, as had key United Nations organizations. In June 2016, UN

Secretary-General Ban Ki-moon told world leaders, "The criminalization of adult consensual sexual relations is a human rights violation . . . [T]he decriminalization of sex work can reduce violence, harassment and HIV risk. Sex workers should enjoy human rights protections guaranteed to all individuals, including the rights to non-discrimination, health, security and safety." The vision that Priscilla Alexander, Selvi, and other pioneers had laid out twenty years ago had now been embraced by the world's leading rights defenders, a development that filled me with hope that in time rationality, truth, and good would win over misinformation and moralistic ideology.

In India, too, there were grounds for despair as well as for hope.

Much as in the US, there was instance after instance of irreparable harm being done to countless women because of the bad old laws criminalizing sex workers and the new antitrafficking zealotry. In September 2014, a well-known actress, Shweta Basu Prasad, was arrested in an antiprostitution sting at a luxury hotel in Hyderabad. Prasad was incarcerated in a government reformatory, sentenced to a six-month term, the media frenzy turning her into a national figure of notoriety.

Civil rights groups and movie industry leaders pressed for Prasad's release, but in depressing contrast the city's leading antitrafficking figure, Sunitha Krishnan—lionized by Nick Kristof and other Western prohibitionists—was quoted in the Indian papers urging that Prasad be held for a lengthy period. It took months to "rehabilitate" victims of trafficking, Krishnan said, though there was not the slightest likelihood that Prasad had been trafficked.

I was angry at the scale of harm and continuing injustice, but I realized, too, that the situation was no longer hopeless. In contrast to the 1980s, when Selvi and other sex workers had been jailed indefinitely with no one speaking up for them, today there were thoughtful people in influential positions committed to their rights and well-being. In late 2014, Lalitha Kumaramangalam, the newly appointed chairperson of the National Commission for Women, spoke out in favor of sex workers' rights, saying, "It is my personal and professional view that sex work should be legalized but the commission must make an informed decision and I am open to listening to all views." In 2018, in an extraordinary statement, the UN special rapporteurs on trafficking and contemporary slavery urged the Indian government to not "conflate sex work with trafficking for the purpose of sexual exploitation."

Most heartening, the Supreme Court's new commitment to defending individual liberty—alongside its longstanding record of protecting marginalized individuals and their socioeconomic rights—meant there was even a possibility that this enlightened court would eventually force the government to decriminalize sex work and give sex workers rights. In a series of rulings from 2013 to 2015, the court overturned the ban on dance bars across Maharashtra State that had been enacted in 2005 by the Hindu-supremacist government, saying that it was an unconstitutional infringement on the women's right to carry on their profession. In 2016, another bench of the court accepted the recommendations of an expert panel it had instituted, making it likely that in its decision it would instruct the government to provide a panoply of social services to sex workers, including guaranteed admission for their children to government schools and meaningful livelihood alternatives, as well as to reform the aspects of the criminal laws that punished them.

❖

In the course of my lifetime, now on the verge of sixty, from all that I had experienced and seen, I had come to two paradoxical conclusions.

One was a saddening one. It was that the actions of a minority of people are what doom the world to the savage, inhumane condition that it is in perpetually, century after century.

The other conclusion was uplifting. It was that the impoverished, the oppressed, the reviled, and the outcast—whether black or untouchable, whether girly boy, faggot, *hijra*, or whore—never stop fighting for dignity and justice. There is hope in this—undying hope. It makes bearable even the most indefinite of sentences—and keeps alive humanity's chances for preservation.

ACKNOWLEDGMENTS

In a book that spans my lifetime, there are countless people and institutions to thank—family, lovers, friends, teachers, and mentors, places that supported me, and the innumerable people who set aside time to speak to me. Many of them will see my gratitude, respect, and affection expressed in these pages.

And then there are thanks specifically regarding this book.

The foremost is to Jacob Gayle, then head of the Ford Foundation's global initiative on AIDS—this book owes everything to Jacob's willingness to support what I candidly told him would be a no-holds-barred account.

Immense thanks go also to Roshmi Goswami, who led the foundation's efforts in India on sexual, reproductive, and women's rights. I have the greatest respect for the Ford Foundation itself for its long history of fighting for the excluded groups and the embattled freedoms that many other funders lack the sense and courage to defend.

I'm grateful also to Canada's International Development Research Centre for an unrelated research grant on poverty that helped me with the broader research for this book. My thanks in particular go to Stephen McGurk and Anindya Chatterjee for their patience regarding that project.

Anna Ghosh, my supportive and indefatigable agent, found this book the perfect home, with Rakesh Satyal at Atria Books. Rakesh has been the most perceptive of editors, and his combination of gently given advice and fulsome praise inspired me to do my very best. I was blessed to have another gifted and sensitive editor for the original, Indian edition, Manasi Subramaniam.

In Vrinda Condillac and Supriya Nair, I had the personal editors that all writers dream of—engaged intellectual companions and the source of tough but infallible advice. To have all that as well as their friendship makes me feel singularly blessed.

My friend Olivier Föllmi, a great photographer and humanitarian, generously allowed me to use the photograph of Tandavan.

My blessings continued. Krishna Kumar pushed me to be outspoken. Sumit Baudh and Aniruddhan Vasudevan were not just inspiring collaborators but also became my soul mates. Joanne Csete—one of the most brilliant, principled, and generous of people—painstakingly read and improved both editions of this book. My beloved brother Bharat worked on virtually every draft, pushing me to do better, his patience and kindness such that he never let on if he was bored.

For everything from comments and encouragement and sharing of their knowledge to other unforgettable kindnesses, I am also indebted to Sohaila Abdulali, Ashok Alexander, Priscilla Alexander, Vivek Anand, Tonuca Basu, Alexia Bedat, Tina Bennett, Rustom Bharucha, DJ and "Bops" Bopanna, Corinne Brenner, Anna Chacko, Jean D'Cunha, Kiran Desai, Akash Dharmaraj, Melissa Ditmore, Pratap Dube, Helena Eversole, Rosemary George, Suzanne Goldenberg, Anjali Gopalan, Gray Handley, Andrew Hunter, Jimmy Jacob, Roshan Jain, Smarajit Jana, Katharina Poggendorf-Kakar, Sudhir Kakar, V.K. Karthika, Saleem Kidwai, Ed Klaris, Rachna Kucheria, Senthil Kumar, Loan Le, Lakshmi Mani, Madhu Mehra, Suketu Mehta, Geeta Misra, Neel Mukherjee, Shyamala Nataraj, Derek O'Brien, Barbara O'Hara, Cheryl Overs, Sophat Phal, Radhika Ramasubban, Gowthaman Ranganathan, Rosemary Romano, Kim Rosenthal, Rahul Roy, Swarup Sarkar, Sankar Sen, Meena Seshu, Vikram Seth, Meenaskhi Shedde, Nimis Sheth, Saudamani Siegrist, Anjum Singh, Sree Sreekumar, Chitra and Ram Subramaniam, Tarun Tahiliani, Tina Tahiliani, Shashi Tharoor, Ellen Tolmie, Nilita Vachani, Ardeshir Vakil, Kamala Visweswaran, and Mithoo Wadia. Thank you all—immensely!

And then there are my boundless thanks to Lorca, more than words can convey, for making every day of the past sixteen years sweeter and more joyous, for making my heart sing, for making me feel singularly blessed.

And finally, there is my indelible debt to my late father, Basant—while I wouldn't have published this book while he was alive, everything good in it is owed to him.

NOTES

The author's notes to this book will be a useful resource for readers. As they are extensive, the publisher has decided to house them online at http://www.simonandschuster.com/indefinite-sentence-endnotes.

These notes contain referenced works, books, and papers that are not directly cited but which would interest readers wishing to delve deeper into particular issues. I've provided commentary for many of the entries.

ABOUT THE AUTHOR

Born in Kolkata, India, Siddharth Dube is widely known for his writing on AIDS, public health, and poverty. He is a graduate of Tufts University, the University of Minnesota's School of Journalism, and the Harvard School of Public Health. He has since been a visiting fellow at the Centre for the Study of Developing Societies in Delhi, scholar-in-residence at Yale University's Center for Interdisciplinary Research on AIDS, senior adviser to the executive director of UNAIDS, and a senior fellow at the World Policy Institute in New York City. Visit SiddharthDube.com.